מבוא

ArtScroll Series®

Rabbi Nosson Scherman / Rabbi Meir Zlotowitz

General Editors

Inspirational stories arranged according to the weekly Torah reading

by Rabbi Shimon Finkelman

Published by

Mesorah Publications, ltd

Shabbos
Stories

FIRST EDITION
First Impression . . . November 1994
Second Impression . . . May 1995
Third Impression . . . November 1995
Fourth Impression . . . April 1997
Fifth Impression . . . July 1999
Sixth Impression . . . March 2003

Published and Distributed by
MESORAH PUBLICATIONS, Ltd.
4401 Second Avenue
Brooklyn, New York 11232

Distributed in Europe by
LEHMANNS
Unit E, Viking Industrial Park
Rolling Mill Road
Jarrow, Tyne & Wear NE32 3DP
England

Distributed in Australia & New Zealand by
GOLDS WORLD OF JUDAICA
3-13 William Street
Balaclava, Melbourne 3183
Victoria Australia

Distributed in Israel by
SIFRIATI / A. GITLER — BOOKS
6 Hayarkon Street
Bnei Brak 51127

Distributed in South Africa by
KOLLEL BOOKSHOP
Shop 8A Norwood Hypermarket
Norwood 2196, Johannesburg, South Africa

THE ARTSCROLL SERIES ®
SHABBOS STORIES
© Copyright 1994, by MESORAH PUBLICATIONS, Ltd.
4401 Second Avenue / Brooklyn, N.Y. 11232 / (718) 921-9000 / www.artscroll.com

ISBN
0-89906-526-0 (hard cover)
0-89906-527-9 (paperback)

Typography by Compuscribe at ArtScroll Studios, Ltd.

Printed in the United States of America by Noble Book Press
Bound by Sefercraft, Quality Bookbinders, Ltd. Brooklyn, N.Y.

৺§ Table of Contents

Preface   ix

Bereishis

Bereishis — The Cholent Miracle   13
Noach — Contaminated Environment   17
Lech Lecha — The Road to Eternity   20
Vayeira — Shalom Bayis   24
            In our Fathers' Footsteps   27
Chayei Sarah — Chance Encounters   28
Toldos — Worlds Apart   33
Vayeitzei — The Strength of Silence   36
Vayishlach — The Primary Weapon   39
Vayeishev — With No Alternative   43
Mikeitz — Trust in Hashem   46
Vayigash — Questions Without Answers   50
            Like One Man, With One Heart   55
Vayechi — The Sword and the Bow   58

Shemos

Shemos — Mark of Greatness   62
Va'eira — An Eagle Takes Flight   66
Bo — For the Sake of a Mitzvah   69
Beshalach — In Merit of Her Faith   73

Yisro — A Lesson for Life   77
        The Source of All Blessing   80
Mishpatim — An Orphan's Pain   84
        Friend or Foe   86
Terumah — A Generous Heart   88
        Miracle of Torah   93
Tetzaveh — The Me'il   97
        Words That Pierce the Heavens   99
Ki Sisa — Reaping the Fruits   101
Vayakhel — Man With a Mission   104
Pekudei — Don't Despair   109

Vayikra

Vayikra — Of Sacrifice and Love   112
Tzav — Gratitude   115
Shemini — Food for Thought   119
        Kindness for All   121
Tazria — For the Sake of a Mitzvah   125
        A Matter of Life and Death   128
Metzora — Soul Talk   132
Acharei — Between Man and His Fellow   135
Kedoshim — The Art of Reproof   138
Emor — Yosse'le Ganav   143
        Beautify the Mitzvah   146
Behar — Mighty Warriors   149
        Service With a Smile   152
Bechukosai — The Joy of Torah Study   154

Bamidbar

Bamidbar — His Children   158
Nasso — Seizing the Moment   163
        Doing Whatever You Can   167

Beha'aloscha — Humility and Greatness   169
Shelach — Garment of Armor   175
Korach — Pursue Peace   179
Chukas — Dead to the World   183
Balak — Human Dignity   187
Pinchas — A Man of Spirit   190
Mattos — Beyond a Shadow of a Doubt   195
Masei — The Time is Now   199

Devarim

Devarim — Thoughtful Rebuke   201
          Fear No Man   203
Va'eschanan — To Love Hashem   206
Eikev — Tefillin in the Camps   212
Re'eh — A Change of Heart   216
Shoftim — A Decision for Life   220
          "Father!"   222
Ki Seitzei — Man of His Word   224
             Kosher Money   227
Ki Savo — Best Investment   229
Nitzavim — Choose Life   232
Vayeilech — The Hidden Hand   235
            Selflessness for Torah   239
Ha'azinu — Treasuries of Wisdom   242
Vezos Haberachah — For Every Jewish Child   246

Preface

> *R' Yitzchak said: It would seem that the Torah should have begun with, "This month shall be for you the beginning of months" (Exodus 12:2), for that was the first commandment given to all Israel. Why, then, does the Torah open with, "In the beginning. . ."?*
>
> *(opening words of Rashi's commentary to the Torah)*

In his *Nesivos Shalom,* Rabbi Shalom Noach Berezovsky, שליט״א, answers the above question as follows: The *Arizal's* famed disciple R' Chaim Vital explains why the development of proper *midos* (character traits) is not reckoned among the 613 *mitzvos.* For example, the Sages speak of arrogance in very harsh terms, yet the Torah contains no prohibition against being arrogant. Proper *midos,* says R' Chaim Vital, are not included among the commandments because they are the foundations upon which all the commandments stand. Without proper *midos,* proper observance of Torah is an impossibility.

As *Nesivos Shalom* explains, the narratives recounted in the Torah from the birth of Adam until the Exodus are not mere stories, recorded for the sake of historical truth. The deeds of the Patriarchs and their descendants are replete with illustrations of lovingkindness, truth, purity, and a host of other sublime attributes. Such qualities are the very foundations of Torah; therefore, the Torah begins with them.

The following Talmudic teaching (*Makkos* 24a) may complement the above insight: The prophet Habakkuk established one principle as a basis for fulfillment of all 613 *mitzvos:* "Habakkuk came and established them [all] upon one, as it is written, *A righteous person will live by his faith (Habakkuk* 2:4). The narratives in the Book of *Genesis* and the first half of

Shemos are replete with lessons of *emunah* (faith); therefore the Torah begins with them.

In fact, all five books of the Torah are filled with vital lessons in character development and faith. The goal of this book is to convey some of these lessons through the medium of stories. It is my hope and *tefillah* that readers of all ages will find its contents meaningful and inspiring.

❀ ❀ ❀

The stories in this volume have been gleaned from a wide range of sources; many appear in print for the first time. Some who related incidents to me are named in the stories themselves. I thank them, as well as the following distinguished rabbis and educators, שליט״א, who kindly shared stories with me: Rabbi Naftali H. Basch, Rabbi Yisroel Belsky, Rabbi Yaakov Bender, Rabbi Moshe Brown, Rabbi Eliezer Ginsburg, Rabbi Shlomo Mandel, Rabbi Menachem Pfeiffer, Rabbi Henoch Plotnik and Rabbi Meyer Scheinberg.

My appreciation to Rabbi Hillel David, שליט״א, for his assistance and guidance whenever I call upon him.

My thanks to Rabbi Boruch B. Borchardt for his gracious assistance.

I would like to take this opportunity to express my appreciation to Rabbi Nisson Wolpin for all that I owe him. A number of stories in this work first appeared in *The Jewish Observer*, which he so ably edits.

In providing material and guiding me to other sources, Rabbi Moshe Grossman has been an invaluable help in this and other projects. A special note of thanks to my brother, Rabbi Mordechai Finkelman, for his assistance.

No words can adequately express my appreciation to Rabbi Nosson Scherman. In this project, as on numerous other occasions, his guidance and insight — always imparted with warmth and patience — have been invaluable to me. Deadlines and other pressures have never prevented Rabbi Meir Zlotowitz from concerning himself with my projects and personal needs. Reb Sheah Brander, as ArtScroll/Mesorah's graphics genius, has once again produced a work of aesthetic beauty. May I offer my *bircas hedyot* that these three great disseminators of Torah continue to benefit the

Jewish people with their incomparable work for many years to come.

My thanks to all the very dedicated people at ArtScroll/Mesorah. I would like to extend a particular note of thanks to Rabbi Avrohom Biderman, who coordinated this project efficiently and patiently; to Reb Eli Kroen and Reb Shlomo Benzaquen for their participation in the graphics; to Mrs. Ethel Gottlieb for her excellent proofreading; and to Mrs. Mindy Breier, Dvory Glatzer, Yehuda Gordon, Udi Hershkowitz and Leah Brachah Lasker for their patient and skillful typing and re-typing.

I am forever indebted to all my *roshei yeshivah* and *rebbeim* from whom I was privileged to learn through word and personal example — and who, in a real sense, are the embodiment of this work's contents.

A significant portion of this book was compiled and written in Camp Agudah, where I am privileged to spend my summers. My thanks to the camp's director, Meir Frischman, its head counselor, Rabbi Simcha Kaufman, and the entire camp administration. I would also like to express my appreciation to Yeshivah Tifereth Elimelech, Yeshivah Darchei Torah, and Camp Torah Vodaath for having granted me the privilege of teaching Torah and being a part of their outstanding staffs.

I am blessed with a father and mother, שיחיו, whose ways and words reflect their beautiful *midos* and deep-rooted *emunah.* May I be privileged to learn from them for many years to come.

My appreciation to my wife's parents for all that they have done for us. May they be granted good health for many years to come.

My wife Tova, תחי׳, has provided me with a home atmosphere that makes my work possible. I thank Hashem for granting me an עזר in the term's full sense. May she see the fulfillment of all her heart's desires.

I thank *Hashem Yisbarach* for permitting me to carry out this project. May we merit the day when the entire Jewish nation will dwell in peace upon its Land, a day when *the earth will be filled with the knowledge of HASHEM, as the water covering the sea bed* — speedily and in our time.

Shimon Finkelman
Kislev, 5755

פרשת בראשית
Parashas Bereishis

The Cholent Miracle

וַיְבָרֶךְ אֱלֹהִים אֶת יוֹם הַשְּׁבִיעִי וַיְקַדֵּשׁ אֹתוֹ.
God blessed the seventh day and sanctified it (Bereishis 2:3).

The Roman Emperor asked R' Yehoshua ben Chana-
nia: "Why does the food which you cook for the
seventh day have a such a wonderful aroma?"

R' Yehoshua replied: "It is because of a spice that we
have — its name is Shabbos. Adding this spice is what
causes the aroma" (Shabbos 119a).

What is [the mitzvah of] "Oneg" [to delight in the
Shabbos]? It is what the Sages said, to prepare for
Shabbos a dish that is exceptionally rich and a drink
that is especially refreshing — each man according to
his means (Rambam, Hilchos Shabbos 30:7).

The phenomenal growth of Torah life in America since the Second World War is one of the great wonders of this long and difficult *galus.* One of the key figures in this miracle was the late Rabbi Elazar Simcha Wasserman, son of the renowned pre-War Torah giant, Rabbi Elchonon Wasserman.

In the early 1950's, Torah life in California was just beginning to take root. Los Angeles had a yeshivah day school but no high school. When a local rabbi sought to establish a *beis midrash* of higher learning, ten students were selected from Mesivta Torah Vodaath to form the student body. Their *Rosh Yeshivah* would be R' Simcha, who was then teaching Torah in Detroit.

For R' Simcha, bringing Torah to the Jews of Los Angeles was not enough. He and his students would have to go out to communities near and far to introduce their fellow Jews to the beauty of Torah.

One such community was in Santa Barbara, California, some one hundred miles from Los Angeles. Beginning in 1969, every Sunday, students of R' Simcha would conduct Talmud Torah classes for boys and girls of all ages. As was his approach in all of the communities where he planted Torah seeds, R' Simcha himself conducted formal classes in Santa Barbara to teach the parents of the Talmud Torah students.

The Eisners were among the families taking part in these classes. Dr. and Mrs. Eisner came to love and revere R' Simcha. In 1974, when the Eisners' son was to become a bar-mitzvah, R' Simcha advised them to host a Shabbaton in honor of the occasion. They would invite all the families involved in the Talmud Torah program. Like a concerned father, R' Simcha guided the bar-mitzvah plans every step of the way, from designing the invitations, to arranging the program beginning on Friday night and ending on Sunday morning.

To make sure that the guests would avoid *chillul* (desecration of) Shabbos, R' Simcha advised that the bar-mitzvah invitation offer a choice: Those who lived out of the immediate vicinity, but were willing to remain in the area for the entire Shabbos, would be provided with a place to stay. The alternative was to attend a *Melave Malkah* after Shabbos, to which one could, of course, drive. Rabbi and Rebbetzin Wasserman themselves planned to come to Santa Barbara after Shabbos to attend the *Melaveh Malkah*.

R' Simcha spent much time mulling over the wording of the bar-mitzvah invitation. While he did not want the Shabbos to be desecrated, he also did not want anyone to be offended by the fact that they could attend the Shabbos festivities only if certain conditions were met. The invitation had to be written in a way that conveyed respect, and R' Simcha made sure that this was the case.

Santa Barbara did not have an Orthodox *shul* at that time. A suitable room in a local hotel was found and the teachers of the Talmud Torah, assisted by their students, constructed an original, decorative *mechitzah* (partition), so that men and women would have their respective areas for *davening*. The plan called for the Eisners to host the Friday night meal in their home, and serve a *kiddush* in *shul* on Shabbos morning, after which everyone would return to the Eisner home for the Shabbos afternoon meal.

On the Thursday before the bar-mitzvah, R' Simcha called Mrs. Eisner to check that everything was set. After reviewing the program and other items, R' Simcha asked that Mrs. Eisner tell him the full menu for the meals and *kiddush*. While she appreciated his concern and involvement, Mrs. Eisner found this request somewhat unusual. Nevertheless, she happily began to list the many foods which she had prepared for the occasion.

When she concluded the menu, R' Simcha said, "Just fine, fine. It sounds wonderful. But only one little thing — *what about the cholent?*"

Mrs. Eisner replied that she had cooked *cholent* only once before, and had not found it an easy venture. She was reluctant to try for only her second time when such a large crowd was involved. "Is it really so important that we serve *cholent?*" she asked.

"Yes," replied R' Simcha. "*Cholent* is a very special Jewish food. A Shabbos experience, especially for those who have never before observed Shabbos, should definitely include *cholent.*"

R' Simcha was not one to burden others with requests that could not be easily carried out. Mrs. Eisner knew instinctively that his advice should be followed. The *cholent* was prepared.

❅ ❅ ❅

The *kiddush* was over and everyone was making their way to the Eisners' home for the afternoon meal. Thus far, everything had worked out beautifully. Even those guests whose relationship to *mitzvah* observance was limited at best, were enjoying themselves thoroughly.

Before the meal could begin, someone told Mrs. Eisner that a woman who had come for Shabbos had said that she was not feeling well and was returning home with her husband.

The Eisners were more than a bit concerned about their friend. At the *kiddush,* the woman had seemed fine. What had happened so suddenly?

On *Motza'ei Shabbos* (Saturday night), the woman's husband called to apologize. He explained:

When the Second World War had erupted, his wife was a little girl. She had spent the war years in a concentration camp, and had emerged physically intact but emotionally devastated. She had suffered a loss of memory. Over the years, she had been to many doctors to seek a remedy for her amnesia, to no avail.

When she had entered the Eisner's home on Shabbos afternoon, she was greeted by a strong smell, one which reminded her of something. Suddenly, she felt herself overcome by emotion as it all came back to her. . .

She was sitting at the Shabbos table in her parents' home. The aroma of her mother's delicious cholent filled the air. Suddenly, the front door was flung open, and Nazi soldiers burst into the room. They murdered her father and mother in front of her eyes and then grabbed her by her hair and dragged her outside. . .

This sudden flood of memories which the *cholent* smell had awakened had so shaken her, that she fled in a frenzy to the security of her home.

Her trauma soon gave way to an incredible sense of relief. The inner turmoil that had plagued her for decades had come to an end. Sweet childhood memories, which had eluded her for so long, now flashed through her mind. Finally, she knew who she was.

❁   ❁   ❁

At the *Melaveh Malkah* that night, Mrs. Eisner related what had transpired to R' Simcha, who responded, "It's not the first time I've heard of a miracle connected with the Shabbos *cholent,* but not always is the hand of Hashem so clearly apparent."

פרשת נח
Parashas Noach

Contaminated Environment

וַיַּרְא אֱלֹהִים אֶת הָאָרֶץ וְהִנֵּה נִשְׁחָתָה,
כִּי הִשְׁחִית כָּל בָּשָׂר אֶת דַּרְכּוֹ עַל הָאָרֶץ.
*And God saw the earth and behold it was corrupted,
for all flesh had corrupted its way upon the earth*
(*Bereishis* 6:12).

*Even animals, beasts and birds lived with species
other than their own* (*Rashi from Sanhedrin* 108a).

When Rabbi Eliyahu Lopian, the famed *Mashgiach* and *tzaddik,* was studying Torah at the great yeshivah of Lomza, Poland, the people of the city were confronted by a perplexing problem. A number of patients who had entered the city's hospital with various ailments had been cured of those ailments — but had contracted some other disease during their hospital stay! This had happened too many times to be considered coincidental. Something was wrong.

After much deliberation, city officials decided to call down a team of experts from Warsaw to investigate the matter. These experts concluded that the source of the problem was the hospital building. A wooden structure, the building was so old that even the senior citizens of Lomza had no idea when it had been built. The walls of the hospital showed their age; in every room, cracks had appeared in various shapes and sizes. It was the germs that had seeped into these cracks which were infecting the hospital's patients with disease.

The experts concluded that the only solution was to demolish the hospital, burn its materials and erect a new hospital in its place. And that is what they did.

Said R' Lopian: Just as in the physical world, germs can pollute the atmosphere and do damage to whoever is in their proximity, so it is in the spiritual world. The collective sins of the generation of the Flood were of such magnitude that the entire world became polluted with the spiritual "germs" created by their sins. This pollution affected even the animals and vegetation. Thus, as the *Midrash* relates, prior to the Flood animals mixed with species other than their own and seeds would produce vegetation other than their own type. The sins of mankind had corrupted all of nature.

❦ ❦ ❦

In 1938, Rabbi Elchonon Wasserman, the great *Rosh Yeshivah* who was martyred in the Second World War, came to America to raise funds for his yeshivah in Baranovich. R' Elchonon's visit had a profound impact on America's Orthodox Jews, while a number of non-religious Jews actually became *ba'alei teshuvah* as a result of his visit.

There was a Jew named Shraga Block who proudly referred to himself as *"dem Rebben's ba'al agalah,"* the *Rebbe's* wagon driver, for he chauffeured R' Elchonon to his many daily appointments during his long stay in New York. Being the holy *tzaddik* that he was, it was R' Elchonon's practice to always look toward the ground when outside in the street, to ensure that he not see a forbidden sight. When he rode in a car, R' Elchonon kept his eyes fixed on the floor of the vehicle; he never looked out the window.

One day, R' Elchonon had an appointment in Manhattan. To get there, Mr. Block drove his car down a Manhattan street which was known as a place where low-class people would loiter and engage in improper behavior. Suddenly, R' Elchonon winced as if he had been stung. "Where are you taking me?" he demanded of Mr. Block. "This place is filled with *tumah* (spiritual impurity). How can one study Torah in such a place?" Mr. Block quickly turned the car off the street.

❧ ❧ ❧

There is a saying that "a person is a product of his environment." In its plain meaning, this saying indicates that a person is influenced by the behavior and attitudes of those with whom he associates. As we have seen, however, the influence of one's environment is far greater. When people behave in a proper way, in a way that reflects the Torah's commandments, then their words and deeds fill the atmosphere with sanctity and everyone in their company will absorb some of that sanctity. And when people are sinful, they fill their environment with *tumah* and all who find themselves in their environment are affected by that *tumah*.

A Jew must strive to find himself in the right places, among the right kind of people.

פרשת לך לך
Parashas Lech Lecha

The Road to Eternity

וַיֹּאמֶר ה׳ אֶל אַבְרָם, לֶךְ לְךָ מֵאַרְצְךָ וּמִמּוֹלַדְתְּךָ וּמִבֵּית אָבִיךָ,
אֶל הָאָרֶץ אֲשֶׁר אַרְאֶךָּ.

*Hashem said to Avram, "Go for yourself from your land,
from your relatives, and from your father's house
to the land that I will show you" (Bereishis 12:1).*

Just as Hashem guided the path of Avraham, so too does He guide the life of every individual Jew. Avraham, prior to embarking on his journey to Canaan, had demonstrated his unflinching devotion to Hashem at Ur Kasdim. Similarly, any Jew who sincerely dedicates himself to Hashem's service can rest assured that Hashem will lead him along the path of truth.

The following story, related by the late *Rosh Yeshivah* of Yeshivah Ner Israel in Baltimore, Rabbi Yaakov Yitzchak Ruderman, tells of a boy who aspired to dwell in the tent of Torah and was guided from Above so that his yearning was fulfilled.

In his days as a yeshivah student in Europe, R' Ruderman met a man who was an outstanding *talmid chacham*, an author of a scholarly work, and also quite wealthy. R' Ruderman asked the man how he had become so great in Torah while amassing a fortune. The man replied, "I merited both through a single joke." And he proceeded to relate the following:

He had been born into a very poor family. His father managed to scrape together enough money to send his son to a *cheder* where he developed a great love for learning. As the years went on, the boy's thirst for Torah grew while his father's earnings dwindled. By the time he turned fifteen, the situation had become desperate; there was simply not enough food on the table to satisfy everyone's hunger.

One day, a sign caught the father's eye. In a neighboring town, there lived a Jew who had a reputation as an exceptionally wise person who could give advice on virtually anything under the sun. People would pay the man sizable sums of money for his advice. It was said that those who followed the man's guidance would often see amazing success in their endeavors.

The sign stated that the wise man, who lived alone, was seeking to hire an attendant who would live in his house and serve as both his secretary and housekeeper. In exchange, the person would be given room and board.

The thought of parting with his son brought tears to the father's eyes, however there was no choice. Now, his son would be properly fed and would be free to pursue his learning when not attending to his chores. As an additional benefit, his son would be living with and learning from a very wise Jew, surely a rare opportunity for someone so young. The father consoled himself with the thought that as soon as his own situation improved, he would bring his son home.

That night, father and son talked together for a very long time. The next day, they traveled to the neighboring town, where the wise man interviewed the boy and agreed to hire him.

It did not take long for the boy to discover that the "wise man" was a charlatan. He claimed to know everything, but, in fact, he comprehended just enough to give the impression that he was knowledgeable. People thought that the man spent his days and nights immersed in Torah, but the boy knew that this was not so.

The boy was dejected, to say the least. He wanted to pack his few belongings and return home, but he felt that he could not do this to his parents when they were having such a difficult time providing for themselves and the other children.

One day, a farmer came to seek the wise man's advice. While they were waiting for the wise man to appear, the farmer asked the boy, "You live here, and obviously you know the wise man better than anyone. Tell me, do you think that I am doing the right thing by paying such a large fee for his counsel? I am seeking advice as to how my fields can yield more produce — and I know that I am taking a risk. There is no guarantee that his advice will work. Do you think that I am making a sound investment?"

The boy thought for a long time before replying. Finally, he said, "I'll tell you: The Torah tells us that robbery was a prime cause of the Flood. If water is what your crops need, then you've come to the right place. Since this is a house of robbery, it's sure to bring lots of rain!"

The farmer did not know how much truth lay in the boy's words, but he laughed hard at the joke. Moments later, the two were startled by the sound of someone clearing his throat. They turned to face the wise man, who stood in the doorway, seething with rage. It was obvious that he had overheard the boy's remarks. The farmer excused himself and hurried from the house, leaving the boy to face his employer alone.

"Get your things and get out of here, you ungrateful scoundrel!" the man shouted. "I don't ever want to see your face again."

Soon the boy was walking down the road, his pack slung over his shoulder. It seemed that he had no choice but to return home — but how would his father feed him? He mulled over his dilemma for a while until he decided to take a break and do that which he enjoyed more than anything — studying Torah.

He entered a *beis midrash* on the side of the road and found it empty. It was early afternoon, when men were at work. He withdrew a volume of *Gemara* from a bookshelf and was soon immersed in the words he so loved.

For a long time the boy continued studying, oblivious to the passage of time. He was unaware that a local businessman had entered the *beis midrash* and had been watching him intently for a long time. Who was this boy, the man wondered. He had never seen anyone so young study alone for so long, with such concentration.

When the boy finally looked up from his *Gemara*, the man greeted him and asked what had brought him to this *beis midrash*. The boy proceeded to relate his sorrowful tale. After taking a few minutes to mull the matter over, the man said, "You know, I have plenty of room and food in my house. It would be my pleasure to have you live with my family."

The boy went home and related to his parents what had transpired. Upon inquiring, the father learned that this man was a highly respected and successful businessman, and was a supporter of Torah. He gladly accepted the man's invitation on his son's behalf.

The next few years flew by. The boy continued to live in the businessman's home and blossomed into an outstanding young *talmid chacham*. When the man's daughter, his only child, became of marriageable age, there was little doubt as to who would be suggested as her match. The boy, now a mature young man, became the businessman's son-in-law and continued to study Torah full-time for many years. When the businessman died, his daughter and son-in-law inherited his fortune.

"And so," the man concluded to Rabbi Ruderman, "because of one joke — the one I told the farmer — I met my future father-in-law, through whom I acquired great wealth — material wealth and, more important, the wealth of Torah knowledge."

פרשת וירא
Parashas Vayeira

Shalom Bayis

וַיֹּאמֶר ה' אֶל אַבְרָהָם, לָמָה זֶה צָחֲקָה שָׂרָה לֵאמֹר
הַאַף אֻמְנָם אֵלֵד וַאֲנִי זָקַנְתִּי?
Then Hashem said to Avraham, "Why is it that Sarah laughed,
saying: 'Shall I in truth bear a child, and I am aged?'"
(Bereishis 18:13).

When Sarah heard the angel (who was disguised as a wayfarer) tell Avraham that she would give birth to their first child a year later, Sarah — at age eighty-nine — laughed in disbelief. She said, "[Shall I . . . bear a child,] *and my husband is aged!"* However, in relating this to Avraham, Hashem quoted Sarah as having said, *"and I am aged!"*

Why did Hashem alter Sarah's words? For the sake of *shalom bayis*, harmony between husband and wife (*Rashi* from *Bava Metzia* 87a).

It seems difficult to understand how Sarah's actual words could have upset the harmony between Avraham and herself. Avraham was ninety-nine years old. What could be wrong with referring to him as aged?

We see from here that marriage requires a special degree of sensitivity on the part of both husband and wife. It is because husband and wife are so close that each is especially sensitive to the comments and actions of the other. Words that may not harm a relationship between friends, could cause hurt between husband and wife. And it is crucial that such distress be avoided. Our Sages teach that when husband and wife live in harmony, the *Shechinah* (Divine Presence) comes to dwell in their home. To whatever degree there is friction in the home, to that degree the *Shechinah* is not present.

This is why Hashem deemed it necessary to alter the words of Sarah (from *Sichos Mussar*).

❦ ❦ ❦

One evening, the renowned *tzaddik* of Jerusalem, Rabbi Aryeh Levin, spoke in a local *shul* on the topic of harmony in the home. Attending the talk was Rabbi Isser Zalman Meltzer, one of the generation's great Torah leaders. R' Isser Zalman was renowned not only for his Torah genius, but for his sterling character as well.

When R' Aryeh had concluded his talk, R' Isser Zalman approached him. "Thank you so much," he said, "I've gained much from your words."

R' Aryeh could not help but laugh. "You, R' Isser Zalman? Why, *you* should be the one speaking about harmony in the home.

"Let me explain," R' Isser Zalman replied. "It is many years since I have begun writing my *Even HaAzel*. [1] My handwriting is poor; the typesetter cannot possibly read it. Therefore, my devoted wife has undertaken the difficult task of transcribing my notes in her own beautiful handwriting.

"In checking over her work, I sometimes find that she has transcribed a word or phrase incorrectly. As you can well understand, this can sometimes change the meaning of the passage, something which no author of *chiddushei Torah* (original Torah thoughts) wants to see happen.

"At times, I may have displayed a slight degree of irritation when such mistakes occurred. Your talk, R' Aryeh, caused me

---

1. On *Rambam's* code of Jewish law, *Yad HaChazakah*.

to think about this. I have resolved to rid myself of such feelings in the future — and yes, I thank you."

※ ※ ※

As *Rosh Yeshivah* of Beth Medrash Govoha, Rabbi Aharon Kotler[1] would commute regularly between his Boro Park apartment and his renowned yeshivah in Lakewood, New Jersey. In his early years in America, R' Aharon would make the trip by train and bus; later, his students would take turns driving him back and forth.

Once, a student was driving R' Aharon from Boro Park to Lakewood. After they had been on the road for about one-half hour, R' Aharon suddenly said, "I'm sorry, but I forgot something very important. We must return to my apartment." Knowing how precious every minute was to R' Aharon, the student asked if perhaps there was some way for the matter to be taken care of without their having to return to Boro Park. "No," replied R' Aharon, "I must take care of it right now."

When they returned to Boro Park, the student followed R' Aharon up four flights of steps to his apartment. R' Aharon unlocked the door, walked into the kitchen where his *rebbetzin* was sitting, said, *"A gutten tag"* ("Good day"), and left.

Years later, the student recalled, "The smile on the *rebbetzin's* face told me that, indeed, the *Rosh Yeshivah* had returned for something very, very important."

---

1. R' Aharon was the son-in-law of R' Isser Zalman Meltzer.

In Our Fathers' Footsteps

וַיֹּאמֶר קַח נָא אֶת בִּנְךָ אֶת יְחִידְךָ אֲשֶׁר אָהַבְתָּ אֶת יִצְחָק וְלֶךְ לְךָ אֶל אֶרֶץ
הַמֹּרִיָּה, וְהַעֲלֵהוּ שָׁם לְעֹלָה עַל אַחַד הֶהָרִים אֲשֶׁר אֹמַר אֵלֶיךָ.

And He [Hashem] said: "Please take your son, your only one,
whom you love — Yitzchak — and go to the land of Moriah;
bring him up there as an offering upon one of the mountains
which I shall tell you" (Bereishis 22:2).

Rabbi Menachem Mendelson, rabbi of *Moshav Komemius* in Israel, related the following story:

Shortly before Rosh Hashanah 5754 (1993), a little girl told her father: "*Abba* (Father), we learned in school that next year is going to be *Shemittah*, when the Land cannot be worked. You will not be allowed to work your vineyard and you must declare its grapes *hefker* (ownerless)."

"My child," replied the father, "what is the matter with you? We live from our vineyard! How do you expect to eat if I do not sell the crop as I do every year? As for not working the vineyard, it will never be the same if I don't tend to it as I always do."

The little girl looked very sad. For a while, she said nothing. Then, a thought entered her mind.

"*Abba*, have you ever heard of Avraham *Avinu* (our father Avraham)?"

"Yes, I have."

"Do you know, *Abba*, that Avraham *Avinu* had a precious son, Yitzchak? And that Hashem told Avraham to offer Yitzchak as a sacrifice? Do you know that Avraham, without any hesitation, hurried to fulfill Hashem's will?"

"I do recall studying that as a child."

"Abba, if Avraham, our forefather, was willing to give up his precious son for Hashem's sake, can't we give up our vineyard for one year?"

Her father was visibly moved. "If that's the way you put it, my dear child, I will do as you say."

פרשת חיי שרה
Parashas Chayei Sarah

Chance Encounters

וַיֹּאמַר, ה׳ אֱלֹהֵי אֲדֹנִי אַבְרָהָם, הַקְרֵה נָא לְפָנַי הַיּוֹם,
וַעֲשֵׂה חֶסֶד עִם אֲדֹנִי אַבְרָהָם.
And he [Eliezer] said: "Hashem, God of my master
Avraham, may You so arrange it for me this day
that You do kindness with my master Avraham"
(Bereishis 24:12).

When Eliezer, the servant of Avraham, went to seek a wife for Yitzchak, he requested of Hashem that Yitzchak's pre-destined wife be shown to him by way of the following test: He would stand by the city's well and ask one of the girls to allow him to drink from her water jug. The girl who would respond, "Drink, and I will even water your camels," would be the one chosen as Yitzchak's wife and a Matriarch of the Jewish nation.

In his prayer to Hashem, Eliezer said, ". . .may You so arrange it for me this day . . . ." The term הַקְרֵה, arrange is related to מִקְרֶה, a chance occurrence. [1] Now, the meeting between Eliezer and Rivkah was anything but a chance occurrence. Why, then, is this term used here?

R' Samson Raphael Hirsch explains that, in fact, the root קרה, occur, is related to קרא, call. A Jew must know that nothing in life is a matter of "coincidence," a "lucky break," or "bad luck." Everything that happens is from Hashem, whether or not His involvement is apparent to us. As in the meeting between Eliezer and Rivkah, what seems to be a chance occurrence is actually a calling from the One Above.[2]

The following story tells how a seemingly chance encounter between a rabbi and a gentile resulted in a Jew discovering the beauty of Torah and mitzvos.

David was a fine Jewish boy, who excelled in his studies and was well-liked by everyone. There was one major problem.

He attended a Catholic school.

He was born and raised in a New England city where there were no religious Jews and no Jewish school. When the quality of education in the local public school deteriorated, David's parents decided that it was no longer suitable for their son. But where would he attend classes instead? There was only one alternative — the local Catholic school. Though Jewish, David's parents knew absolutely nothing of their rich and glorious heritage. They were not enthusiastic about enrolling their son in a Catholic school, but neither were they very troubled by it.

David completed elementary school and continued on in the Catholic school's high school division. He was an "A" student and his life was totally secular.

---

1. See Vayikra 26:21.
2. See the commentary of R' Hirsch to Bereishis 49:1.

Then he entered Father McKenzie's English class.

One day, Father McKenzie assigned the class a book report on a great historical personality. Each student could select the personality of his or her choice. David went to the local library and scanned the shelves, searching for a name that had some meaning to him. The name "Maimonides" caught his eye. Maimonides, he knew, was a great figure in Jewish history. That was all he knew of the great Jewish leader and thinker known to us as *Rambam*. [1] David decided that, as a Jew, he had more in common with Maimonides than with Abraham Lincoln, Winston Churchill, or some other famous personality. He took the book home and began reading.

Three weeks later, the graded book reports were returned to the students. When David was called to come forward and pick up his report, Father McKenzie told him, "David, I want you to remain after class. There's something we have to discuss."

Class ended and David stood before his instructor. "David," the priest said, "you're the first student I've ever had who did a book report on a Jew. Why did you select Maimonides?"

"Because I'm Jewish," the boy answered quietly.

"You're Jewish?" Father McKenzie responded in astonishment. "Then what are you doing in a Catholic school?"

"My parents wanted me to get a quality education, and the public schools don't seem to be offering that any more."

The priest was silent for a while. Finally, he said, "Are you familiar with Jewish practice and ritual?"

"No," replied David, somewhat embarrassed. "Nothing at all, as a matter of fact. My home is one hundred percent secular. I don't know Hebrew any more than I know Chinese."

Father McKenzie lapsed into silence once again. Then, he picked up a pencil, wrote something on a piece of paper, and handed it to his student. "David," he said, "let me give you some advice. If you ever decide to learn about your religion, visit Jerusalem and look up this address."

---

1. An acronym for Rabbeinu Moshe ben Maimon.

That conversation awakened David to the realization that his life was empty of real meaning. If being Jewish was important, then what was he doing in a Catholic school? And if his Jewishness did not matter, then what *did* matter? The fact that he had been drawn to the book on Maimonides meant that deep inside him, his Jewishness was important to him. He had to find out what being a Jew was really all about.

As his high school graduation approached, David asked his parents for a graduation gift for which they were not prepared — a trip to Israel. Not that they had anything against visiting Israel. But what was wrong with London, Rome, or Tokyo? Why not make Israel one brief stop in a journey through Europe and the Middle and Far East? But no, David was insistent. He wanted to visit only Israel.

Upon arriving in Jerusalem, David checked his bags in a hotel and then withdrew a scrap of paper from his pocket — the paper which Father McKenzie had given him. He showed someone the address and asked for directions. Soon, he found himself standing before a structure with a sign, "Yeshivah Sha'ar HaEmes"[1] above its entrance.

David took a deep breath and opened the door.

Four years later, there was a knock on Father McKenzie's door. Standing in the doorway was a young man who was obviously a religious Jew.

"Yes. . .?" the priest asked warily.

"It's David . . . David Stone. Remember. . .? The guy who did the book report on Maimonides?"

It took a few moments for the information to register. "Yes . . . of course!" Father McKenzie finally exclaimed. "Why, David, you must have looked up that address in Jerusalem! I see they've turned you into a real yeshivah boy!"

"No, sir," David replied softly. "They didn't *turn me* into this. With G-d's help, and the help of some very wonderful people, I've turned myself into this.

1.The yeshivah's name, as well as that of the boy in the story have been changed.

"I've come here today for two reasons. Firstly, I have to thank you for giving me the address of the yeshivah. And that brings me to my second reason for coming here. How did you know the address and why did you give it to me?"

"It's very simple," said the priest. "When I was a young man studying for the priesthood, I traveled around the world to see the great religious shrines of my people. I spent most of my time in Rome and Jerusalem. I was curious to see the Wailing Wall which you Jews hold so dear, so while in Jerusalem, I went to the Wall one afternoon. I was clad in a tee-shirt and jeans, and looked like a typical tourist.

"As I stood by the Wall, a young rabbi approached me. Assuming that I was Jewish, he invited me to join him for a cup of coffee, and then offered to show me a Jewish school of higher learning for young men with limited or no religious background. Intrigued, I could not bring myself to tell him the truth, that I was actually a Catholic, studying to become a priest!

"I was really taken aback by the reception I received at the yeshivah. The people were so warm and friendly, so eager to help me get started on the road of religious observance.

"To make a long story short, I stayed at the yeshivah for three months before returning to the States. This may sound strange, but those were three of the most enjoyable months of my life.

"I've always felt guilty about my stay at the yeshivah. After all, for three months, I was taught by the rabbis and the more advanced students, I ate the yeshivah's food, slept in its dormitory — and gave them nothing in return! Worse, I fooled every one of them into thinking that he was helping a Jewish kid find his roots. It really was not right of me.

"When I learned that you were Jewish, and saw how you showed some interest in your Jewishness, I told myself that if I were to totally hide my experience from you, I would only be adding to my guilt. I had no choice but to give you that address.

"Let me tell you, David, you made a wise decision in going there."

An understatement, to say the least.

פרשת תולדות
Parashas Toldos

Worlds Apart

וְיַעֲקֹב נָתַן לְעֵשָׂו לֶחֶם וּנְזִיד עֲדָשִׁים, וַיֹּאכַל וַיֵּשְׁתְּ וַיָּקָם וַיֵּלַךְ,
וַיִּבֶז עֵשָׂו אֶת הַבְּכֹרָה.

Yaakov gave Eisav bread and lentil stew,
and he ate and drank, got up and left;
and Eisav disgraced the birthright (Bereishis 25:34).

Hashem had chosen Avraham as the father of the nation that would one day receive the Torah and live by its sacred teachings. This promise passed from Avraham to Yitzchak. Hashem's blessing to Avraham specified that the Torah would be bequeathed to one, but not both, of Yitzchak's children.[1] This is why the birthright, was so important to Yaakov, for he knew that whoever owned the birthright would inherit the spiritual blessings that Hashem had bestowed upon Avraham.

Eisav readily gave up the birthright to Yaakov, because he lived to enjoy this world; the World to Come did not concern

---

1. See *Rashi* to *Bereishis* 28:15.

him. The birthright, and the Torah which it represented, had no place in Eisav's way of life. He lived to satisfy his physical desires, not to serve his Creator by observing His *mitzvos*.

Maharal points out that the value of the letters of the word בְּכֹר, *firstborn,* allude to what the birthright represented. ב is equal to 2; כ is equal to 20; the second number when counting by tens; and ר is equal to 200, the second number when counting by hundreds. The birthright signified the right to the Torah, the privilege of becoming Hashem's chosen nation. It meant realizing that the main world is the *second world* — the World to Come, where souls bask in the splendor of the Divine Presence and reap the rewards of doing *mitzvos* in this world. Yaakov, who understood the value of Torah and appreciated the incomparable reward of the World to Come, valued the birthright, while Eisav spurned it.

One of the most famous converts to Judaism in recent centuries was Avraham ben Avraham, the *ger tzeddek* of Vilna. In an age when the Catholic Church was extremely powerful and conversion to Judaism was strictly forbidden, this young man, the son of a Polish count, left his native country and secretly became a member of the Jewish people. Day and night, he pored over the teachings of Torah with an unquenchable thirst and commitment.

Eventually, Avraham ben Avraham returned to his native Poland, where he settled in a village and studied Torah throughout the day in a local *beis midrash.* The Polish authorities caught up with him; he was arrested and senten-ced by the Church to be burnt at the stake. According to a tradition related by Rabbi Aharon Kotler, the Vilna *Gaon* sent a message to Avraham ben Avraham in prison in which he offered to use his knowledge of *Kabbalah* to free him. The *ger tzeddek* responded, "Since I first recognized the true G-d, I prayed that I might be granted the opportunity to die *al kiddush Hashem* (for the sanctification of G-d's Holy Name). Now that I have been granted the opportunity, I do not want to forgo it."

It was on the second day of Shavuos some two hundred years ago that his pure soul ascended to Heaven with the cry of *Shema Yisrael* on his lips.

The Chofetz Chaim would say the following in Avraham ben Avraham's name:

Our Sages teach that when the Torah was to be given, Hashem offered the Torah to the other nations, but each refused it because at least one of the Ten Commandments contradicted that nation's sinful way of life. This, said Avraham ben Avraham, means that *the majority* of that nation rejected the Torah. However, there were individuals who did want the Torah, but were outnumbered. These souls reappear in later generations as righteous converts.

One year, on the second day of Shavuos, the Chofetz Chaim's saintly son-in-law, Rabbi Tzvi Hirsh Levinsohn, related the following:

As the brutal Church guards were leading Avraham ben Avraham to his death, they taunted him, "You probably plan to get even with us when you get to the next world — or don't you?"

Calmly and sincerely, he replied, "When I was a little boy, I enjoyed fashioning small soldiers out of clay. Once, I made ten or twelve handsome soldiers and arranged them in a row on the front lawn of my family's estate. Then, along came some peasant children and trampled them to pieces! I ran to my father and with tears rolling down my cheeks, I told him of the 'catastrophe' that had occurred. 'Father,' I pleaded, 'you have power — you must punish those awful children at once!' My father refused to become involved in the matter. I vowed to myself that when I would grow up and have power of my own, I would take revenge.

"Well," Avraham ben Avraham asked his tormentors, "do you think that I took revenge when I grew up? Of course not. After all, the only thing they had done was to ruin something of little value — nothing more than dried mud!

"And I say the same to you. You are about to take my body of flesh and blood, which in any case was destined to return to the earth at some point in time. On the other hand, you cannot in any way harm my soul, which lives on forever. Why then should I seek revenge from you in the next world? In Heaven, where the true purpose of life is crystal clear, I shall not give any thought to your wicked ways."

פרשת ויצא
Parashas Vayeitzei

The Strength of Silence

וַיְהִי בַבֹּקֶר, וְהִנֵּה הִיא לֵאָה.
And it was, in the morning,
that behold it was Leah! (Bereishis 29:25).

The *Midrash*[1] relates that upon the destruction of the first *Beis HaMikdash*, the souls of Avraham, Yitzchak and Yaakov came before Hashem to plead for mercy on behalf of the Jewish people. Their efforts, though, did not succeed. Then Rachel came before Hashem and said:

---

1. *Midrash Rabbah,* introduction to *Megilas Eichah* §24.

"It is known before You that Your servant Yaakov wanted to marry me and worked for seven hard years for that purpose. But my father Lavan decided to deceive Yaakov and give my older sister Leah to him instead. My heart ached and I could have revealed the truth to Yaakov before it was too late, but I did not want to see my sister, Leah, humiliated. I suppressed all my feelings and emotions and revealed to Leah the secret signs that Yaakov and I had made up between ourselves as guarantees against my father's trickery.

"Dear G-d, please see how I acted, though I am a mere mortal of flesh and blood! I overcame my natural feelings and gave to my sister what was rightfully mine! In that merit, please do not forsake my children."

Hashem responded: "Hold back your voice from crying, and your eyes from weeping, for your efforts will bear fruit, and your descendants will return to their Land."[1]

A well-known rule of Heavenly judgment is *midah k'neged midah* (measure for measure); the punishment fits the crime. This applies in a positive sense as well. The more forgiving Jews are toward each other, the more love they display toward one another, the more forgiving is Hashem of their misdeeds and the more love He showers upon them.

There are times when our feelings are hurt by others and we feel a tremendous urge to respond the same way. There are also times when others are awarded something that we feel deserving of and we have a strong desire to speak up and demand what, to our minds, is rightfully our own. These are moments when Hashem looks down from Heaven and takes careful note of our reaction. Do we have the inner strength to remain silent in the face of insult, in order that argument and senseless hatred be avoided? Can we refrain from demanding what we think is our own, so that the other person not be hurt and possibly embarrassed?

Rachel's silence was an incredible display of self-sacrifice. She knew full well that by giving up the opportunity to marry

---

1. See *Yirmiyahu* 31:15.

Yaakov, she was losing the opportunity to be the mother of the nation that would receive the Torah and carry out Hashem's will on this earth. Yet Rachel was not deterred by this. In making her decision, she saw before her one decisive factor — the tremendous shame that her sister would experience were Lavan's trickery to be revealed as Leah stood under the wedding canopy.

And because of Rachel's self-sacrifice, Hashem promised that the Jewish people would be redeemed from exile.

❧ ❧ ❧

It was the first day of the Six Day War in 1967. Jerusalem was coming under shelling from the area of the Old City, which was still under Jordanian control. The basement dining room of the Mirrer Yeshivah, which was not far from the pre-War border, was now a very crowded bomb shelter. Men, women, and children filled the large room, frightened by the warning sirens and the occasional sounds of explosions. The yeshivah students and their *rebbeim* were joined by the others in reciting chapter upon chapter of *Tehillim.* The mood was grim.

Shells began whistling overhead, striking dangerously close to the yeshivah. Then, it happened. A direct hit! The entire building shook from the force of the explosion. People thought that this was the end and shouted *Shema Yisrael.*

Among the assembled was a woman whose husband, a scoundrel, had deserted her some twenty years earlier without giving her a *get* (bill of divorce) so that she would be free to marry another man. Since the day of her husband's desertion, the woman had supported herself and her children by washing other people's clothing. Her life was one of sheer misery.

As the people cried out what they thought might be their final words, the voice of this woman was the loudest of all. She was shouting something else. *"Ribono shel Olam,"* she cried, "my husband abandoned me twenty years ago. I have suffered so much — but I forgive him! Just as I have forgiven him, please forgive the Jewish people for all we have done wrong."

Soon after, the shelling stopped. Not much time passed before the Israeli army broke through the Jordanian border defense and captured the Old City.

Among those present during the shelling was Rabbi Chaim Shmulevitz, the Mirrer Yeshivah's legendary *Rosh Yeshivah.* In his talks in the years that followed, Reb Chaim would shed tears when describing this woman's plight. He was convinced, he would say, that it had been her sincere words of forgiveness which had saved them all.

פרשת וישלח
Parashas Vayishlach

The Primary Weapon

וַיִּוָּתֵר יַעֲקֹב לְבַדּוֹ, וַיֵּאָבֵק אִישׁ עמוֹ עַד עֲלוֹת הַשָּׁחַר.

Yaakov was left alone and a man wrestled with him until the break of dawn (Bereishis 32:25).

The Torah tells of the struggle between Yaakov and the angel of Eisav, who is Satan. Why did Satan choose to do battle with Yaakov and not with Avraham and Yitzchak who preceded him?

Rabbi Elchonon Wasserman explained this with a parable: A war cannot be considered won as long as both sides still have their weapons. However, when one side is disarmed and has nothing left with which to fight, the war is surely over.

There is only one way for man to achieve victory in his struggle with Satan: *I [Hashem] have created the evil inclination and I have created Torah as its antidote* (*Kiddushin* 30b). As long as the Jewish people study Torah diligently, there is hope that they will abandon their sins and return to Hashem with a full heart. However, when the Jewish people grow weak in their study of Torah, the primary weapon against the *yetzer hara* has been lost.

Each of the Patriarchs excelled in a particular area. Avraham was the Pillar of *Chesed* (Kindness). Yitzchak was the Pillar of *Avodah* (Service to Hashem). Yaakov was the Pillar of Torah. His struggle with Satan foretold that in later generations, Satan's primary efforts against our people would be directed toward weakening our study of Torah.

❦ ❦ ❦

In Eastern Europe at the turn of the nineteenth century, there lived a boy named Yosef, known by the nickname 'Yosse'le.' Yosse'le had a great deal of potential, and a lot that could hinder that potential. He was bright, astute, insightful; but also adventurous, restless and impulsive. He could not sit still for more than a moment.

Yosse'le's father recognized his son's unusual mental abilities and hired the choicest of Torah teachers. He prayed fervently to Hashem that his son grow to be a great Torah scholar. As time went on, however, it became increasingly clear that Yosse'le's unbridled nature was winning. He could not keep his mind focused on the *sefer* in front of him, and teaching him was an impossible chore.

Much to his parents' dismay, Yosse'le found himself without a *rebbi*. All day he roamed the streets getting into mischief. As Yosse'le approached bar-mitzvah, his father and mother wept over their son.

One day, Yosse'le heard a mother scolding her child, "What do you think, you are going to become another *Yosse'le*, roaming the streets and getting into mischief? No! We will not permit this!"

Yosse'le froze. So this is how he was perceived — the symbol of mischief, of trouble, of failure!

That was the turning point in Yosse'le's young life. He headed straight for home and informed his parents that he was ready to turn over a new leaf. But there was one condition.

"I do not want to remain at home and study with other boys my age. I know that I have above-average ability, and I will use that ability to the fullest. I want to study in Volozhin."

The Yeshivah of Volozhin was founded in 1803 by Rabbi Chaim Volozhiner, famed disciple of the Vilna *Gaon.* The studies in the yeshivah were very advanced, and one was required to know at least two orders of *Shas* to gain admission. Yosse'le's degree of knowledge did not even come close.

His father tried to dissuade him, but Yosse'le was very determined. He was going to Volozhin, and he would succeed, somehow. His mother helped him pack his few belongings, his father gave him some money and his blessings. With bated breath, they bid farewell to their son.

Yosse'le arrived in Volozhin and introduced himself to the *Rosh Yeshivah*. No, he told R' Chaim, he did not know very much in the way of Torah. But he was resolved to do everything humanly possible to grow great in Torah knowledge. R' Chaim Volozhiner had little trouble perceiving the boy's sincerity and iron-willed determination, and he assigned a number of qualified students as Yossel'e's tutors until he had progressed enough to enter a class.

From then on, Yosse'le channeled every ounce of concentration toward the study of Torah. Before long, he had joined the 'eighteen-hour group,' a contingent of dedicated students who studied for eighteen hours a day, every single day. Yosse'le remained in Volozhin for many years and rose to become one of R' Chaim's most outstanding disciples.

One day, Yosse'le received a letter from home. His father's

tailor shop had been ravaged by fire. The family was virtually penniless. Yosse'le was needed at home.

He brought the letter to his *rosh yeshivah* who read it carefully. R' Chaim's feelings for the devastated family were obvious. He reached for a quill to write a letter of condolence. Turning to Yosse'le, R' Chaim said, "It is indeed an extremely difficult situation. However, my advice is that you remain here in the yeshivah."

Over the next few months, more letters arrived, each one worse than the previous one. The situation at home was becoming intolerable. When was Yosse'le coming home?

R' Chaim's reaction did not change. He was dismayed, he sympathized, he offered suggestions, and he even sent some money. But his advice to Yosse'le was still the same — remain in yeshivah.

Years passed. One day, a delegation from Yosse'le's town arrived. Their *rav* had died and they were seeking a replacement. R' Chaim sent for Yosse'le. When Yosse'le entered the room, R' Chaim rose to his full height as a sign of respect. Turning to the delegation, R' Chaim said, "Do you remember Yosse'le? He is truly an outstanding *talmid chacham*. Your city can take pride in him. He will make an excellent *rav*."

When Yosse'le went to take leave of his *rosh yeshivah,* R' Chaim gazed at him lovingly and said, "Take note, my son, of how precious your Torah study is in Heaven. Satan tried everything he could to deprive the world of your study. However, you persevered, and today you are ready to lead a community as an outstanding *talmid chacham*.

"Remember well that which has transpired. Satan would do everything in his power to prevent one *ben Torah* from realizing his potential in Torah."

פרשת וישב
Parashas Vayeishev

With No Alternative

וַתֹּאמֶר, הַכֶּר נָא, לְמִי הַחֹתֶמֶת וְהַפְּתִילִים וְהַמַּטֶּה הָאֵלֶּה.
*And she [Tamar] said, "Identify, if you please,
whose are this seal, this wrap, and this staff"*
(Bereishis 38:25).

T he righteous Tamar did not shame Yehudah publicly by identifying him as the one with whom she had lived [a fact of which Yehudah, at that point, was unaware]. She reasoned: "If, upon recognizing his seal, wrap and staff, he admits it voluntarily, well and good; if not, let them burn me, but let me not publicly disgrace him." From here, our Sages derive, "One should let himself be thrown into a fiery furnace rather than shame his neighbor in public" (*Sotah* 10b).

❦ ❦ ❦

It was a cool night in Jerusalem and the hour was late. Rabbi Isser Zalman Meltzer was sitting in his small apartment studying Torah together with Rabbi David Finkel, a much younger scholar with whom he was very close. Their learning was interrupted by a knock on the door.

A young man wished to speak to the *Rosh Yeshivah.* He apologized for coming at that late hour. The matter could not wait, he explained.

R' Isser Zalman led the visitor into another room so that they could talk privately. A few minutes later, R' Isser Zalman came out of the room looking very upset. He was muttering to himself: "How can such a thing be allowed to happen? How can one be lenient in such a matter?" R' Isser Zalman walked past his *rebbetzin* and study partner without even a glance and entered another room so that he could be alone.

R' Isser Zalman was a frail man and his *rebbetzin* became quite concerned whenever she saw her husband become agitated. She asked R' David Finkel to enter the room and find out what exactly was troubling her husband. R' David found R' Isser Zalman sitting on a bed, muttering to himself, 'Oh, my head! It feels like it is about to burst. . ."

"What is the matter?" asked R' David anxiously.

"Please, I need to be alone," was R' Isser Zalman's very uncharacteristic answer. Now, R' David became even more concerned. "Please, *Rosh Yeshivah,* perhaps I can help. . ."

"I need to be alone. Please leave the room," came the reply.

Some time passed. Finally, R' Isser Zalman came out of the room, his face flushed with emotion. He hurried back into the room where his visitor still sat. *Rebbetzin* Meltzer and R' David sat anxiously as they heard R' Isser Zalman pounding his fist on the table and shouting, "Such a thing cannot be! To spill the blood of a fine Jewish daughter! Absolutely not!"

Soon the door opened and R' Isser Zalman emerged, followed by the young man. "Well, if this is how the *Rosh Yeshivah* feels. . ." the young man was saying.

"Certainly, certainly!" R' Isser Zalman interjected. "I have no doubt that this is correct. *Mazal tov,* and in a year from now, you will inform me of the *bris."*

When the young man left, R' Isser Zalman turned to his *rebbetzin* and explained:

The young man had become engaged to a fine religious girl. During the engagement, she had been examined by a doctor who determined that she could not have children. The young man had come to ask R' Isser Zalman if he should break the engagement, since according to the doctor, their marriage would never be blessed with children.

Reb Isser Zalman's initial reaction was that the young man had no choice but to break the engagement. However, he then began to ponder how the girl would feel once the engagement would be broken. What grief, what humiliation! To break the engagement would be like spilling the blood of this wonderful girl.

After thinking the matter through some more, R' Isser Zalman came to the conclusion that the girl's feelings must be the deciding factor. The engagement must not be broken.

One year later, R' Isser Zalman was *sandak* for the couple's newborn boy (from *B'Derech Eitz Chaim*).

פרשת מקץ
Parashas Mikeitz

Trust in Hashem

וַיַּעַן יוֹסֵף אֶת פַּרְעֹה לֵאמֹר בִּלְעָדָי, אֱלֹהִים יַעֲנֶה אֶת שְׁלוֹם פַּרְעֹה.
Yosef answered Pharaoh, saying,
"That [to interpret dreams] is beyond me;
it is God Who will respond with Pharaoh's welfare"
(Bereishis 41:16).

At the conclusion of *Parashas Vayeishev,* Yosef correctly interpreted the dreams of two of Pharaoh's servants who were with him in prison. At that time, Yosef requested of the *Sar HaMashkim* (Chamberlain of the Cupbearers) that upon his release from prison, he should mention Yosef's worthiness before Pharaoh. However, this did not happen. "Yet the *Sar HaMashkim* did not remember Yosef, but he forgot him" (*Bereishis* 40:23). Our Sages teach that because Yosef placed his trust in Pharaoh's servant he was punished by having his prison sentence extended for another two years.

What had Yosef done wrong? Are we not required to do whatever we can to help ourselves, and only then rely on

Hashem to do the rest? Would any of us have done differently had we been in Yosef's situation?

The Chazon Ish explained that there are many levels of trust in Hashem. For the average person, Yosef's request of the Chamberlain of the Cupbearers would have been perfectly in order. For Yosef, however, it was a mistake. He had lived in Egypt for twenty years, one Jew among a population of very sinful people. He had remained Yosef *HaTzaddik* by being constantly aware of Hashem's Presence; not for a moment did he forget that wherever he went, Hashem was with him. For Yosef, it was a mistake to rely on the help of a human being. He should have relied on Hashem alone to end his imprisonment.

It may be that Yosef made amends for his mistake with his very first words to Pharaoh. Pharaoh had said to him, "I dreamt a dream, but no one can interpret it. Now I heard it said of you that you comprehend a dream to interpret it." Yosef responded, "That is beyond me; it is G-d who will respond with Pharaoh's welfare." Yosef was telling Pharaoh that he deserved no credit for his correct interpretation of the Chamberlain of the Cupbearers' dream, for Hashem had placed the interpretation into his mind.

It would seem that if Yosef had been taken from prison solely because of his ability to interpret dreams, he would have better assured his freedom by remaining silent. It would be to his advantage to allow the king to think that he was a man of supernatural power, and that his own abilities had made it possible for him to interpret the dreams correctly.

However, Yosef, the man of oustanding faith and trust in Hashem, could not permit this. He could not remain silent as Pharaoh spoke his praise. Yosef saw no alternative but to speak the truth: it was Hashem, and not he, Who was the true interpreter of dreams.

❦ ❦ ❦

The Brisker *Rav,* Rabbi Yitzchak Zev Soloveitchik, achieved a very high level of trust in Hashem. Whenever anyone expressed concern over the need for money or some other thing, the Rav would say, "When you really need it, it will be there." And he lived by this teaching.

At one point, the *Rav* was taking two pills a day of a certain medication manufactured in Switzerland. One day, he found himself with only two pills remaining, and had no idea when the next shipment would be arriving. Someone suggested that he take one pill on that day, and leave the other for the following day. The *Rav* disagreed. "If I need two pills today, then I must take two pills today. I'm not worried about tomorrow. 'When you really need it, it will be there.' "

The next morning, a total stranger knocked on the *Rav's* door, bearing a package which had been handed to him the previous day at the airport in Switzerland. Inside was a fresh supply of pills.

❧ ❧ ❧

In the summer of 1939, the *Rav* and his eldest son, R' Yosef Dov ('R' Berel') spent a few weeks in Otvotsk, Poland, a resort spot for many *rabbanim* and *roshei yeshivah.* On September 1, 1939 (24 *Elul* 5699), World War II erupted with the German invasion of Poland. The *Rav* and his son fled to Warsaw, where they took refuge with a Jewish family.

Food became very scarce; each morning, bread lines which stretched for blocks would form in the heart of the city, as people waited for their meager rations. A man who had fled the *Rav's* town of Brisk took it upon himself to supply the *Rav* with a daily provision of bread. While the amount was less than one would eat under normal conditions, it was enough to provide minimal nourishment and still leave some over for the next day, in case of emergency. The *Rav,* however, did not leave anything over. He reasoned, "If I eat the full provision today, I will have more strength to serve Hashem today. I'm not worried about tomorrow."

The eighth of *Tishrei* was the only time that the Rav was in doubt as to what to do. The next day would be *erev* Yom

Kippur, when it is a *mitzvah* to eat.[1] Perhaps, for the sake of a *mitzvah*, one should leave over some food? The *Rav* decided to leave over a portion of his bread.

The next day, a woman who was formerly from Brisk surprised the *Rav* with a delicious meal which she had prepared especially for him. She explained that one item was missing from the menu — *challah*. On the previous night, a German bomb had hit her home. Miraculously, the house suffered no damage — except for the oven, which blew up with her *challos* inside.

The *Rav* saw this as Heaven's way of demonstrating that he should not have left over any bread. Had he placed his trust in Hashem, he would have had fresh *challah* for the *mitzvah* of eating on *erev* Yom Kippur.

---

1. See *Shulchan Aruch, Orach Chaim* 604:1.

פרשת ויגש
Parashas Vayigash

Questions Without Answers

וַיֹּאמֶר יוֹסֵף אֶל אֶחָיו, "אֲנִי יוֹסֵף . . ."
And Yosef said to his brothers, "I am Yosef . . ." (Bereishis 45:3).

When Yosef said, "I am Yosef," Hashem's master plan suddenly became clear to the brothers. They now understood why Pharaoh's viceroy — their own flesh and blood — had acted as he did. Furthermore, everything that had transpired during the past twenty-two years, from the time Yosef had dreamt his prophetic dreams, suddenly became clear as well.

So, too, will it be at the time of Mashiach's arrival, when Hashem will reveal Himself and announce, "I am HASHEM." The veil will be lifted from our eyes and we will understand all that transpired in our nation's history (the Chofetz Chaim).

Baruch did not understand. His father did not understand. Baruch and his family lived in Russia in the early 1900's, and Baruch studied Torah in one of the great *yeshivos* of that era. Life had been very peaceful for Baruch. His father was a wealthy businessman and had provided for his family's every need. Baruch had been taught Torah by the finest teachers and was a young budding *talmid chacham.* His parents hoped that within a few years their son would marry and raise a generation that would be another link in their family's golden chain.

Then came the draft notice. Baruch remembered the day well. How could he forget it? He had been home from yeshivah to be with his family for the *yomim tovim.* A registered letter addressed to him, bearing a government stamp, had arrived. He was to report in three weeks for induction into the Russian army.

He had been overcome with dread. For a religious Jew, the army was far more than a place of physical danger. The Czars of Russia were known for their rabid anti-Semitism. In the nineteenth century, the infamous Cantonist decrees of Czar Nikolai had taken thousands of young Jewish boys away from their families to spend as much as twenty-five years in the Russian army where they were taught to reject every detail of their glorious Jewish heritage. By the time Baruch had been born, those decrees had been rescinded, but the Russian army was known for its hatred of Jews and their Torah. Being a soldier could mean being forced to desecrate the Shabbos, to eat non-kosher food and to live in the company of vulgar, rough gentiles who often came from the very lowest levels of society. In short, for a Jew to be a Russian soldier was a matter of spiritual danger.

It is no wonder, then, that religious boys used any and every means to avoid army service. Some would go so far as to intentionally cause their bodies injury so that they would be declared physically unfit to serve.

There was another way to avoid the draft: bribery. Army doctors were often willing and eager to write a false medical report for the right price. Thus, boys from wealthy homes were usually able to avoid army service. Of course, there was no guarantee. One had to hope that the doctor responsible for his checkup would be willing to accept the bribe and that the ruse would work.

Baruch's father was one of the wealthiest Jews in his city. So, while Baruch was understandably upset by the draft notice, he knew that there was good reason to think that he would be granted an exemption. His father assured him that he would make the doctor an "offer" that he would not refuse.

It was common for boys who had received draft notices to seek a blessing from the generation's greatest *tzaddik*, the holy Chofetz Chaim. A deeply religious man, Baruch's father did not rely on his bribery efforts alone. He purchased train tickets for both himself and his son, and the two headed for the small Polish town of Radin.

The Chofetz Chaim was then in his seventies, but his mind had lost none of his sharpness. People from near and far would stream to his small home to seek his blessing, counsel, and prayers.

Baruch's father greeted the Chofetz Chaim and explained Baruch's situation. He concluded, "Please bless my son that he should be successful in avoiding army service."

The Chofetz Chaim was silent for a few moments. Then, in his soft, gentle voice, he said, "And what is so bad if he will learn how to shoot?"

Baruch and his father thought that they had not heard correctly. They respectfully asked the *tzaddik* to repeat himself — and he did. "And what is so bad if he will learn how to shoot?"

"*Rebbe,*" Baruch's father pleaded anxiously, "we're talking about the Russian army! Anti-Semites! Desecration of *Shabbos!* Non-kosher food! Danger to the body and the soul! Please, *Rebbe,* a blessing!"

The Chofetz Chaim was silent.

Baruch and his father left the Chofetz Chaim's house in a daze. What had he meant? Certainly he was aware of the dangers facing a religious Jew in the Russian army. And countless yeshivah students had come before the Chofetz Chaim for the same reason, and had been granted the blessing they had requested. Why was Baruch different?

A difficult question, with no apparent answer.

Two days later, Baruch was at the induction center for his physical exam. He entered the examination room and showed the doctor his identification card. The doctor smiled and said, "Ah, yes. Your father spoke with me the other day. There shouldn't be any problem. I'll write out a report which will declare you absolutely unfit to serve as a soldier." The doctor picked up his clipboard and began to write.

Suddenly, the door of the room swung open and in walked an army officer. Looking the tall, well-built Baruch up and down, the officer said, "I like this fellow! Good, strong build. He'll make an excellent soldier! Make a note on his report that I want him assigned to my battalion." The officer turned and left.

"I give you my word, this never happened before," the doctor told Baruch as soon as the door had closed. "Never in all my years as an army doctor did an officer enter the room while an examination was in progress." The doctor now removed the report sheet from his clipboard and tore it into shreds. "I'm really sorry — for both of us, that is. There's no way I'm going to risk filling out a false report when the officer ordered that you be assigned to his batallion. Of course, I'll return your father's money. Now, let me examine you so that I can write a true report . . ."

Late that night, Baruch and his parents sat around the kitchen table as if in mourning. They simply could not believe that all this had really happened. "You know," Baruch's father finally said, "I sincerely believe in that which our Sages teach: 'A *tzaddik* decrees and Hashem fulfills that decree.' It seems that the Chofetz Chaim decreed that you, Baruch, should serve in the army and learn how to shoot a rifle — and Hashem has fulfilled that decree. The question is, why is it necesssary for you to learn how to shoot? It is a question for which I have no answer."

Baruch fought on the front lines in World War I. He earned the admiration of his comrades as an excellent sharpshooter and as an expert at repairing broken guns. When his army service had ended, he returned home still a yeshivah *bachur.*

But the unusual happenings that led to his induction remained a troubling, unanswered mystery.

Twenty-five years passed. Baruch was residing in Poland when the Second World War erupted. The German beasts forced the Jews of his town into a cramped, ten block area, which they surrounded with barbed wire.

Life in the ghetto was unbearable. As the days wore on, food and drink became more and more scarce and Jews were either shot or taken away, never to be heard from again.

One day, Baruch approached two of his friends. "I've been observing the movements of the Nazi guards near the ghetto fence. There is one spot that is not well-guarded. It might be possible to cut a hole in the fence during the night and flee to the forest.

"Only through a miracle can we possibly survive in this ghetto. I feel that it is worth the risk to attempt an escape. I'm going to try tonight. You're both invited to join me."

That night, the three met at the appointed spot. Using wire-cutting tools, Baruch cut a hole in the fence and the three crawled out to freedom. Ten minutes later, they found themselves in the forest. They paused for a few minutes under a tree to catch their breath and rest from the incredible tension which they has just endured.

As they rested, there was a rustling sound in the bushes nearby. Moments later, the three defenseless Jews stood face to face with a tall, fierce-looking figure who aimed his rifle directly at them.

"Jews! Again, some Jews trespass into our territory! Well, your bravery has not done you much good, useless souls that you are. . ."

The man spoke Polish, and it was obvious who he was. . .

"Wait!" Baruch exclaimed. "You're a Polish Partisan, fighting against the accursed Germans. Please don't harm us. We're all on the same side, trying to overcome a common enemy. Let us join your group and we will serve as loyal soldiers!"

The Partisan sneered derisively. "Serve us loyally! Sure, you Jews will promise anything to save your skins. You're all half-starved and have never picked up a gun in your lives. How in the world can you help us? No, all you'll do is deplete our resources and be a burden to us."

"You're wrong!" Baruch responded. "I fought in the Russian Army in the First World War. I was a sharpshooter, and became an expert at repairing weaponry. Let me demonstrate my skills and you'll see that I'm telling the truth."

The Partisan was intrigued and marched the three deeper into the forest where they encountered other Partisans. Baruch was given a rifle to repair and was given a chance to show his shooting skills. He passed both tests with flying colors. The Partisans were obviously impressed and welcomed him into their ranks.

"What about my two friends?" Baruch asked. "It's a package deal. If you accept me, you have to accept them as well."

Baruch and his friends survived the war in the forests of Poland, fighting the Germans in numerous skirmishes. When the war ended, Baruch thanked Hashem for the miracles which had brought about his survival — especially the fact that he had learned how to shoot.

❧ ❧ ❧

Like One Man, With One Heart

כָּל הַנֶּפֶשׁ לְבֵית יַעֲקֹב הַבָּאָה מִצְרַיְמָה שִׁבְעִים.
*All the souls of Yaakov's household
who came to Egypt — seventy (Bereishis 46:27).*

The Chofetz Chaim writes (*Shemiras HaLashon, Sha'ar HaTevunah* — ch. 6):

The Hebrew word for "souls" is *nefashos*. Yet, in this verse, the singular form, *nefesh*, is used, alluding to the fact that in

Heaven, the souls of the people of Israel are like one. Each Jewish soul, while part of one whole, is distinct and unique, like a person whose body is a single unit comprised of many individual parts, each with its own distinct and unique function.

The Chofetz Chaim translates this point into practical terms:

"If another Jew refuses to do a favor that you have asked of him, or even if he has caused you heartache or has shamed you in some way, do not seek revenge or bear a grudge. For who is 'oneself' and who is 'one's fellow'? — both stem from the same source, as it is written, 'And who is like Your nation, Israel, one nation on earth?' " (*I Divrei HaYamim* 17:21).

❀ ❀ ❀

The year 1911 saw the entire Jewish world in an uproar over the infamous "blood libel" case against Mendel Beilis, an unassuming Russian Jew who was falsely accused of murdering a Christian child in order to use its blood for Jewish ritual. Well aware that it was virtually unheard of for an observant Jew to commit any sort of violent crime, the prosecution sought some sort of "proof" that the Torah permits such crimes against people of other faiths.

Someone uncovered the following Talmudic statement (*Yevamos* 61a): " 'Now you, My sheep, the sheep of My pasture — you are Adam [Man]' (*Yechezkel* 34:31) — You [Israel] are called Adam, but the nations of the world are not called Adam." Is this not conclusive proof, claimed the prosecution, that the Jews view the gentiles as sub-human? And if gentiles are sub-human, then did it not follow that for a Jew to kill a gentile for his blood is no worse than to slaughter an animal for its meat?

A response to this accusation was provided by Rabbi Meir Shapiro, then a relatively unknown *Rav* in the Eastern Galician town of Galina and the future *rav* of Lublin and originator of the *Daf Yomi*. He explained: The term "Adam — Man" as used in the Talmudic passage in no way indicates that non-Jews are not considered "man." Rather, it indicates that the Jewish people stands alone as a nation that is, in a real sense, like *one man.*

When a person has an inflammation in his foot, one cannot say that the man's foot hurts, but the rest of him feels fine. A person's entire body is affected by a disorder in a single limb. Similarly, the souls of the Jewish people are bound up with one another. When one Jew is hurting, all Jews, even those who do not know him or her personally, feel the person's pain and suffering in a way that simply is not found among any other nation on earth. Only the Jewish nation is like a single soul.

❀ ❀ ❀

Our Sages teach that the Second Destruction came about because of senseless hatred among Jews (*Yoma* 9b). The Chofetz Chaim comments: If senseless hatred destroyed an existing *Beis HaMikdash*, surely it has the power to prevent the third *Beis HaMikdash* from being built!

Our Sages also teach that the Jewish people arrived at Sinai to receive the Torah "like one man with one heart" (see *Rashi* to *Shemos* 19:2). Without unity, says *Ohr HaChaim,* the Jewish people could not have received the Torah.

Tana D'Vei Eliyahu (I, ch. 28) states: "The Holy One, Blessed is He, said to Israel: 'My beloved children! Is there anything I lack that I should have to ask it of you? All I ask of you is that you love one another, that you honor one another, that you respect one another. In this way, no sin, robbery, or base deed will be found among you, so that you will remain pure forever.' "

פרשת ויחי
Parashas Vayechi

The Sword and the Bow

וַאֲנִי נָתַתִּי לְךָ שְׁכֶם אַחַד עַל אַחֶיךָ,
אֲשֶׁר לָקַחְתִּי מִיַּד הָאֱמֹרִי בְּחַרְבִּי וּבְקַשְׁתִּי.
*And as for me, I have given you Shechem — one
portion more than your brothers, which I took
from the hand of the Emorite with my sword
and with my bow (Bereishis 48:22).*

*With my sword and with my bow — with my prayer
and with my beseeching (Targum Onkelos).*

*Prayer is like a sword because it can pierce the very
Heavens. It is like a bow because just as an arrow's
swiftness, power and distance depend on the pressure
which the archer exerts on the bow, so too, the power
of a person's prayer depends on his sincerity and how
intense is his concentration (Maharal).*

In the first half of this century, there lived a *Rav* in
Pittsburgh, Pennsylvania named Rabbi Moshe Shimon
Zivetz. R' Zivetz was a renowned *talmid chacham* and authored
a number of *sefarim*.

R' Zivetz' name was well-known in Torah communities
everywhere. One of the greatest Torah genuises of his
generation was the *Imrei Emes*, Rabbi Avraham Mordechai

Alter of Ger. The *Imrei Emes* had one of the largest Torah libraries in the world; it numbered tens of thousands of *sefarim* and he was familiar with the contents of every single *sefer.*

When a great scholar named Rabbi Moshe Nachum Yerushalmski died, the *Imrei Emes* purchased his entire library. In a letter written shortly thereafter, he wrote, "When I merited, with the help of Hashem, to acquire the *sefarim* left behind [by R' Yerushalmski], I rejoiced over having acquired the *sefarim* . . . by the *gaon,* R' Moshe Shimon Zivetz, may Hashem lengthen his days and years."

In 1931, Rabbi Yaakov Yitzchak Ruderman arrived in America, where he would later found Yeshivah Ner Israel in Baltimore. When R' Ruderman emigrated from Europe, he was already regarded as one of the generation's most outstanding young *talmidei chachamim* and had authored a work entitled *Avodas Levi.* R' Ruderman felt it proper to mail a copy of his *sefer* to R' Zivetz, whose *sefarim* he had studied. A few weeks later, R' Ruderman received a letter from R' Zivetz thanking him for the *sefer.* Along with the letter was a check made out to R' Ruderman in the amount of fifty dollars.

R' Ruderman did not understand. He was grateful that his *sefer* had found favor with this great *talmid chacham* — but why the fifty dollars? If R' Zivetz had meant to pay for the cost of the *sefer* (which had been sent as a gift), a few dollars would have been sufficient. Fifty dollars was a huge sum in those days. What had prompted R' Zivetz to send it?

Some time later, R' Ruderman visited Pittsburgh and stayed at the home of R' Zivetz. He thanked R' Zivetz for the letter and check. "It seems to me, though," he continued, "that the *Rav* was far too generous in sending me so large a sum."

There was silence for a while as R' Zivetz pondered his reply. "I will tell you," he finally said. "I have been *Rav* here for many years and *baruch Hashem,* the people here appreciate me very much.

"Some time ago, I was visited by the board members of our congregation. They expressed their appreciation to me for all that I had done for them over the years. They said that while they hoped that I would serve as their *Rav* for many more years, they realized that the day might soon come when it would simply be too taxing on me to continue to lead them. I would want to retire — but from what would I live?

"A meeting of all the congregation's members had been held — without my knowledge, of course — to discuss this matter. At the meeting, it was suggested that everyone contribute some money toward a retirement fund for my sake. Everyone was asked to contribute whatever they could.

"The chairman of the board presented me with a check for the full amount that had been raised at that meeting. I could not believe my eyes — twenty thousand dollars!

"I did not feel comfortable accepting this gift, but my congregants would have it no other way. They made it clear that the money was mine and I was free to do with it as I saw fit.

"I took the check and deposited it in a savings account, not knowing exactly what I was going to do with it. Should I leave it in the account so that interest could accrue, or should I invest it in some high-dividend venture? Or, perhaps I should purchase something like gold or silver which would almost certainly increase in value as time went on?

"Over the next few weeks, something very disturbing began to happen. All my life, I was always able to *daven* (pray) with proper concentration. When I would pray the *Shemoneh Esrei*, I was able to focus on the meaning of each and every word.

"But now, things were different. I would begin *Shemoneh Esrei* and before I knew it, my mind was on my money. This happened not once or twice, but many times. My *davening* just wasn't the same anymore.

"I gave the matter some thought, and finally decided that as long as I possessed this small fortune, I would not be able to overcome my problem. I never had money before and now that I did, I was overwhelmed by it. There was only one thing that I could do so that I could once again *daven* properly — I would have to get rid of the money.

"To return the money was not an option. I knew that my beloved congregants would never accept it. I had to find some other way to be rid of of it. So it is a couple of years now that I have become a generous philanthropist. In years past, when a *rosh yeshivah* would arrive from Europe to raise money for his yeshivah, I would write out a check for ten dollars. Now, I give a minimum of a hundred. For a poor bride, I do the same. Whereas in years past, I would send five dollars for a *sefer* such as your own, I now send fifty.

"*Baruch Hashem,* it will not be much longer before all of the money will have been used up. I can now *daven* with a clear mind."

❧ ❧ ❧

Rabbi David Yitzchak Isaac Rabinowitz, the *Rebbe* of Skolye, was blessed with a sweet voice. This quality, complemented by the deep feeling of love and awe of Hashem that permeated his prayers, made him a natural choice to lead the *tefillos* on Rosh Hashanah and Yom Kippur. In 1938, after he had fled Nazi-occupied Austria, the *Rebbe* settled in New York's Lower East Side. It would be some time before the *Rebbe* would again be leading a congregation of his own, so the *Rebbe* found himself a local *shul* where he felt comfortable *davening*. The congregation wasted no time in asking the *Rebbe* to lead the services on Rosh Hashanah. The *Rebbe* consented.

On the first day of Rosh Hashanah, the *Rebbe* had reason to return to his apartment during the break between *Shacharis* and *Mussaf.* He walked through the door to find that the apartment had been ransacked by thieves. Among the belongings he had brought from Europe were irreplaceable family heirlooms, including silver wine goblets and the like, that had belonged to some of his famous chassidic ancestors. Now they were gone.

The *Rebbe* later recalled, "I returned to *shul* to lead the *tefillos*. The loss that I had suffered was put completely out of my thoughts. It was as if nothing at all had happened."

With classic humility, the *Rebbe* mentioned this story toward the end of his life as one of his "few sources of merit."

פרשת שמות
Parashas Shemos

Mark of Greatness

וַיְהִי בַּיָּמִים הָהֵם, וַיִּגְדַּל מֹשֶׁה וַיֵּצֵא אֶל אֶחָיו וַיַּרְא בְּסִבְלֹתָם.

*It happened in those days that Moshe grew up
and went out to his brethren and observed
their burdens (Shemos 2:11).*

*He observed their burdens — in what way? He
would see their suffering and weep, saying, "Woe is to
me for you! If only I could die for you!" There is no
labor more strenuous than molding bricks, yet Moshe
would shoulder their burdens and help each one of
them (Shemos Rabbah 1:27).*

The *tefillin* worn by all Jewish males over the age of
thirteen are made in accordance with the opinion of
Rashi. Rabbeinu Tam, one of the *Ba'alei HaTosafos*, disagreed
with *Rashi* as to the order in which the Torah portions inside
the *tefillin* should be arranged. There are many people,
especially among those of Chassidic origin, who at the
conclusion of *Shacharis* each morning remove their *tefillin*
D'Rashi (of *Rashi*) and don *tefillin D'Rabbeinu Tam* for a short
while.

The legendary Chassidic leader, R' Elimelech of Lyszensk, author of *Noam Elimelech,* put on *tefillin D'Rabbeinu Tam*. One year, however, a period of two weeks went by in which R' Elimelech did not wear these *tefillin*. When his *chassidim* noticed that after these two weeks had elapsed, their *Rebbe* was wearing the *tefillin* once again, they asked him why he had changed his custom during the past two weeks. He explained as follows:

One evening, a particularly large flow of visitors came to his door. Some had come to ask that he bless them, others had requested that he pray for the sick, while still others had come seeking advice or *tzedakah*. R' Elimelech had answered everyone patiently, though he had not a moment to himself the entire evening. When the last petitioner had left, it was well past midnight.

Wearily, R' Elimelech recited *Shema* and retired for the night. He had been asleep only a few minutes when there was banging on his window. "*Rebbe, Rebbe!* Sarah, the baker's wife, is in the midst of childbirth and is having a difficult time. Please pray for her!"

"My initial thought," R' Elimelech told his *chassidim,* "was one of irritation. 'Am I not entitled to an hour's rest?' I thought to myself. Immediately, however, I was overcome with dismay for having allowed such a thought to enter my mind. I chided myself, 'Is this how one reacts when he hears that another Jew is in difficult straits and is in need of prayer? Is this how I would have reacted were the woman in childbirth my own daughter? Certainly not!

"I later said to myself: 'Regarding the wearing of *tefillin D'Rabbeinu Tam, Shulchan Aruch* states (*Orach Chaim* 34:3): *This should be done only by one who is renowned for his piety.* Now, can a Jew who, even for a moment, does not feel the pain of his brethren — can such a Jew consider himslf *one who is renowned for his piety?*

"I told myself that surely I was unworthy of donning *tefillin D'Rabbeinu Tam.* And so, for two weeks I refrained from putting them on. During these two weeks, I worked on developing a stronger feeling for the needs and sufferings of my people.

"Now, I feel that I am ready to don the *tefillin* once again."

❦ ❦ ❦

When Rabbi David Zaretsky was a young man, he paid a visit to the Chofetz Chaim in Radin. The Chofetz Chaim was then past ninety and extremely weak. R' Zaretsky extended his hand in greeting and introduced himself to the *tzaddik*. He then said, "I have a sister in Argentina, a young woman who is a true *bas Yisrael*. She has taken ill and is in need of a blessing for a speedy recovery." He then went on to describe the nature of her illness.

The Chofetz Chaim turned his aged body toward the wall and cried out, "*Ribono shel Olam!* Your precious daughter, who faithfully follows Your every command, has taken ill. Please, *Ribono shel Olam*, grant her a full and speedy recovery so that she can serve You in joy and tranquility." Tears streamed down the Chofetz Chaim's cheeks as he prayed on her behalf.

R' Zaretsky later reflected: "This woman was my very own sister, and of course she was very dear to me. Naturally, I prayed for her and asked others to pray as well — but until that point, I had not brought myself to shed a single tear for her sake. Yet, this *tzaddik*, who never met my sister, shed tears for her as soon as he learned of her illness. . ."

❦ ❦ ❦

In the early 1980's a yeshivah student came to the Ponovezher *Rosh Yeshivah*, Rabbi Eliezer Menachem Shach, to discuss a serious personal problem. R' Shach spoke with the student for a long time before concluding that the *bachur* needed to discuss the matter further with a certain individual who lived in Jerusalem. R' Shach picked up the phone and called that person. It was the thirteenth of *Nissan*, the day preceding *bedikas chametz*, the search for the *chametz*. R' Shach apologized for troubling the person at such a busy time and proceeded to explain the *bachur*'s dilemma. By the time R'

Shach finished, the person understood why the matter could not wait and agreed to meet with the boy in his home that night.

"Fine," said R' Shach, "so we'll be there tonight."

"We?" asked the man. "Surely the *Rosh Yeshivah* is not planning to accompany the *bachur* from Bnei Brak to Jerusalem?"

"Yes, I am," R' Shach replied. "He is very distressed and is desperately in need of moral support. It would not be good for him to go alone and he does not want anyone else to know about his problem."

"But it is a big trip for the *Rosh Yeshivah* — and the *Rosh Yeshivah* must guard his health! And tonight is the night of *bedikas chametz*! Forgive me for arguing, but I feel very strongly that the *Rosh Yeshivah* should let the *bachur* come alone."

"I'm coming with the *bachur*."

There was silence for a few moments. Finally, the man whom R' Shach had called took a deep breath and said, "I hope that the *Rosh Yeshivah* will forgive me for what I am about to say; I will say it only because of my deep concern for the *Rosh Yeshivah*'s health.

"I will see the *bachur* tonight, but when I open the door I want to find the boy there alone."

Rav Shach did not respond.

That night when the man answered his doorbell's ring, he found the *bachur* standing there alone. He welcomed him in and the two spent a few hours talking together. When the *bachur* left, the man felt satisfied that, indeed, he had helped him.

The next morning, a neighbor asked the man, "What was going on in your house last night?"

"Nothing unusual," the man replied. "Why do you ask?"

"Because *HaRav* Shach, שליט״א, was pacing back and forth near your house for a couple of hours! I did not have the nerve to ask him what was going on. . ."

פרשת וארא
Parashas Va'eira

An Eagle Takes Flight

וְהוֹצֵאתִי אֶתְכֶם מִתַּחַת סִבְלֹת מִצְרַיִם . . . וְלָקַחְתִּי אֶתְכֶם לִי לְעָם.

I shall take you out from under the burdens of Egypt . . .
and I shall take you to Me for a people
(*Shemos* 6:6-7).

I n this *parashah*, the process of redemption unfolds. Pharaoh and his wicked people are to be subjected to ten miraculous plagues, after which Pharaoh will not only allow the Jews to leave Egypt, but will even *implore* them to leave as quickly as possible.

Our Sages teach that the Jews in Egypt were sunk in מ״ט שַׁעֲרֵי טוּמְאָה, *forty-nine levels of impurity*. In fact, when the Angel of the Sea was commanded by Hashem to let the sea split, it argued, "These [the Egyptians] and those [the Jewish people] are both idol worshipers!" How, then, were the Jews worthy of redemption? The answer to this can be explained by way of a parable, told by Rabbi Dov Kushilevsky:

※ ※ ※

Once there was a farmer who spent his entire life on a chicken farm. His father had owned the farm until his death, at which time he, the son, had taken over. The farmer's whole life revolved around his work. As far as he was concerned, there was not much else to this world except chickens and eggs.

One day, for no apparent reason, the farmer decided,to leave the boundaries of his farm and go for a walk in the forest. As he walked, he came upon a hatched egg, with a baby bird sitting next to it. How excited he was! A baby chick right here in the forest! It never dawned upon the farmer that the bird could be anything but a little chicken. In fact, it was a baby eagle.

The farmer happily scooped up his find and brought the eaglet back home with him, where, naturally, he placed it in a coop with some of his chickens.

Now an eagle, as we know, is the highest flying bird and is quite bold. But in that chicken coop, a strange thing happened. The eaglet, having only chickens to learn from, behaved like a chicken. It would flap its wings a bit, but never spread them in the way that eagles do. It pecked at the food thrown at it just as the chickens did. And it never attempted to fly, because it never saw any of its neighbors fly. A very strange eagle, indeed.

One day, a stranger showed up at the farm. The man introduced himself as a hunter passing through town and asked if he could spend the night on the farm. The farmer obliged and proudly took his guest on a grand tour. When they came to a particular coop, the hunter's mouth opened wide in shock. "Why, there's an eagle there among those chickens!"

The farmer did not understand. "I don't know what you're talking about. There's nothin' but chickens in them coops!"

"Don't you see?" the hunter countered. "That one over there. He looks different from all the rest. He's certainly no chicken. I'm a hunter and I can assure you that that's an . . ."

"And I've been raising chickens since before you were born!" the ignorant farmer shot back. "I know a chicken when I see one and that's a chicken! Now, if you want to spend the night on my property, you'd better stop making me angry!"

The hunter kept quiet after that. That night, he only pretended to go to sleep. There was no way that he was going to allow the eagle to remain cooped up with a bunch of chickens! To force it to live like that was downright cruel!

An hour past midnight as everyone else slept, the hunter stealthily made his way to the chicken coop. He tiptoed over to the coop in which the eagle was kept, opened the door and carefully took the bird out. "Come, little fella," the hunter whispered, "let me show you what you really are."

He hurried down the road and headed for a mountain that lay ahead in the distance. By the time he reached the mountain's peak, the first rays of sunlight were shining forth above the horizon. The hunter held the eagle in both his hands and said, "You are not a chicken, my friend. You are an eagle. Now, flap those wings and soar above the clouds in the way that I know you can."

The bird hopped along at first, still unwilling to change its habits. But as it moved about with freedom for the first time in its life, the eagle began to fly, first for only a few yards and then, gradually, for greater distances. Finally, the eagle flew as only an eagle can, and disappeared into the horizon. The eagle was an eagle once more.

❀   ❀   ❀

The Jews in Egypt had sunk to the forty-ninth level of impurity, but this did not indicate what sort of people they *really* were. Their sins were the result of their enslavement to a wicked nation, to a people whose very essence was impure. The inner core of the Jews, on the other hand, was pure and holy. The Jews proved this when, before leaving Egypt, they were commanded to defy the Egyptians and slaughter a lamb, which the Egyptians worshiped, as a *Korban Pesach.* The Jews tied the lamb to their bedposts, slaughtered it, placed its blood on their doorposts, and roasted it out in the open. In faithfully fulfilling every detail of this *mitzvah,* the Jews proved who they really were. They were Hashem's people, descendants of Avraham, Yitzchak and Yaakov, and were ready and willing to heed Hashem's call.

The eagle had shown that, indeed, it was an eagle.

פרשת בא
Parashas Bo

For the Sake of a Mitzvah

שִׁבְעַת יָמִים מַצּוֹת תֹּאכֵלוּ.

For seven days you shall eat matzos (Shemos 12:15).

Chaim looked out the door of his barracks as he surveyed the thawing Siberian landscape. He had a problem to solve, and it needed to be solved quickly. Pesach was only days away.

When World War II erupted, he had been studying at Yeshivah Etz Chaim of Kletzk, headed by Rabbi Aharon Kotler. At that time most of the yeshivah's students, together with their revered *Rosh Yeshivah,* had made their way to Vilna, where they came under the protective wings of Rabbi Chaim Ozer Grodzensky and the *Va'ad HaYeshivos.* Chaim, however, was not among that group. He had fallen into the hands of the Germans, but miraculously had escaped.

Chaim had then made his way to Lublin where he was reunited with his parents and younger brother. The Russians were then in control of Lublin and they offered Chaim's family the choice of becoming Russian citizens or being sent to Siberia. It was a difficult decision, because neither alternative was without its dangers. Chaim's parents decided that Siberia was the lesser of two evils. Life in Siberia would be no paradise, but at least there was a possibility of being freed some day. Were they to become Russian citizens, the Communists would never allow them to leave Russia.

Chaim, his father and brother were assigned to the same barracks in the labor camp, and for this they would be eternally grateful. The fact that they were together made it somewhat easier to bear the backbreaking work, harsh treatment and bitter weather conditions.

Observing *mitzvos* was, of course, strictly against camp rules. But this did not prevent Chaim from wearing *tefillin* every weekday during his four years of imprisonment. Once, when a guard threatened to take away his *tefillin*, Chaim shouted, "Shoot me instead!" and the guard left him alone.

But now, as Chaim looked out the door, one thing gnawed at his mind. Peasch was only days away and his family did not know how they could possibly avoid eating *chametz* and survive.

Amazingly though, they did have *matzah* and wine for the *Seder.* Many weeks before, they had received a food package from the *Va'ad Hatzalah*, the American-based Orthodox Rescue Committee. It contained flour and some grapes. Though desperate for food, the family had decided to save the items for Pesach. They left the grapes to ferment, and then made wine which they carefully stored until the *yom tov.* The flour was taken out into the forests one day, where a crude oven was built out of stone. Joyfully, they had baked six *matzos,* three for each *Seder.*

But what would they do for the rest of Pesach? The main staple of the labor camp diet was coarse bread. Without it, they would almost surely die of starvation.

As he continued to ponder this dilemma, Chaim suddenly had an idea. There was only one possession which his family still owned that had any substantial value for making deals in the labor camp. It was his father's fur-lined coat. The coat provided excellent protection from the frigid conditions which prevailed during the winter months. Surely they could find a gentile who would buy the coat in exchange for some fruits or vegetables. But would Chaim's father, worn and haggard from suffering and deprivation, be willing to part with this valuable possession?

Chaim carefully broached the subject to his father. His father's eyes lit up. "Of course, Chaim! What an excellent idea. Here, take the coat and make a good deal for us."

Chaim wasted no time in making his way around the camp grounds. He spotted a Russian riding a wagon, loaded with sacks of onions and potatoes.

"How much do you want for some onions and potatoes?" asked Chaim. "Forget it," came the reply. "Money has little value here in Siberia. Whatever offer you make me will not be enough."

"What about this?" countered Chaim as he showed the man the coat. A few minutes later, an exhilarated Chaim was carrying two sacks, one of potatoes and the other of onions, back to the barracks.

A few nights later, the men in Chaim's barracks gathered around a table to conduct the *Pesach Seder*. A clean white sheet served as a tablecloth, on top of which was a few cups of wine and the *matzos*. An elderly *talmid chacham* was honored with leading the *Seder* and he recited much of the *Haggadah* from memory. The men felt as if transported to another world. Even in this dark, difficult prison, they were able to feel the taste of freedom which is so integral to the *Seder* night.

"The guard is coming!" shouted the man who had been standing watch at the door. The others jumped from their seats, threw themselves into bed and pulled their sheets over themselves, But there was no time to clear the table upon which lay the *matzos* and wine.

"Who is responsible for this?" shouted the guard as he overturned the table. "I know!" He walked up and down the barracks until he came to Chaim's bed. The sheet was torn from on top of him, and his feet, still in boots, were revealed. "Aha!" cried the guard. "I might have known. Get out of bed. We have better accommodations for you."

Chaim was marched outside into the cold Siberian night wearing nothing but his shirt, pants and boots. After a long walk, he was led into a dingy stone building and thrown into a cell.

He lay there on the floor, trying to tell himself that he was hallucinating. It couldn't be true. Just minutes earlier he had been in a state of spiritual ecstasy. Now, he was lying in a dark, cold cell not knowing what his fate would be. Chaim began to weep. *"Ribono shel Olam,"* he cried, "we tried so hard! We sacrificed so much in order to fulfill Your precious *mitzvos.* We were willing to suffer hunger so that we could save the flour and wine for this night. My father was willing to deprive himself of badly needed warmth so that we would not eat *chametz* on Your holy *yom tov.* We suffered physically, but our joy in giving up so much for Your *mitzvos* was boundless. Will I now be left to die in this horrible cell?" Chaim continued to weep until he fell into a deep sleep.

That night, his grandfather, who had died years before, appeared to him in a dream. "Do not cry, my dear Chaim," his grandfather said. "The reward for your *mesiras nefesh* (self-sacrifice) for the *mitzvos* of Pesach has been stored for you for when you will arrive in the Next World. Many years will pass before you will enjoy that reward — for you, your parents and brother will one day leave Siberia. You will yet see the light of freedom."

The next morning, Chaim was released from his cell and sent back to his barracks without explanation. When the war ended, he and his family were freed. They settled in America, where Chaim raised a family that to this day is a credit to Hashem and His Torah.

פרשת בשלח
Parashas Beshalach

In Merit of Her Faith

וַיַּרְא יִשְׂרָאֵל אֶת הַיָּד הַגְּדֹלָה אֲשֶׁר עָשָׂה ה' בְּמִצְרַיִם,
וַיִּירְאוּ הָעָם אֶת ה', וַיַּאֲמִינוּ בַּה' וּבְמֹשֶׁה עַבְדּוֹ.

Israel saw the great hand that Hashem inflicted
upon Egypt; and the people revered
Hashem, and they had faith in Hashem
and in Moshe His servant (Shemos 14:31).

Why does the Torah state following the splitting of the Sea that the Jews had faith in Hashem? Did they not have faith in Him when they departed Egypt after מַכַּת בְּכוֹרוֹת, the slaying of the Egyptian firstborn? In fact, the Torah testifies to their faith even *before* the Ten Plagues had begun. After returning to Egypt from Midian, Moshe related to the Jews what Hashem had spoken to him and he also performed certain miracles. There, the Torah states: וַיַּאֲמֵן הָעָם, *And the people had faith (Shemos 4:31).*

The answer to this is that there are infinite levels of *emunah*, faith in Hashem. When Hashem instructed Moshe to return to Egypt to lead the Jews and begin the process of redemption,

Moshe protested, *"But they will not believe me..."* (*Shemos* 4:1). Hashem responded that the Jews were *ma'aminim b'nei ma'aminim*, believers, sons of believers (*Shemos Rabbah* 3:12). They were descendants of Avraham, of whom it is written, *And he had faith in Hashem* (*Bereishis* 15:6).

As the Ten Plagues progressed and the various stages of redemption unfolded, the Jews' faith grew. By the time they departed Egypt on the fifteenth of *Nissan,* their hearts were permeated with *emunah*. Nevertheless, from their reaction upon seeing the approaching Egyptian armies as they headed toward the sea, it is clear that they had not yet attained the highest level of faith: *Pharaoh approached; the children of Israel raised their eyes and behold! — Egypt was journeying after them, and they were very frightened; the Children of Israel cried out to Hashem* (*Shemos* 14:10).

Hashem's response was that now was not a time for prayer. The Jews now had the opportunity to rise to the highest level of faith. To earn this, they would have to demonstrate unshakable trust in Hashem as they faced a terrifying situation. *Hashem said to Moshe: "Why do you cry out to Me? Speak to the children of Israel and let them go forth!"* (*ibid.* v. 15; see *Rashi*). The Jews heeded the call. Led by the prince of the Tribe of Yehudah, Nachshon ben Aminadav, they entered the sea fearlessly — and then it split (*Sotah* 37a). What was their reward? *They had faith in God and in Moshe His servant.* They had attained the highest level of faith *(Nesivos Shalom).*

❦ ❦ ❦

Rabbi Dovid Yitzchak Isaac Rabinowitz, the *Rebbe* of Skolye, was a *gaon* and *tzaddik* of rare distinction. His every waking moment was totally dedicated to Hashem's service. The major part of his day was spent studying Torah, *davening,* and meeting privately with the many who came to him for blessings, advice or simply to pour out their troubles to someone who they knew cared deeply for every Jew.

He became *Rebbe* in Vienna upon the passing of his father in 1917 and served as *Rebbe* until his own passing in 1979. In

1938 he arrived in America, where he lived for the rest of his life.

Toward the end of the *Rebbe*'s life, a well-known *Rosh Yeshivah* came to him for a blessing for his child, who was to undergo surgery for a serious condition. It was the first time that the two had ever met. Later, the *Rosh Yeshivah* told someone, "Never in my life did I see a person make someone else's troubles like his own to the degree that he [the *Rebbe*] did."

In Vienna, when the *Rebbe* was yet a young man, a woman who had never been to him before, came with a tragic story. Her seven-year-old daughter, an only child, had contracted a rare disease for which there was no known cure. Her daughter was lying in a hospital bed, deathly ill. The woman began to cry and begged the *Rebbe* to promise her that her daughter would recover. The *Rebbe* was overcome with compassion for the woman, but was taken aback by her request. Gently, he said, "How can I promise such a thing? It is Hashem and Hashem alone Who can heal your child. It is beyond me to make such promises."

The woman, however, would not accept this. Her weeping now became more intense and she replied between sobs, "*Rebbe,* I know that it is Hashem alone Who can heal my child. But I also know that the words of *tzaddikim*, who are very close to Hashem, carry great weight in Heaven. If you will assure me that my daughter will recover, Hashem will ensure that your words come true. Please, *Rebbe,* do not refuse the plea of a broken-hearted *Yiddishe mama* (Jewish mother)!"

The *Rebbe* was silent for a few moments as he pondered the matter. Finally, he said, "What does a Jew do in a time of distress? He says *Tehillim.* That is what I shall do. I give you my word that as you soon as you leave, I will begin to recite *Tehillim* for the sake of your daughter."

Though this was not exactly what the woman had requested, she was calmed by the *Rebbe*'s words. She thanked the *Rebbe* and turned to leave for the hospital. The *Rebbe* reached for his *Tehillim.*

The doctors informed the mother that, according to their estimations, her daughter would die that night between the hours of two and four. Since the disease with which the child had been stricken was a rare one, her case aroused the interest of the hospital's leading physicians. Shortly before 2:00 A.M., the child's bed was surrounded by doctors who wanted to observe what would happen as the end neared.

Four o'clock came and the girl was unconscious, but still alive. The heartless doctors turned to the child's mother and said, "Well, our calculations can be off by an hour or two. But there is no doubt that your daughter will not survive the night."

At 7:00 A.M., the child opened her eyes. A few days later, she was discharged from the hospital, having fully recovered. She grew to marry and raise a fine Jewish family.

Many years later, an aged Skolye *Rebbe* wept as he told this story. He concluded with classic humility: "Believe me, I did nothing, nothing at all. It was in the merit of that woman's pure faith that her daughter recovered. She believed with such certainty that, despite the doctor's predictions, the child could recover if such was Hashem's will. And that is why it happened."

פרשת יתרו
Parashas Yisro

A Lesson for Life

וַיִּשְׁמַע יִתְרוֹ, כֹהֵן מִדְיָן חֹתֵן מֹשֶׁה,
אֶת כָּל אֲשֶׁר עָשָׂה אֱלֹהִים לְמֹשֶׁה וּלְיִשְׂרָאֵל עַמּוֹ.
And Yisro, the priest of Midian, the father-in-law
of Moshe, heard all that God did to Moshe
and to Israel, His people (Shemos 18:1).

The Torah informs us that before becoming a Jew, Yisro had been a priest in Midian, a man whom the people of Midian revered and, perhaps, idolized. The *Midrash* tells us that before coming to Midian, Yisro had been among the close advisers of Pharaoh, King of Egypt. Yet Yisro was willing to forfeit the honor and power to which he had grown accustomed, and instead trek through the wilderness to join the Jewish people. The miracles of the Exodus had convinced him that life could only have meaning if he became a member of G-d's chosen nation and learned to live by their teachings. Any other way of life would be empty and without purpose.

❧ ❧ ❧

Allon was among the best pilots in the Israeli Air Force. Of course, becoming a pilot had not been easy. The testing and training which an Air Force pilot must undergo are the most difficult of any in the military. But Allon had made it, and for five years, he flew combat missions in an Israeli version of the American Skyhawk jet. In one mission over Lebanon, a ground-to-air-missile came dangerously close to blowing his jet apart.

One day, in a moment of calm, Allon mulled over his accomplishments and what lay in store for him. True, he was bravely risking his life time and again for the sake of his people and his Land. Nevertheless, he felt that there was something missing in his life. He knew that in the not-too-distant future, his age would require that he retire from active combat duty — with honors, of course. And what meaning would life have then? Could it be that G-d created this magnificent, wondrous world merely for man to eat, drink, work and relax?

Allon decided to speak to a rabbi. Before long, he applied for a six-month leave of absence from the Air Force. Allon spent his leave at Yeshivah Ohr Somayach in Jerusalem. When the six months were over, Allon was a full-fledged *ba'al teshuvah,* with an unquenchable thirst for Torah. He signed out for a longer leave. Eventually, he married a *ba'alas teshuvah* and took permanent leave of the Air Force so that he could study Torah full-time.

When leaving the Israeli Air Force, a pilot is required to be interviewed by a commanding officer. The officer who interviewed Allon could not hide his indignation. "What's this business about leaving us so that you can study? You're one of our best pilots; we've taught you everything you need to know — what else is there to learn?"

"You're making a mistake," Allon replied calmly. "I've discovered that for the Jewish people to survive, we need to know a lot more than how to fly Skyhawks. There is a vast Torah to learn, and *that* is the key to our survival."

As the interview drew to a close, the general asked one final question: "Don't you feel that you gained from being an Air

Force pilot? After all, we trained you, we molded you — we made you into something very, very special. Who doesn't look up to an Air Force pilot?"

"Yes," Allon replied thoughtfully. "I gained tremendously from my Air Force experience. I was privileged to defend my fellow Jews from their enemies, and surely, that is something very special. But I gained even more. Let me explain.

"You see, had I been a paratrooper, running over rough terrain with sand blowing in my face, I might have looked up at those Skyhawks and thought: maybe life as a paratrooper is somewhat unfulfilling, but if I could be a pilot flying one of those Skyhawks, then surely, I would feel that nothing was lacking in my life.

"Had I been a tank commander, sweating away in a clanking metal cabin, I might have thought the same: the pilots streaking overhead in their Phantoms have reached the ultimate; there cannot be a better, more fulfilling life.

"But now that I've flown those jets, I realize that even being an Air Force combat pilot is not the ultimate goal in life. Only Torah can give my life real meaning and my soul true fulfillment.

"I appreciate this lesson. Thank you."[1]

_____

1. From *Anatomy of a Search* by Akiva Tatz (Mesorah Publications).

The Source of All Blessing

זָכוֹר אֶת יוֹם הַשַּׁבָּת לְקַדְּשׁוֹ
Remember the Shabbos day to sanctify it (Shemos 20:8).

C havah looked out the window, a worried expression on her face. "It's getting late," she muttered to herself. "Why isn't he home yet?"

Zev, the yeshivah *bachur* who boarded in Chavah's home, could not help but notice the woman's anxiety. "Don't worry," he assured her. "There is still plenty of time until Shabbos begins. I'm sure your husband will be home soon."

Chavah shook her head. "You don't understand," she replied. "I'm sure he'll be home before Shabbos. But that's not good enough. I like to have everything ready for Shabbos with plenty of time to spare. That's how it's been in our house for years. Let me explain."

❧   ❧   ❧

Chavah and her husband Yaakov had been childless for many years until finally their prayers were answered. They were blessed with a baby boy, whom they named Berel. Their joy knew no bounds — for a few months' time. Then they began to realize that something was wrong. Berel was not developing the way a child should. He grew slowly, he could not do most of the things that children his age could do, and he always seemed to be sleepy and lethargic. After examining Berel, the family doctor recommended that the infant be seen by a specialist in Vilna.

In Vilna, the specialist offered a grim prognosis. "Your baby has a serious heart defect. Don't waste your money by taking him to other doctors. Nothing can be done for him. He has but a few months to live."

Father and mother returned to their lodgings devastated. This child was the answer to their most fervent hope and wish. It was for little Berel that they had prayed and shed tears since their marriage many years before. And now, he was to be taken from them — after but a few short months? Chavah could not bear the pain. As she cried out in anguish, her whole body shook with uncontrollable weeping.

Her cries were interrupted by a knock on the door. A kindly man in the room adjacent to her own had heard Chavah's cries and was concerned. Yaakov, fighting back his own tears, explained the cause of his wife's anguish. The neighbor said, "You know, the town of Radin is not far from one of the stops on the train back to Mir. Why don't you go there and speak to the holy Chofetz Chaim? If any person on this earth can help you, surely he is the one."

Yaakov thanked the man for his suggestion and said that indeed, they would go to the Chofetz Chaim.

As Chavah, holding little Berel in her arms, followed her husband up the path which led to the Chofetz Chaim's front door, their hearts filled with hope. How great was their disappointment when the person who answered their knock told them, "I am truly sorry, but the *Rav* is feeling very weak today. No one may see him." The person politely wished them a good day and closed the door.

The distraught couple felt themselves drowning in a sea of despair. What were they to do now? Suddenly, Yaakov recalled something. "Chavah, remember Reuven Dov, the *bachur* who stayed at our house four years ago? He has since married a granddaughter of the Chofetz Chaim and, as I recall, is living here in Radin. Perhaps he can help us."

It did not take them long to locate Reuven Dov. He welcomed the couple warmly. Reuven Dov could not hide his tears upon hearing what had brought them to Radin. He remembered well how wonderfully this couple had treated him during the year's time he had lived in their home. He was determined to help them. "Come," he told them, "let us return to my grandfather's house. I will do my best to have permission granted for you to see him."

An hour later, Yaakov, Reuven Dov and Chavah — still holding little Berel — were seated before the *tzaddik* of the generation. When the couple had finished relating all that had transpired, the Chofetz Chaim responded humbly, "But why have you come to me? If it is large sums of money that you need, so that you can seek greater doctors, surely I am not the one to turn to. . ."

Chavah burst into tears. Reuven Dov exclaimed, "*Zaide* (Grandfather)! It is an only child!"

The Chofetz Chaim was silent for a few moments. Then, turning to Chavah, he said gently, "My daughter, accept upon yourself to greet the Shabbos Queen early. This means that by noon on Friday, the Shabbos tablecloth should already be spread out, with the Shabbos candles properly arranged on the table. Also, be sure to light the candles each week no later than *licht bentchen tzeit* (candle-lighting time — eighteen minutes before sunset)."

Chavah solemnly accepted upon herself to follow these instructions for the rest of her life.

No sooner did the couple return home than Berel began to thrive. He developed a better appetite; his cheeks, which had always been pale and drawn, now turned pink and became rounder. He slept less and was more active during his waking hours. Neighbors commented to Chavah that Berel had grown, and indeed he had.

The next time Berel was brought to the family doctor for a checkup, the doctor could not believe his eyes. So amazed was he that he bought the couple train tickets to Vilna so that the specialist who had given them no hope could see the miracle with his own eyes.

Upon examining Berel, the specialist declared, "You people are fooling me. This is not the same child that you brought me last time. It cannot be." Yaakov and Chavah insisted that it was, and told the doctor of their visit to the Chofetz Chaim. Though the doctor was not Jewish, he had heard of the *tzaddik* from Radin who often came to Vilna for the sake of Torah causes.

Finally, the doctor said, "It seems that the Chofetz Chaim can bring about something which we doctors cannot. You see, doctors can try to repair a damaged heart, but we cannot create a new heart out of nothing. I give you my word that the last time you brought your little boy here, he had almost no heart at all. What has happened can only be called a miracle."

❦ ❦ ❦

As Chavah finished telling her story, she breathed a sigh of relief, for her husband had just turned the corner of their street. "Now," she told her boarder, "you understand why I am so anxious that my husband come home early on Friday afternoon."

To welcome the Shabbos, come, let us go, for it is the source of all blessing (from the Friday night *Lechah Dodi*).

פרשת משפטים
Parashas Mishpatim

An Orphan's Pain

כָּל אַלְמָנָה וְיָתוֹם לֹא תְעַנּוּן.
*You shall not cause pain to
any widow or orphan (Shemos 22:21).*

It was a very difficult time for the *Rebbetzin*. Her husband, Rabbi Yosef Dov ("R' Berel") *HaLevi* Soloveitchik, the revered *Rosh Yeshivah* of Yeshivas Brisk in Jerusalem, was seriously ill. The *Rebbetzin* was doing everything she could so that R' Berel would be as comfortable as possible. Every few minutes she would come to her husband's bedside to see if there was something he needed.

One day, R' Berel told his wife, "Reb Yosef Loibler is not here."

Thinking that she had not heard correctly, the *Rebbetzin* asked her husband to repeat what he had said. "Reb Yosef Loibler is not here," he repeated.

The *Rebbetzin* did not understand.

The next day, R' Berel Soloveitchik, one of the great *gaonim* of the generation, passed away. During the week of *shivah,* the *Rebbetzin* repeated her husband's strange words to his illustrious brother R' David (himself a revered *Rosh Yeshivah*). R' David nodded his head knowingly. He explained:

He and his late brother were great-grandsons of R' Yosef Dov *HaLevi* Soloveitchik, author of *Beis HaLevi* and after whom R' Berel had been named. During his lifetime, the *Beis HaLevi* had been referred to by the nickname "Yosheh Ber."

As a young boy, Yosheh Ber came home from yeshivah one day and declared, "I cannot learn Torah by this *rebbi* any longer!" He explained that that morning, there had been a contest in class. The *rebbe* had tested the boys on their studies and had offered a prize for the one who offered the most correct answers. Two boys had tied for first place. One boy was the son of a wealthy member of the town's Jewish community. The other boy was an orphan; he had no father. The *rebbi* had awarded the prize to the rich man's son.

Yosheh Ber became emotional as he asked his father, "How can I study Torah from a person who is not sensitive to the feelings of an orphan?"

While Yosheh Ber's father knew that the *rebbi* had erred, he nevertheless felt that this did not disqualify the *rebbi* as a Torah teacher. He also knew that it was in his son's best interest to continue studying under that *rebbi*, at least for the time being. That same day, Yosheh Ber's father went and bought a prize, which he brought to the house of the *rebbi*. The next day, the *rebbe* told the class that the previous day, he had had with him but one prize and, at random, had given it to the other boy. Now, he proudly presented a prize to the orphan boy as well. Yosheh Ber was somewhat calmed by this and he continued to study under the *rebbi*.

Some time later, young Yosheh Ber fell seriously ill and lapsed into a coma. While everyone prayed, they feared the worst. Miraculously, the boy opened his eyes one morning and improved little by little until he had completely recovered. He then told his father that while unconscious, he had seen the Angel of Death coming to take his soul. As the angel approached, its path was blocked by R' Yosef Loibler, the deceased father of the orphan boy. "Stop!" R' Yosef Loibler had declared. "Let this boy live! It was he who spoke up for my little boy when his feelings had been so terribly hurt."

The Angel of Death backed off and Yosheh Ber awoke shortly thereafter.

And so, as his great-grandson, R' Berel Soloveitchik, felt his end drawing near, he remarked that there was no Reb Yosef Loibler to ask that he be granted a new lease on life in this world.

Friend or Foe?

לֹא תִשָּׂא שֵׁמַע שָׁוְא.

Do not accept a false report (Shemos 23:1)

This verse prohibits us from believing lashon hara (Rashi).

P eople who speak *lashon hara* tend to rationalize their sinful behavior with the contention that the listener wanted to hear the gossip and that he obviously enjoyed it. Moreover, the two remained good friends after their discussion. Could one really be guilty of causing his listener harm when he obviously had such a good time? The Chofetz Chaim explained the fallacy of this type of thinking with the following parable:

A swindler arrived in a certain town and disguised himself as a respected leader of the community. When a visitor arrived in the town, the swindler welcomed him like an old friend and invited him to a local inn where the two could enjoy each other's company. At the inn, the swindler said, "It's been so many years since the last time we saw one another. My joy is indescribable. This calls for a celebration! Please, go to the counter and tell the manager to serve us the very best of everything he has to offer! Of course, I'll pay the bill."

The two wined and dined until they had both eaten more than their fill. At that point, the swindler slipped out the door, leaving his "guest" with the enormous bill to pay. The poor fellow explained to the manager what had transpired, but to no avail. "All I know," said the manager, "is that you came to the counter and ordered all that food and drink. Whatever happened between you and that other fellow is of no concern to me. Pay up!"

One who listens to *lashon hara* is like the visitor in our parable. The listener is happy and feels no ill will toward the speaker, who seems to be entertaining him free of charge. The listener sees the speaker as his dear confidant, who tells him private information that he might not divulge to others. But all this is only in this world, while "the shop is open, and the Merchant extends credit" (*Avos* 3:20). In the next world, however, where "the ledger is open . . . and the collectors make their rounds" one will have to stand judgment for having listened to and believed slanderous talk.

פרשת תרומה
Parashas Terumah

A Generous Heart

‎. . . מֵאֵת כָּל אִישׁ אֲשֶׁר יִדְּבֶנּוּ לִבּוֹ תִּקְחוּ אֶת תְּרוּמָתִי.

. . . from every man whose heart will move him,
you shall take My gift (Shemos 25:2).

We know that buildings which are needed for national concerns, such as the Congressional building or Post Office, are funded by taxes and other forms of government revenue. The *Mishkan* was built as a place where Hashem would rest His *Shechinah* (Divine Presence) and in which the Jewish People would serve Him. It was the "headquarters" of our service to the One Above. Why, then, was it built through private donations? Why was it not funded through a national tax?

Rabbi Zalman Sorotzkin writes *(Oznayim L'Torah)* that the main quality of the *Mishkan* was the generosity through which it was built. It was precisely because its every piece of gold and every scrap of wood was given with a pure and sincere willingness of heart that Hashem desired to rest His Presence in it.

R' Sorotzkin writes that it is this generosity which makes every *beis haknesses* so special. The fact that every *beis haknesses* is built by Jews who willingly give of their resources to glorify Hashem's Name, makes the prayers uttered in these places so pleasing to Hashem.

The generosity of heart that Jews demonstrate, both in building Torah institutions and in helping individual Jews, is a quality that is unique to the Jewish people.

❦ ❦ ❦

Rabbi Stein,[1] an executive director of a well-known yeshivah, rang the Millers'[1] doorbell one evening. He was welcomed in graciously by Mr. Miller, who invited him to have a seat at the table where supper was about to be served. Rabbi Stein's apologies were quickly brushed aside. "I'm sure you're here for an important reason — how can I help you?" asked Mr. Miller. Rabbi Stein explained that his yeshivah was in a very difficult financial situation and was desperately in need of funds. Mr. Miller summoned one of his children to fetch his checkbook.

After being handed a generous check, Rabbi Stein rose to leave. "I just want to apologize again for coming at such an inconvenient time."

"You don't understand," Mr. Miller replied. "You came at the *best* time. You know, Rabbi Yitzchak Hutner[2] calls me from time to time to request a donation for his yeshivah. Once, when he called during supper, I told him, 'I am very organized in how I give *tzedakah*. I always set aside ten percent of my earnings and distribute it in a very systematic way. I would probably give this donation even without the *Rosh Yeshivah*'s phone call — but I appreciate the call very much. You see, I would never interrupt my supper to pay an electric bill or a gas bill. But I *do* interrupt my supper to give *tzedakah* — and this is an important lesson for my children to learn.'

---

1. A fictitious name.
2. Late *Rosh Yeshivah* of Yeshivah and Mesivta Rabbi Chaim Berlin.

"And so," Mr. Miller concluded, "I really thank you, Rabbi Stein, for ringing my doorbell as we were about to sit down to eat. You couldn't have come at a better time."

❀ ❀ ❀

R' Chaim Gelb was a Williamsburg baker and a one-man *chesed* institution. Many vividly recall the sight of R' Chaim hurrying about at weddings, a *yarmulka* filled with coins in his outstretched hand as he raised money for the poor.

As a young couple, R' Chaim and his wife had accumulated $10,000 in their savings account. It was then that they decided to dedicate their lives to the *mitzvos* of *tzedakah* and *chesed*. During the year that followed, their entire savings was disbursed to the poor and to Torah institutions.

To R' Chaim, it was not enough to give money to the poor, they had to be shown love and respect as well. As our Sages teach, the comfort one offers a poor person is even greater than the money one gives him (*Bava Basra* 9b). When R' Chaim married off his daughter, it was natural for R' Chaim to invite the poor people who were regular guests at his home. But R' Chaim did more. He sat the poor people at the head table!

When R' Chaim's granddaughter went to enroll her son in a renowned yeshivah in which all the classes were said to be full, the head of the yeshivah welcomed the boy with open arms. He explained, "Today, our yeshivah is well-established, and is forced to turn away many applicants. But I have not forgotten the day when we first opened many years ago. We had few students, and almost no money. Your grandfather, my good friend R' Chaim, came to present me with a donation — the very first we received from anyone. He said, 'A yeshivah needs students, but it also needs money — *if there is no flour, there can be no Torah*' (*Avos* 3:21).

"I have never forgotten his generous and thoughtful gesture. Now I can repay him in some way."

R' Chaim was not one to speak about his accomplishments. Thus, in his younger years, there were some who wondered what exactly he did with all those nickels and pennies he collected. It therefore came as a surprise to some when the legendary *Menahel* of Mesivta Torah Vodaath, R' Shraga Feivel Mendlowitz,[1] accepted R' Chaim's invitation to join him at his home one Shabbos for *Shalosh Seudos.* Only later did it become known that in the 1930's during the Great Depression, R' Chaim raised thousands of dollars for the yeshivah, and it was this money which allowed it to stay open.[2]

❧ ❧ ❧

Rabbi Naftali Riff served for many years as *Rav* of Camden, New Jersey. He was an outstanding *talmid chacham* and had a place in his heart for every Jew. He would seek out the poor in his area and strive to help them to the best of his ability.

Late one night, he went to a nearby neighborhood to slip an envelope containing money under a poor person's door. A policeman drove by and saw R' Riff bending down at the door. Not knowing the *Rav,* the officer suspected him of trying to break in. Before R' Riff could explain himself, the poor man, who had heard the commotion, opened the door. R' Riff knew that his explanation would cause the poor man some embarrassment. Therefore, he remained silent.

It did not take long for the poor man to figure out what had happened. He asked the officer to step aside with him so that he would be out of the *Rav*'s earshot. The poor man told the officer, "This man is a rabbi; all he wanted to do was help me out by slipping some money under my door. In fact, if you'll look over your shoulder, you'll notice that he is trying to drag the money back with his foot so that it won't be discovered."

The officer looked over his shoulder, then apologized to R' Riff and drove off.

❧ ❧ ❧

Rabbi Eliyahu Moshe Shisgal, late son-in-law of Rabbi Moshe Feinstein, was another outstanding *talmid chacham* who combined greatness in Torah with boundless *chesed.*

---

1. See chapter to *Parashas Vayeilech.*
2. From *A Life of Chessed* by Rabbi David Fisher (Mesorah Publications).

When R' Shisgal taught Torah at Mesivta Torah Vodaath, the poor of Williamsburg would wait along the path he regularly walked, knowing that no matter how many times they asked for a donation, he would never refuse them. He would give and give until his pockets were empty — literally. This created a problem because R' Shisgal needed bus fare for the ride over the bridge which connects Williamsburg to the Lower East Side of Manhattan where he lived. R' Shisgal finally solved the problem by setting aside a pocket in his coat where he kept only his bus fare. This way, he made sure to always leave that money for himself. The rest could be given to the poor.

❧ ❧ ❧

Mr. Harry Hershkowitz was a great supporter of many charitable causes, including Yeshivah and Mesivta Torah Vodaath, whose building bears his name.

As Director of Internal Revenue for the southern district of Manhattan, Mr. Hershkowitz worked closely with prominent judges, lawyers and other important people in New York City. When Mr. Hershkowitz married off a daughter, many dignitaries were in attendance.

In the middle of the wedding meal, Mr. Hershkowitz asked that the band stop playing for a few minutes. He took the microphone and said, "Friends, though I have married off a child tonight, my happiness is not complete. How can my heart be filled with joy when I know that in this very city, there are Jewish fathers and mothers who do not have the money with which to feed and clothe their young children? Please, I ask all of you to come forward and contribute generously to help these unfortunate families . . ."

Who is like Your people Israel, one nation on earth?

Miracle of Torah

וְעָשׂוּ אֲרוֹן עֲצֵי שִׁטִּים.

*They shall make an Aron (Ark)
of acacia wood (Shemos 25:10).*

*R' Levi said: We have a tradition from our forefathers
that the space taken up by the Aron is not included in
the dimensions of the Sanctuary [miraculously, it did
not take up any room] (Megillah 10b).*

Throughout this long and bitter exile, one factor above all has given the Jew the strength to overcome any obstacles or suffering — the study of Torah. In the words of Rabbi Chaim Ozer Grodzensky, *Rav* of Vilna and leader of Lithuanian Jewry in the pre-Holocaust years:

"From the day that Israel was exiled from its land, the everlasting and unbroken chain of Talmudic study and transmission was never broken. In the days of religious persecution, decrees, oppression, and wanderings, they toiled with self-sacrifice to prepare a dwelling place for Torah ... To those that merited it, the study of Torah was always a potion of life ...."

R' Saadiah Gaon said that our nation is a nation only through Torah. Israel's survival, since the First Destruction, as a nation of Torah is one of the great miracles of Jewish history. The miraculous nature of the *Aron*, in which the *Luchos* (Tablets) were kept, alludes to the miracle of Torah.

This miracle stretches from the very beginning of the first exile following the destruction of the first *Beis HaMikdash* and continues to this very day.

Eleven years before the First Destruction, Nevuchadnezzar took Israel's King Yehoyachin from his seat of royalty in

Jerusalem and imprisoned him in Babylon. At that time, ten thousand of Israel's best people were taken away. The prophet relates:

"And [Nevuchadnezzar] carried away into exile all Jerusalem, and all the leaders, and all the mighty warriors, ten thousand exiles, and all the craftsmen and the gate watchmen (הֶחָרָשׁ וְהַמַּסְגֵּר) . . . And the King of Babylon took them into exile to Babylon" (*II Melachim* 24:14,16).

Charash and *Masger*, Craftsmen and Gate Watchmen, were a group comprised of one thousand of Israel's most distinguished Torah scholars, including several prophets.[1] Nevuchadnezzar's plan was simple. By removing Jersualem's leading scholars and *all the leaders and all the mighty warriors* (i.e. its civil and military leadership) he would ensure that the Jews of the Holy Land would never again flout his authority.

Unwittingly, Nevuchadnezzar brought about the failure of his own plans. The *Charash* and *Masger* and those that accompanied them built the foundations of a flourishing Torah community in exile. When the *Beis HaMikdash* was destroyed and the Jewish nation driven from their Land, they found a community of Torah personalities in Babylon, waiting to guide and teach them. The survival of the Jewish people as a nation of Torah had been ensured.

The building of Torah in America during and after the Second World War was guided by a handful of great *gaonim* and *tzaddikim* whom Heaven spared from the fires of the Holocaust. One such personality was the Telshe *Rosh Yeshivah*, Rabbi Eliyahu Meir Bloch.

R' Elya Meir arrived in America in 1941. Soon after, he visited one of the few *sefarim* stores that existed there at that time, and asked the proprietor for a *Sefer Ketzos HaChoshen,* a classic work on *Shulchan Aruch* and major Talmudic topics.

---

1. The letters חרש (*Charash*) can also mean *silence* (as in חֶרֶשׁ). The word hints that as soon as these men opened a learned discussion all the others became as though speechless (*Sanhedrin* 38a). The root of מַסְגֵּר is סגר, *closed*. Once they had closed a *halachic* discussion it was never reopened, for none were able to cast doubt on their ruling (ibid.).

The proprietor climbed a ladder and from a high, dusty shelf pulled down a volume which was obviously years old. "Take good care of this, Rabbi," the man said. "This is probably the last volume of *Ketzos HaChoshen* that will ever be sold in America." With a terrible war raging in Europe and few yeshivos in existence in America, it seemed that the future of Torah study was bleak.

But R' Elya Meir knew better. With a voice full of conviction he declared, "And I say that thousands more of this very *sefer* will yet be sold in this land!" History has proven R' Elya Meir correct.

Without a doubt, a turning point in the Torah miracle at that time was the arrival in America of Rabbi Aharon Kotler. As a young man, R' Aharon was already renowned as one of the outstanding Torah personalities of his day. R' Chaim Ozer Grodzensky would sometimes send *chiddushei Torah* (original Torah compositions) to R' Aharon, who was twenty-five years his junior. R' Chaim Ozer would say of him, "He is the future *gadol hador* (leader of the generation)."

R' Aharon's yeshivah in Kletzk, Poland, was one of Eastern Europe's great citadels of Torah. Upon arriving in America, R' Aharon made it clear that he was determined to establish a yeshivah in the style of the one in Kletzk, where young men would study nothing but Torah, day and night. R' Aharon also made it clear that his yeshivah would not only be for *talmidim* who aspired to become *rabbanim* or *roshei yeshivah.* The study of Torah *lishmah*, for its own sake, was the sacred privilege and obligation of every Jewish male. And Torah, R' Aharon taught, was like the *Aron* — above time and place. The Torah that was studied so intensively in Europe would be studied in America in exactly the same way.

Many dismissed R' Aharon's goal as a dream that could not possibly materialize. Many also failed to appreciate the inestimable merit of helping to ensure the survival of Torah.

Once, R' Aharon approached a wealthy man for a donation and instead was shown great disrespect. Mr. Amos Bunim, who had accompanied R' Aharon on this visit, chastised the man,

"Is this how you would have spoken had the Chofetz Chaim approached you for a donation?"

Later, R' Aharon told Mr. Bunim, "That man is to be pitied. To support the study of Torah is a great *zechus* (source of merit). How unfortunate that this man has not merited this *zechus.*"

Many, however, were moved by R' Aharon's inspiring words and personality. Through their generosity, he established Beth Medrash Govoha in Lakewood, New Jersey with a small group of students. Today the "Lakewood Yeshivah" has fifteen hundred students, in addition to yeshivos and *kollelim* throughout North America and beyond which were founded and staffed by Lakewood alumni. R' Aharon's dream has become a reality that will continue to bear fruit for all time.[1]

---

1. For more on the building of Torah in America, see chapters on *Parashas Pekudei* and *Parashas Vayeilech.*

פרשת תצוה
Parashas Tetzaveh

The Me'il

וְעָשִׂיתָ אֶת מְעִיל הָאֵפוֹד כְּלִיל תְּכֵלֶת
*You shall make the Me'il [Robe] of the Ephod
entirely of turquoise wool (Shemos 28:31).*

One of the eight garments worn by the *Kohen Gadol* (High Priest) was the *Me'il*, Robe. The Talmud (*Arachin* 16a) states that the wearing of the *Me'il* atoned for the *lashon hara* spoken by the Jewish people. The Chofetz Chaim (*Shemiras HaLashon*, part II) explains how the various aspects of this garment allude to a number of concepts relating to *shemiras halashon,* guarding one's tongue.

The *Me'il* was made entirely of turquoise wool. The Sages teach that turquoise wool is similar in color to the sea, the sea is similar to the sky, and the sky is reminiscent of Hashem's Throne of Glory (*Menachos* 43b). The Sages also teach (*Tana D'vei Eliyahu* I, ch. 18) that the *lashon hara* which a person speaks in this world ascends to the Throne of Glory, bringing harm to the speaker and to the Jewish people as a whole.

Thus, the color of the *Me'il* serves as a reminder of the negative power of *lashon hara*.

"Its [the *Me'il's*] opening shall have a border all around of weaver's work" (*Shemos* 28:32). When argument erupts, says the Chofetz Chaim, one should imagine that his lips are woven together, so that he cannot open his mouth to offer words of strife.

"It [the neck of the *Me'il*] shall be for it like the opening of a coat of armor — it may not be torn" (ibid.). As *Rashi* explains, in Biblical times, the neck of a coat of armor was folded over within so that it would not tear.

Why must the Torah inform us that the *Me'il's* neck was similar to that of a coat of armor? The Torah could have stated simply, "Its head shall be folded over within, it may not be torn."

The Torah is teaching us that the best weapon against argument or insult is to keep one's mouth sealed. The nature of argument is that sharp words are countered with sharper words; and ultimately, a verbal dispute may become physical. However, if one responds with silence, his adversary will gradually calm down and his caustic talk will cease.

Words That Pierce the Heavens

You shall make on its [the Me'il's] hem pomegranates of turquoise, purple and scarlet wool, on its hem all around, and gold bells between them, all around; a gold bell and a pomegranate, a gold bell and a pomegranate on the hem of the robe, all around (Shemos 28:33-34).

The ringing bells on the hem of the *Me'il* allude to the sounds of *tefillah* (prayer)[1] and to Torah study.[2] Those who are careful to avoid *lashon hara* and other forbidden talk are assured, "Its sound shall be heard when he enters the Sanctuary before Hashem. . ." (ibid. v.35) — that their prayers and Torah study will find favor in Heaven.

Rabbi Yehudah Zev Segal, the late Manchester *Rosh Yeshivah,* was referred to by the Steipler *Gaon* as "the pillar of *tefillah* in our generation." R' Segal invested his prayers with incredible effort and concentration. Every word was expressed with proper intent and enunciated clearly. Once, R' Segal fainted while reciting *Shacharis.* When he came to, those attending him wanted to be sure that he had not suffered a stroke and that his mind was functioning properly. They asked him at what point in his *davening* he had fainted. R' Segal replied: "Between the words תְּהִלּוֹת and לָאֵ־ל עֶלְיוֹן." Even after having fainted, he could recall clearly which word he had said and which he had not, for no word was uttered without intense concentration.

---

1. As stated in *Alsheich.*
2. As stated in the Chofetz Chaim's *Sefer Shemiras HaLashon.*

Those who were privileged to observe him as he prayed would say that they would consider it a great accomplishment if their *Ne'ilah* prayer on Yom Kippur was like R' Segal's typical weekday *Shemoneh Esrei*. He uttered every *Shemoneh Esrei* amid heartfelt tears as he prayed for the needs of individuals and for the Jewish people as a whole.

Thousands of Jews around the world sought R' Segal's blessings and prayers, because they were convinced that Hashem would fulfill the will of this great *tzaddik*. Years ago, when a young man told Rabbi Moshe Feinstein that a relative of his was seriously ill, R' Moshe said, "There is a Jew in Manchester who can help you." He was referring to R' Segal.

Once, a brilliant yeshivah student became stricken with a serious illness. The boy's parents contacted R' Segal and requested that he pray for their son's recovery. In the course of the conversation, the parents mentioned that they had already decided that their son, who had completed high school, would leave yeshivah to pursue a career. R' Segal told them, "Your son can develop into an outstanding *talmid chacham*. Dedicate him to the study of Torah and he will recover from his illness." Later that day, someone standing near R' Segal as he was praying heard him say, *"Ribono shel Olam,* I promised!"

That very day, the boy's doctor broke his leg and was replaced by a doctor who was considered less qualified. The second doctor recommended a different treatment which proved successful. The boy recovered fully, and went on to become an outstanding *talmid chacham.*

It is not coincidental that R' Segal, "the pillar of *tefillah* in our generation," was also the pillar of *shemiras halashon* in our generation. It was he who developed a daily learning schedule, used world-wide, for the study of the laws and concepts of guarding one's tongue from speaking the forbidden. In fact, R' Segal requested that he be buried with his *shemiras halashon* calendar, saying, "This is my passport to the World to Come."

Virtually everyone who brought his personal suffering to R' Segal's door was advised to strengthen himself in the area of *shemiras halashon*. When someone would joyfully report that his or her problem had been solved, R' Segal would say that it was the merit of the Chofetz Chaim, who authored the classic texts on *shemiras halashon,* that had brought about the salvation.

Others, however, felt that it was the combination of the Chofetz Chaim's merit and the merit of the Manchester *Rosh Yeshivah,* whose avoidance of forbidden speech made his words of *tefillah* so very powerful.

פרשת כי תשא
Parashas Ki Sisa

Reaping the Fruits

רְאֵה קָרָאתִי בְשֵׁם, בְּצַלְאֵל בֶּן אוּרִי בֶן חוּר לְמַטֵּה יְהוּדָה.
See, I have called by name Bezalel, son of Uri,
son of Chur, of the tribe of Yehudah
(Shemos 31:2).

B ezalel, son of Uri, son of Chur, was endowed with a G-dly spirit and was granted knowledge of the wisdom with which Hashem created heaven and earth. It was with this spirit and wisdom that Bezalel built the *Mishkan*, where Hashem would rest His *Shechinah* (Divine Presence) on this earth.

How did Bezalel merit this? Obviously, he must have been an exceptionally great person in a generation of great people. However, it was not his merit alone that earned him this privilege.

It is unusual that the Torah mentions not only the name of Bezalel's father, but also his grandfather, Chur. Chur was the son of Miriam, Moshe's sister. Our Sages tell us that when the Jews began worshiping the Golden Calf, Chur rebuked them. Caught up in the frenzy of their sin, the people killed Chur.

Chur's *mesiras nefesh* (self-sacrifice) was not for nought. The building of the *Mishkan* was a sign that the people had been forgiven for the terrible sin of the Golden Calf, and that Hashem would once again rest His Presence among them. And it was in the merit of Chur's *mesiras nefesh* that his grandson, Bezalel, was chosen for this lofty task *(R' Yehudah Zev Segal).*

A Jew's self-sacrifice for Torah and *mitzvos* never goes unrewarded. The reward may come in the next generation, or even later, but ultimately, it will come.

❧ ❧ ❧

In Lithuania in the last century there lived a G-d-fearing couple of very modest means. They had very little in the way of furniture and clothing, but were very wealthy in Torah and *mitzvos.*

The wife owned only a few dresses and had very little to wear on Shabbos and *yom tov.* One day, the husband decided that it was time for his wife to buy a new dress. They would put aside a few cents each week until there would be enough money to purchase the dress. Many weeks went by before the amount needed had been saved. The woman had already gone to a seamstress and picked out the dress that she wanted. She wrote down the address of the shop, and the type of dress she wanted and handed the note to her husband, who was only too happy to buy the dress and bring it home to his very special wife.

As he walked through the town's streets, the man noticed a commotion. A man selling *sefarim* was surrounded by many customers. The dealer was offering one specific *sefer* for sale —

a new edition of *Masechta Bava Metzia* with the commentary of R' Shmuel Strashun, better known as the *Rashash*, printed at the end of the volume. This was the first printing of a *Gemara* that contained the *Rashash's* commentary.

The man picked up a volume and inspected it. What a work of beauty! Learning from it would be a delight, and would afford one the opportunity of having the commentary of the *Rashash* at his fingertips!

He was not thinking of his own learning. His mind was on his teenage son, a diligent yeshivah student. His son would begin learning *Bava Metzia* in about a month's time and needed a *Gemara* to take with him to yeshivah. The man asked the dealer the price. It was almost as much as the dress cost.

The man stood in silence, pondering what to do. Of course, this money was intended for his wife, not his son. But what would his wife say were she standing here? There was no time to go home and ask her; the volumes were being sold quickly; only a few remained. The dealer would leave town and probably not return for another six months.

"I know my wife better than anyone," he thought. "Surely, she would be willing to undergo any sacrifice for the sake of our son's learning." Having reached that decision, he handed the dealer the money and asked him to wrap up a *Gemara*.

On his way home, the man met the city's *rav*, who asked him what he was carrying. When the man explained what he had purchased and why, the *rav* excitedly asked if he could come home with him to see his son's reaction when he would be given the *Gemara*. The two walked up the path that led to the couple's home.

Suddenly, the husband stopped. "What's wrong?" asked the *rav*. The husband replied, "I bought the *Gemara* after coming to the conclusion that this is what my wife would want me to do. But what if I'm wrong? What if she will be hurt and upset?"

But it was too late for second thoughts. He took a deep breath, knocked on the door and opened it. The man greeted his wife and placed the package on the table. Slowly, he told her what it contained and how he came to purchase it.

His wife smiled broadly and said, "Oh, I'm so delighted! This is the most wonderful gift that I have ever received!"

❦ ❦ ❦

The above story was told by Rabbi Avraham Kalmanowitz, legendary Torah leader and head of Mirrer Yeshivah both in Europe and in America. Those who know say that the husband and wife were R' Kalmanowitz' parents and that their teenage son was none other than R' Kalmanowitz himself.

פרשת ויקהל
Parashas Vayakhel

Man With a Mission

וַיָּבֹאוּ כָּל אִישׁ אֲשֶׁר נְשָׂאוֹ לִבּוֹ.
Every man whose heart inspired him came
(*Shemos* 35:21).

The building of the *Mishkan* and its vessels, the making of its tapestries, and the weaving of the garments of the *Kohanim* required incredible skill and craftsmanship. Yet, the generation that departed Egypt and entered the Wilderness found itself without any such craftsmen. The Egyptians, of course, did not train the Jews in any crafts, nor did they allow them to develop their talents on their own.

Who, then, were the craftsmen of the *Mishkan* and all the vessels?

Ramban writes that there were Jews who, though unskilled, did have natural ability and they were inspired to volunteer for whatever had to be done. They were infused with faith that Hashem would help them to do whatever was necessary to fulfill the task — and so it was.

There are times when the community is badly in need of help but no one feels qualified to come forward and provide that assistance. A Jew must know that when he seeks to benefit the community *lesheim Shamayim* (for the sake of Heaven), he is granted special *siyata diShmaya* (help from Above), and can often accomplish things that seemed to be above and beyond his capabilities.

❧ ❧ ❧

R' Binyomin Wilhelm, founder of Yeshivah Torah Vodaath and other worthy institutions, succeeded where many others failed. He succeeded because he was a man of deep *emunah* (faith) and iron-willed determination. Most important, he was always ready to give of his time and energy, even when some might have argued that the problem could not be solved.

R' Binyamin was born in Poland around the year 1885 and was orphaned at the age of eleven. He then went to live with his grandfather in a one-room apartment. One morning, Binyamin awoke to discover that his grandfather had died suddenly during the night. Now he was alone in the world. He did not attend yeshivah because there was no organized system of yeshivos as it exists today. Every father had to see to it that his son learned with a *melamed* (Torah teacher) who was paid directly by the parents of his students. If a boy's father could not afford to pay the *melamed*, or the boy was an orphan, he very often grew up ignorant of Torah.

When he was sixteen, Binyamin received a letter from a friend who had emigrated to America and was living in New

York. The friend knew of Binyamin's tragic situation and implored him to join him in the "new country." Binyamin soon boarded a ship without a penny in his pocket. He paid his way by working in the ship's kosher kitchen.

Upon arriving in New York, Binyamin was welcomed by a small group of old friends. At a get-together, he and his friends solemnly vowed to always live faithfully by the Torah and never to compromise on a single *mitzvah* or *halachah*, no matter how great the pressure. This was at a time when finding a job in America was almost impossible for those who kept Shabbos, and when kashrus supervision in America hardly existed.

Binyamin opened a successful hardware business, married a deeply religious girl from a fine home and settled in New York's Lower East Side. He attended Torah classes every day, and through intense study and effort, developed into a respected *talmid chacham*.

In the early part of this century, the Lower East Side boasted the largest Jewish population in America. Most of its Jews lived in crowded apartment buildings. Across the river in neighboring Willamsburg lived another large concentration of Orthodox Jews. Willamsburg had many blocks of large single family homes, something which was quite appealing for a young, growing family. R' Binyamin and his wife moved there in 1917 and were very happy in their new dwelling. But there was one major problem. In the Lower East Side, Yeshivah Rabbi Jacob Joseph had already been founded, but in Williamsburg there were no yeshivos. R' Binyamin's oldest son was four years old; R' Binyamin was determined that his son receive the Torah education that he himself had been denied.

He approached a number of prominent Jews living in Willamsburg. They all responded the same way: Their neighborhood was not the place for a yeshivah. Though they were religious, they were resigned to sending their children to public school, where they could receive a quality secular education. Yeshivos, they felt, belonged to the "old world" of Europe. One man pointed to the palm of his hand and told

R' Binyamin, "When hair will grow here, there will be a yeshivah in Williamsburg."

One day, a man met R' Binyamin in the street and asked if he had had any success in his quest to start a yeshivah. When R' Binyamin responded in the negative, the man said, "R' Binyamin, take my advice. Stop asking others to start a yeshivah; start one yourself."

Over the next four months many nighttime meetings were held in R' Binyamin's home. His wife served herring and *kichlech* in the hope of attracting a crowd. But the meetings were not successful and it seemed as if the predictions of failure were correct.

It is customary in many *shuls* to read the entire Book of *Devarim* on the night of Hoshanah Rabbah. Such was the custom in the *Poilisher Shteibel*, one of the largest and most prominent congregations in Williamsburg. On the night of Hoshanah Rabbah in 1917, R' Binyamin made his way to the front of the *Poilisher Shteibel* and pounded on the *bimah* for attention. He said, "I will not permit the reading to commence until we resolve an urgent matter — the future of our children. Many are convinced that they can continue sending their children to public school and watch them grow up as Torah Jews. This is a grave error. Without Torah our children will not be Torah Jews. And without a yeshivah, they will have no Torah."

At the conclusion of his address, R' Binyamin asked for pledges toward founding a yeshivah. One of the *shul's* wealthy members, Mr. Aharon Goldman, wrote out a check for one thousand dollars, and a furrier named Mr. Wolf pledged five hundred dollars, both enormous sums in those days. Many others came forth with smaller pledges.

As news of R' Binyamin's Hoshanah Rabbah "protest" spread, people came forward to offer their participation in a founder's committee. A few months later, a building on the corner of Marcy Avenue and Keap Street was rented. Forty-five children were registered for the yeshivah, which was to open its doors the following September.

But when September arrived, the picture became clouded once again. With only forty-five children spread across five grades, there was not enough tuition to pay the necessary *rebbeim*, secular studies teachers and office staff. At a committee meeting held a few days before Yom Kippur, the committee voted to postpone the yeshivah's opening for one more year. The only dissenting vote was R' Binyamin's. "How can we wait another year?" he demanded. "What of the children who might become lost to us *this year*, and might never be brought back? How can we face the *Ribono shel Olam* on Yom Kippur after having made such a fatal decision?"

After hearing R' Binyamin's heartfelt plea, the committee decided to postpone a final decision until after Yom Kippur.

R' Binyamin spent the Holy Day in a most unusual manner. He arose early on Yom Kippur morning, and instead of going to *shul, davened* alone in his house. He spent the rest of the day going from *shul* to *shul* making appeals — not appeals for money, but for children. He appealed to fathers and mothers to save their children, and future generations, by registering them in the yeshivah that was soon to open. When the fast had ended, R' Binyamin returned home after a very successful day. Forty-five more children would now be enrolled in the yeshivah. With projected income from tuition now doubled, the committee voted to open the yeshivah in a few days. Yeshivah Torah Vodaath had been born.[1]

---

1. Across the street from the yeshivah's original home on the corner of Marcy and Keap lived a wealthy Jew named Yisrael Belsky. R' Binyamin prevailed upon Mr. Belsky to enroll his five-year-old son Berel in the yeshivah and to add a donation for two thousand dollars. Years later, R' Berel Belsky, who went on to study in Radin under the Chofetz Chaim, became R' Binyamin's son-in-law.

פרשת פקודי
Parashas Pekudei

Don't Despair

אֵלֶּה פְקוּדֵי הַמִּשְׁכָּן, מִשְׁכַּן הָעֵדֻת. . .

*These are the reckonings of the Mishkan,
the Mishkan of Testimony. . . (Shemos 38:21).*

*A testimony for Israel that Hashem had overlooked
the sin of the Golden Calf, for He rested His Shechinah
among them (Rashi).*

s Rabbi Yehudah Zev Segal, the Manchester *Rosh
Yeshivah*, explained, the Jewish people were demoralized following the terrible sin of the Golden Calf. In the depths
of their hearts, they found it difficult to believe that they could
be forgiven for this sin. Then, Hashem commanded that a
Mishkan be built: "And they shall make a Sanctuary for Me so
that I may dwell among them" (*Shemos* 25:8). The fact that the
Shechinah (Divine Presence) would rest among them was clear
proof that they had achieved forgiveness. Their hearts were
joyous once again.

Our Sages note that the verse does not read "And they shall
make a Sanctuary for Me so that I may dwell *in it* [בְּתוֹכוֹ].

Rather, it reads ". . . so that I may dwell *among them* [בְּתוֹכָם]"
— meaning, within each and every Jew (*Seder Olam Rabbah* 6).
A Jew, by living his life according to the Torah, becomes a
Mishkan in which the *Shechinah* dwells.

And just as the *Shechinah* returned to the Jewish people
after they had sinned so grievously, so does It return to a Jew
who has sinned and later mended his ways. A Jew who has
sinned must never allow himself to think that he is beyond
hope, that he can never do proper *teshuvah* for his past
mistakes.

The great Chassidic leader R' Aharon of Karlin once said:
"To despair is not a sin, but despair can lead to worse things
than any sin could."

A Jew can always turn himself around and start anew. That
is what the gift of *teshuvah* is all about.

In *Kreina D'Igresa,* the collected letters of the Steipler *Gaon,*
the Steipler responds to the letter of a yeshivah student who
expressed feelings of despair for sins he had committed:

". . . Most important of all is that you toil in the study of
Torah, the Torah of the living G-d, Blessed is His Name. Toil in
the study of Torah with intense effort, with the goal of
understanding all the fine details of a given topic . . .

"Do not say: 'My soul is sullied; the Torah cannot attach
itself to me,' Heaven forfend to think this way! Every word,
every bit of logic of Torah is *kodesh kodashim* (holiest of
holies). . . When Torah becomes ingrained in one's mind,
he becomes sanctified beyond measure with the sanctity of
Torah . . .

"The study of Torah for the sake of Heaven is the best means
of correcting the damage caused by past sins. This is
especially true of study that is intense and energetic, for it
atones like a sacrifice in the *Beis HaMikdash* . . . ."

❦ ❦ ❦

Rabbi Yaakov Pasternak served as *Rav* of Congregation
Ahavath Achim in Brooklyn and eighth grade *rebbe* at
Yeshivah Dov Revel in Queens. To those who knew him, he will

always be remembered as a loving teacher who cared for every Jew like his very own child.

At eighth grade graduation one year, a student approached R' Pasternak and the yeshivah's principal, R' Nochum Kaplan. "Goodbye for life," the boy told them. "I'll probably never see either of you again." The boy had failed miserably in his studies and had shown a total lack of interest in anything relating to Torah and *mitzvos.*

For years, the boy was not heard from. Then, R' Kaplan received a letter from the boy, addressed to himself and R' Pasternak. The boy wrote how he had drifted very far from his roots, abandoning even the most basic *mitzvos.* The letter continued, "Remember, Rabbi Pasternak, how you had once told me that whatever you had taught me was not for naught, because ultimately it would have its desired effect? Well, you were right. I am ready to come back."

Today, the boy is studying in a yeshivah in Jerusalem.

פרשת ויקרא
Parashas Vayikra

Of Sacrifice and Love

וַיִּקְרָא אֶל מֹשֶׁה, וַיְדַבֵּר ה' אֵלָיו מֵאֹהֶל מוֹעֵד לֵאמֹר.

He [Hashem] called to Moshe, and Hashem
spoke to him from the Tent of Meeting, saying
(Vayikra 1:1).

Τhere is a widespread custom for young children to begin their study of *Chumash* with this verse. The Book of *Vayikra* deals with the laws of the Temple service and ritual purity. As the *Midrash* puts it: יָבֹאוּ טְהוֹרִים וְיִתְעַסְּקוּ בִּטְהוֹרִים, *Let the pure [children] come and engage in the [study of] the laws of purity (Vayikra Rabbah 7:3).*

Sefer Avnei Ezel says that this custom is also a message to parents: The opening of the Book of *Vayikra* deals extensively with *korbanos* (Temple sacrifices). A parent must be prepared to make sacrifices so that his children can study Torah. If a child's success in Torah means giving up certain luxuries in order to pay tuition or a private tutor, or ridding the home of items that can hinder a child's growth in Torah, a parent must be prepared to do just that.

One of the outstanding *Roshei Yeshivah* of our generation is from a family that is not distinguished for its Torah scholarship. A former classmate of this *rosh yeshivah* once commented: "Only Hashem knows how his parents merited to raise such a son. But one thing I do know: When he was still a yeshivah *bachur*, he attended a family wedding that ended in the early hours of the morning. As soon as the wedding was over, his father drove him back to yeshivah — some three hundred miles round trip. The man appreciated the fact that his son did not want to be late for his learning period that morning."

❀   ❀   ❀

In the early years of this century, in the city of Ostrov, Poland, there lived a young couple and their two little boys. They lived in utter poverty, and so the husband and wife finally decided that there was no choice but to emigrate to America, where hopefully life would be somewhat easier. The husband sailed to America where he hoped to quickly find an apartment and a job, and then have his family join him.

But matters did not work out as planned. World War I erupted and travel across the Atlantic was suspended. It would be ten years before this family would be reunited.

In the meantime, the wife worked a few hours a day in order to support her two sons and herself, and also pay her sons' *cheder* (elementary school) tuition.

As time went on, the woman realized that she had a problem on her hands, one that any parent would hope to have. One of her sons was exceptionally bright and diligent; the *cheder* lessons were simply too easy for him. What he needed was a private *rebbi* for at least a few hours a day who would teach him on an advanced level.

But how would she pay the *rebbi*'s fee? The only solution would be for her to find another job. And that is what she did.

Each night, after her sons were tucked safely in bed, the woman would deliver cans of milk to villages on the outskirts of Ostrov. It was wartime, and the roads were especially dangerous, but nothing could deter her. She had a mission to accomplish, and with Hashem's help, she would succeed.

When the war ended, she and her sons emigrated to America, where the family was reunited. As the years passed, her young prodigy blossomed into an outstanding *talmid chacham*. He is the renowned *Rosh Yeshivah*, Rabbi Chaim Pinchus Scheinberg, head of Yeshivah Torah Ohr in Jerusalem.

❧ ❧ ❧

Our Sages state that the Book of *Vayikra* opens with the words וַיִּקְרָא אֶל מֹשֶׁה, *He called to Moshe,* to teach that Hashem summoned Moshe lovingly, saying, "Moshe, Moshe," whenever He wished to speak with him.

We may suggest that this, too, is implied in the custom of children beginning their study of Torah with the Book of *Vayikra.* Just as Hashem called lovingly to Moshe, so too, must a parent or teacher speak lovingly to a child when teaching him or her the proper way to behave.

When the mother of Rabbi Avraham Pam was about eight years old, she decided to fast on the Tenth of *Teves,* one of the four fast days which are related to the destruction of the *Beis HaMikdash.* She knew that were her parents to know of her plans, they would insist that she eat. To circumvent this problem, she spent the fast day at the home of friends and did not return home until nightfall after the fast had ended.

Upon coming home, she found that her father, who was the city's *Rav,* was being paid a visit by one of the community's distinguished members. When the man heard what the *Rav's* daughter had done, he became angry. "She deserves quite a punishment!" he declared. "Oh, would I give it to her if she were my daughter!"

The *Rav* did not respond. His daughter was given supper and then went off to her room to go to sleep. Soon after, her father entered the room, and took her into his arms. "*Mein kind* (My child)," he said, "I realize that you wanted to do a *mitzvah.* Nevertheless, you have made a mistake. If someone is commanded to fast, and he fasts, then he has done a *mitzvah*. But when one does not have to fast, it is not a *mitzvah* to fast. One is not permitted to deprive his body unnecessarily of the nourishment it needs. With Hashem's help, in a few years you will fast, and then it will be a real *mitzvah*. Now, you must be very tired, so go to sleep, and sleep tight. Good night!"

R' Pam's mother lived past ninety. In later years she would say that her father's words on that night warmed her all the days of her life.

פרשת צו
Parashas Tzav

Gratitude

אִם עַל תּוֹדָה יַקְרִיבֶנּוּ. . .
If as a thanksgiving offering he shall offer it. . . (Vayikra 7:12).

When the *Beis HaMikdash* stood, a person who survived a life-threatening crisis was required to offer a קָרְבָּן תּוֹדָה, *thanksgiving offering.* From a chapter in *Tehillim,* [1] the Sages derive the four experiences which necessitate this

---

1. Ch. 107.

offering: travel through a desert, release from prison, recovery from serious illness and a voyage at sea. Nowadays, one who experiences any of the above recites the בְּרְכַּת הַגּוֹמֵל, *thanksgiving blessing*. [1]

Hakaras hatov, gratitude, is surely not limited to our relationship with Hashem. It is also fundamental in our relationship toward our fellow man. According to *Ramban*, a lack of *hakaras hatov* is at the root of the prohibition against accepting male converts from Amon and Moav (*Devarim* 23:4-5). These two nations owe the Jewish people eternal gratitude, for it was Avraham who rescued Lot, the forefather of these two nations, when he was taken captive in war. Instead of showing gratitude, Amon and Moav did not even provide our ancestors with bread and water on their way to *Eretz Yisrael*. Those who lack the quality of *hakaras hatov* cannot be part of the Jewish people.

❦ ❦ ❦

It was the custom of Rabbi Aharon Kotler to eat the Shabbos meal with his *talmidim* in the dining room of his yeshivah. A *talmid* related how upon eating the soup, R' Aharon, on at least one occasion, asked one of his students to summon the cook who was busy in the kitchen. R' Aharon thanked the cook and commented on how delicious the soup had been.

❦ ❦ ❦

It was the practice of Rabbi Eliyahu Lopian to stand in the doorway of his home for a few moments and gaze upon the set table when returning after *Ma'ariv* on Friday nights. This was his way of showing recognition for his wife's many hours of toil in preparing the Shabbos foods and whatever else was needed for the honor of Shabbos.

❦ ❦ ❦

One summer, Rabbi Yonasan Shteif, the Veiner *Rav,* was taking a walk in the Catskill Mountains. The day was extremely hot and humid. As he walked, a light breeze began to blow.

---

2. See *Shulchan Aruch, Orach Chaim* 219:9.

R' Shteif stopped and exclaimed, "*A dank, Ribono shel Olam, far dem vint,* Thank you, Hashem, for the wind."

❁   ❁   ❁

Rabbi David Yitzchak Isaac Rabinowitz, the *Rebbe* of Skolye, spent his days and nights deeply immersed in the study of Torah. He rarely ventured out of the building in which his apartment and *shul* were housed. In the summer, however, he would spend a few weeks in the Catskill Mountains where his frail body could rejuvenate itself amid the fresh country air.

After his *rebbetzin* passed away, it became necessary for someone to accompany the *Rebbe* to the Catskills and care for his needs. For two consecutive summers, the *Rebbe's* nephew, Rabbi Shmuel Leifer, was assigned this task. The following summer, R' Leifer, then but a teenager, spent the summer in a learning camp in the Catskills.

One day during that third summer, a car drove up to the camp where Rabbi Leifer was staying. Out of the car stepped the *Rebbe,* whose own place of lodging was a half-hour drive from the camp. A crowd quickly formed, to greet the *tzaddik* and to learn the reason for this surprise visit. When R' Leifer greeted his uncle, the *Rebbe* said, "I came for one purpose — to thank you for taking care of me during the past two summers." He then handed his nephew an envelope containing spending money.

❁   ❁   ❁

According to *Sefer HaChinuch, hakaras hatov* is a primary reason for the *mitzvah* to honor one's father and mother. *Sefer HaChinuch* further notes that when a person strives to feel appreciation toward people, he ultimately comes to appreciate the infinite goodness of Hashem.

❁   ❁   ❁

Rabbi Dovid Bender was a rare individual. He was loved and revered by the students of Yeshivah Torah Vodaath where he was *Menahel.* His children remember him as someone who, among his other outstanding qualities, fulfilled the *mitzvah* to honor one's parents in a very exceptional and unusual way.

In his later years, Rabbi Bender's father, R' Avraham, emigrated to *Eretz Yisrael*. R' Dovid never missed an opportunity to send his father anything that might bring him *nachas* (pleasure from his offspring). If one of his children came home from yeshivah with a good grade on a test, the test paper was immediately air-mailed to his father. A snapshot of one of the children was also sent out immediately. Had the fax machine been invented at that time, there is no doubt that a steady flow of *nachas*-material would have traveled between the Bender home in Williamsburg and R' Avraham Bender's apartment in Tel-Aviv.

One year, R' Avraham traveled to America to visit his son and grandchildren. On the day on which R' Avraham's plane was to arrive at Idewild Airport (today Kennedy Airport), his grandchildren were ready bright and early, clad in their Shabbos finery. They were all going to the airport to welcome *"Der Zeide."*

They arrived at the airport and rode to the top of an observation deck that overlooked the runway on which the plane would land. Finally, the moment arrived, as the plane from Israel came down the runway and rolled to a stop. As R' Avraham stepped out of the plane, he heard a familiar voice shouting in the distance, *"Papa, Papa!"* He looked up at the observation deck and was able to make out the figure of his beloved son, who was oblivious to the stares of those around him. R' David could not wait the extra ten or fifteen minutes it would take to be able to embrace his father. He had to express his love for him *now* and he continued to shout, *"Papa, Papa . . .!"* R' Dovid's children recall how their grandfather responded with a smile that radiated joy and *nachas*.

R' Dovid Bender passed away suddenly at age fifty-three. His family in Bnei Brak decided that it would be best to keep the news from his aged father for as long as possible. This was no simple task, especially since R' Dovid had always been in frequent touch with his father. Finally, the family realized that the news could not be kept from him any longer. Afraid of how the news might affect R' Avraham's health, relatives in Bnei Brak arranged for a doctor to be on hand when he was informed.

Upon hearing the news, R' Avraham reacted by saying the following: "In truth, I must first express my *hakaras hatov* to the *Ribono shel Olam*. You see, when my dear son Dovid was three years old, he contracted a serious illness. Doctors were concerned that he might not survive. Yet, not only did he recover, but he lived another fifty years, and left behind sons and daughters. For this, I express my deepest *hakaras hatov* to the *Ribono shel Olam.*"

Then he sat down on the floor and cried.

פרשת שמיני
Parashas Shemini

Food for Thought

זֹאת הַחַיָּה אֲשֶׁר תֹּאכְלוּ . . .
These are the creatures that you may eat . . . (Vayikra 11:2).

Rabbi Noach Weinberg, *Rosh Yeshivah* of Yeshivah Aish HaTorah in Jerusalem, tells the following story:

There was a nursing home in America where only three residents were Jews. The Jewish director served them only strictly kosher food. One day, a government inspector came to check that all was in order at the home. A ninety-five-year-old woman complained to him, "I'm not happy here. I want to eat the same food as everyone else, but the director won't let me."

The inspector demanded an explanation, and was told the truth by the director: As an observant Jew, he was forbidden to feed another Jew non-kosher food. He assured the inspector that the kosher food served was of the highest quality, and that the woman's complaints were unfounded.

The inspector was unimpressed. "I don't care how good the kosher food tastes. That woman has a right to eat whatever she wants. The next time I come here, I expect to find that she's being served the same food as everyone else."

The director knew that there was no way he could obey the inspector's instructions. What he had to do was convince the woman to drop her demand for non-kosher food.

"You know," he told the woman, "our kosher food is actually tastier than our non-kosher food. It's also healthier. In fact, it's even more expensive!"

"I don't care if it's tastier," replied the woman. "At my age, I can hardly taste anything at all. As for health, how much longer do you think I have to live anyway? I want to be like everyone else — I want to eat what they eat."

So the director tried a different approach. He spoke to this woman, who had been non-religious all her life, about the beauty of Torah and *mitzvos*. His words had their desired effect. Eventually, the woman began to observe Shabbos, recite blessings over food, pray each day — and, of course, eat only kosher.

Upon being told this story by the director, Rabbi Weinberg asked him what exactly he had said that convinced this woman to become a *ba'alas teshuvah*. The man replied:

"I'll tell you the truth, I don't really know. I can't remember what I said. All I know is that I begged, pleaded, explained, coaxed . . . You see, I *had* to get that woman to keep kosher, or they would have closed my nursing home down. I simply had no choice . . ."

Rabbi Weinberg reflected: If only we would reach out to every non-religious Jew with the urgency that this young man felt when he spoke to the old woman! If only we would feel that we have no choice, that we simply cannot rest until we've led our brethren onto the path of Torah and *mitzvos*. With this approach, surely, we would meet with success.

Kindness for All

וְאֶת אֵלֶּה תְּשַׁקְצוּ מִן הָעוֹף . . . הַחֲסִידָה.
*These shall you abominate from among
the birds . . . the chasidah (Vayikra 11:14,19).*

Why is it called "chasidah" (חֲסִידָה)? Because it shows kindness (חֶסֶד) towards others of its species in sharing food with them (Rashi from Chullin 63a).

Eating non-kosher food harms a Jew in a spiritual way. It contaminates the soul and makes it difficult for the person to be connected to that which is holy.

Ramban comments that all non-kosher birds possess a cruel nature, as is evident by the way they tear apart their prey. However, this presents a problem. Why is the *chasidah* deemed non-kosher, if it demonstrates such compassion in sharing its food with others?

R' Yisrael of Rizhin answered that, as the Sages put it, the *chasidah* does kindness *with its friends,* with birds of its own species. It does not share with other types of birds.

This explanation contains an important lesson. For a person to help only those that are like him, who dress, speak and think the way he does, is not at all admirable. A Jew must seek to extend a helping hand to all types of people, including those whose way of life may differ from his own.

❀ ❀ ❀

With the outbreak of World War II, thousands of refugees streamed into the city of Vilna, the capital of Lithuania. Most of these refugees were yeshivah students, who came to Vilna at the behest of the city's great *Rav,* Rabbi Chaim Ozer Grodzensky. R' Chaim Ozer was founder of the *Va'ad HaYeshivos,* which helped support the great yeshivos of Eastern Europe between the two world wars. Since Poland had been invaded by the Germans from one side and by the Russians from the other, R' Chaim Ozer saw Vilna, which was part of independent Lithuania, as the yeshivah students' best avenue of escape. The students and their *roshei yeshivah* looked to R' Chaim Ozer for guidance. As soon as he sent word for them to come, they were on their way.

With the outbreak of war and the influx of refugees, flour became scarce in Vilna. R' Aharon Bakst, *Rav* of Shavli, sent the *Va'ad HaYeshivos* a wagonload of flour. R' Aharon Berek, the *Va'ad*'s secretary, hired bakers to bake bread around the clock. So desperate was the general populace that the freshly baked bread had to be brought to the *Va'ad* headquarters under police escort.

Officially, the bread was for the yeshivah students, for whom R' Chaim Ozer and the *Va'ad* had assumed responsibility. But no one who asked for bread was refused.

Ten years earlier, a group of non-religious Jews in the city had initiated a plot to unseat R' Chaim Ozer as *Rav* of Vilna. At that time, the Chofetz Chaim — then ninety-one-years-old — assisted by the Chazon Ish, had defended the honor of R' Chaim Ozer and ensured that he remain in his position. Now, the instigator of that shameful campaign, who had been a constant thorn in the side of the city's Torah community, asked the *Va'ad* workers for bread. The request was forwarded to R' Aharon Berek, who responded with a statement of the Sages: אֵין בּוֹדְקִין לִמְזוֹנוֹת, *One does not scrutinize [a person's credentials] when he asks for food* (Bava Basra 9a). The bread was given.

❧ ❧ ❧

In the 1920's, a secularist leader in *Eretz Yisrael,* who was known for his outspoken criticism of the Torah community, suddenly became critically ill. He was brought to the British Missionary Hospital in Jerusalem which, as its name indicates, was owned and operated by Christian missionaries. The hospital was open *only* to Jews, for its real purpose was not to heal the sick but to introduce Jews to gentile beliefs. Near every bed was a copy of the "New Testament" and the walls of each room were decorated with religious proclamations. Jerusalem's rabbinate had issued a strict ban against even setting foot into the Missionary Hospital.

After being in the hospital for four weeks, the secularist's condition had deteriorated to the point where doctors declared that there was no hope for recovery. The man's family realized that the only ones who could help them at that point were the doctors at Shaarei Zedek Hospital. Shaarei Zedek had been founded by Jerusalem's Torah community; its staff, headed by the legendary Dr. Moshe Wallach, was known to be the best in the country. The family feared, however, that the patient would not be granted admittance into Shaarei Zedek, since he had ignored the rabbinate's ban and was known as a forceful opponent of the Torah community.

The family concluded that their only hope was to speak to the city's revered *Rav,* Rabbi Yosef Chaim Sonnenfeld, who was known for his kindness and love toward every Jew. Someone was chosen to represent the family, and he went to R' Yosef Chaim's humble home in the Old City.

As the man made his way through the streets of Jerusalem, a terrific thunderstorm struck. Wet and shivering, the man entered the *Rav's* home and found him deeply immersed in study. The visitor apologized and related the entire story.

R' Yosef Chaim promptly closed the *sefer* before him, donned his coat and prepared to leave for the hospital. Outside the thunderstorm was still raging, so the visitor blocked the door, refusing to allow the *Rav* to go out in such treacherous weather. "I only asked for a letter, not that the *Rav* should go out in the storm," he said. To this, R' Yosef Chaim replied, "When a Jewish life is in danger, a letter is not enough. I must personally attend to fulfilling this great *mitzvah.*"

As the visitor later related: "Still speaking, the *Rav* dashed out of the room and in a moment he was up the steps. Young as I was, I had trouble keeping up with this seventy-five-year-old man. No sooner had we set out than the rain became torrential. I advised the *Rav* to wait until it let up a bit. In response, he only quickened his pace, exclaiming, 'Can a few drops of rain deter a person who is going to save a Jewish life?'

"I breathlessly followed the *Rav* until we reached the Jaffa Gate. There we boarded a carriage and ordered the driver to get us to the hospital as quickly as possible. The *Rav* drew his worn *Tehillim* from his pocket; I sat transfixed by the glow on his face as he quietly prayed."

As soon as they arrived at the hospital, R' Yosef Chaim wasted no time in arranging for the patient's immediate admittance. Two weeks later the man was released from the hospital having fully recovered. Knowing how agitated the man became whenever the Torah community came under discussion, his friends decided not to tell him of R' Yosef Chaim's involvement in his case.

During a speech at a groundbreaking ceremony one year later, this secularist declared, "We will build the land in our own way and with our own strength. We will build this land by waging a fight to the death against the black arm of Rabbi Sonnenfeld and his cronies!"

Seated in the audience was the messenger who had come to R' Yosef Chaim on that stormy day to seek his help on the man's behalf. Upon hearing the man's terrible remarks, he jumped up and shouted, "How dare you! Have a little respect for the saintly rabbi to whom you owe your very life!"

He then made his way to the podium and explained to the crowd how R' Yosef Chaim had interceded to save the life of the man who had vowed to destroy him.

פרשת תזריע
Parashas Tazria

For the Sake of a Mitzvah

וּבַיּוֹם הַשְּׁמִינִי יִמּוֹל בְּשַׂר עָרְלָתוֹ.

On the eighth day, the flesh of his foreskin shall be circumcised (Vayikra 12:3).

Rabbi Yosef Chaim Sonnenfeld, the saintly *Rav* of Jerusalem, was a skilled *mohel* and never refused an invitation to perform the *mitzvah* of *bris milah*. He was fond of describing this *mitzvah* as an opportunity to add one more Jew to Hashem's sacred army. At every *bris* he performed, R' Yosef Chaim's face shone with joy.

He performed this *mitzvah* with true self-sacrifice. Nothing could stop him from attending a *bris,* not even Arab riots and disorders which sometimes made walking from neighborhood to neighborhood extremely dangerous.

In the year 1919, Jerusalem was hit by a snowstorm the likes of which its residents had never seen. The storm began on Monday and it continued for three entire days — by Wednesday nearly three feet of snow had fallen. Walking outdoors was extremely hazardous, since it was impossible to tell where the sidewalks ended and the streets began, or where low walls and fences might be buried beneath the snow. Worst of all was the danger of falling into one of the many open pits and wells which were scattered throughout the city.

A *bris* was scheduled for Wednesday morning in Meah Shearim, quite some distance from R' Yosef Chaim's apartment in the Old City. Early Wednesday morning, when the streets were still entirely deserted and it seemed that no one would dare venture outside, the people of Meah Shearim were startled by a strange sight. In the distance, an old man appeared to be making his way through the field of snow; each step was obviously being made only through strenuous effort. The figure was that of R' Yosef Chaim.

Word of R' Yosef Chaim's arrival quickly spread from window to window and house to house. One of the *Rav's* grandsons ran through the snow to greet his grandfather. R' Yosef Chaim was glowing with joy at having been able to reach his destination and perform the *bris.*

His grandson asked, "*Zeide* (Grandfather), why did you strain yourself so? Couldn't they have called a *mohel* who lives nearby? There was no reason to fear that the *bris* would be postponed."

"On the contrary," R' Yosef Chaim answered, "it was precisely because of the difficulties of journeying through the snow that I feared the *bris* might be postponed. Since I had already agreed to perform the *bris,* the baby's parents would certainly begin the day by waiting for me. Even as the hours would pass without my appearing, other *mohelim* would have been reluctant to accept an honor which had already been accorded to someone else. I feared, therefore, that there was a real possibility of the *bris* not taking place on the eighth day — unless I would come. Thank G-d, I have arrived safely."

❦ ❦ ❦

Rena was waiting anxiously. Where were they already?

Finally, there was a knock on the door. Rena's husband, Uri, entered with a little bundle in his arms. Behind him was a man they had only recently met. He was known simply as Reb Avraham.

"Mazal tov, Mrs. Baruchov," said Reb Avraham. "Everything went just fine."

"Yes," added Uri. "Reb Avraham performed the *bris* and everything went as planned. *Baruch Hashem,* no 'surprise guests' showed up. Here, Rena," and he undid the blanket around the infant whom he held, "hold our little Yosef. Finally, our child has a Hebrew name."

Rena picked up the small crying infant, kissed him on the cheek . . . and fainted.

Under the Communists, circumcising an infant was considered an act of "religious coercion." The Communists, always "concerned" for the rights of their citizens, declared it a crime to perform a *bris* until a boy turned eighteen, at which time he could decide for himself whether or not he wanted to be circumcised. Of course, until a boy turned eighteen, the Communists did a very good job of brainwashing him to despise religion and even to deny belief in the existence of a Creator. When they turned eighteen, most Jewish boys had not the faintest notion what *bris milah* was about.

Rena had been raised in a religious home and understood the importance of *bris milah.* She knew that a Jewish boy without a *bris* was a spiritually impaired soul. However, she knew that it would be impossible to have her child's *bris* performed on the eighth day. First, a qualified *mohel* had to be found who was willing to undertake the great risk of performing this *mitzvah.* Then, a plan had to be formulated through which the circumcision could be done in utmost secrecy. It would not be easy.

Rena did not know how long it would be until her son could enter into the covenant of the Patriarch Avraham. She did however know one thing. The longer her son's *bris* was delayed, the greater was the danger that she would grow accustomed to his being uncircumcised. And what if it would be months or even years before the *bris* could be performed? The need to fulfill the *mitzvah* might, G-d forbid, become forgotten . . . .

Rena decided to do something that would allow her no rest until her baby would have his *bris*. She promised herself that she would not kiss her little boy until he was circumcised.

And so, from the day that he was born, Rena cuddled her baby, held him on her shoulder, rocked him to sleep — but never once did she kiss him.

And now, as she held her little Yosef in her arms, all the love and emotion that had been welling up inside of her for so long burst forth as she kissed him for the very first time.

And then she fainted.

A Matter of Life and Death

וְהַצָּרוּעַ אֲשֶׁר בּוֹ הַנֶּגַע, בְּגָדָיו יִהְיוּ פְרֻמִים וְרֹאשׁוֹ יִהְיֶה פָרוּעַ
וְעַל שָׂפָם יַעְטֶה, וְטָמֵא טָמֵא יִקְרָא . . . בָּדָד יֵשֵׁב, מִחוּץ לַמַּחֲנֶה מוֹשָׁבוֹ.
And the person with tzara'as in whom there is the affliction —
his garments shall be torn, the hair of his head shall be unshorn,
and he shall cloak himself up to his lips; he is to call out,
"Contaminated, contaminated!" . . . He shall dwell in isolation;
his dwelling shall be outside the camp (Vayikra 13:45-46).

The Sages teach that the terrible affliction of *tzara'as* is a punishment for the sin of speaking *lashon hara* (evil talk). The term מְצֹרָע (one who is afflicted with *tzara'as*), say the Sages, is a contraction of מוֹצִיא שֵׁם רַע, *one who spreads slander*

(*Arachin* 15b). *Tzara'as* is a condition which indicates that the person has sinned grievously toward his fellow man and that he must mend his ways.[1]

The Torah is unusually stringent with regard to the laws of *tumah* (ritual impurity) that pertain to the *metzora*. This underscores the extreme severity of the sin of *lashon hara*.

Rambam writes (*Hilchos Tumas Tzara'as* 16:10): "The Torah states: *And the person with tzara'as...his garments shall be torn, the hair of his head shall be unshorn, and he shall cloak himself up to his lips;* [2] *he is to call out, 'Contaminated, contaminated!'* The purpose of this proclamation was to warn people to stay away from him lest his *tumah* contaminate them, and to inform others of his anguish so that they would pray for him. The *metzora's* isolation and disgrace would humble him, and would inspire him to regret his sin. He would resolve that from then on, he would refrain from committing this bitter sin, and he would beg forgiveness of those of whom he had spoken disparagingly in the past."

From among the various types of *tumos* (ritual impurities) mentioned in the Torah, only *tzara'as* forces the person to live in isolation.

"Why was the *metzora* singled out to live in isolation? Because [through his evil speech] he caused ... friends to become distant from one another" (*Arachin* 16b).

The laws of *tzara'as*, says the Dubno *Maggid*, are a lesson to the *metzora* about the power of speech. A person afflicted with *tzara'as* cannot become *tamei* unless the *Kohen* who examines

---

1. Contrary to its common translation, *tzara'as* is not leprosy or some other physical disease, but the physical manifestation of spiritual disease. As R' Samson Raphael Hirsch writes, if *tza'aras* were some biological disorder and the *metzora's* isolation was a form of quarantine to prevent the disease from spreading, then some of its related laws are inexplicable. For example, if the symptoms of *tzara'as* are found on a newlywed during the festive week following marriage, the *Kohen* does not pronounce the person *tamei* (impure) so as not to interfere with the festivities. Also, the Torah states that if one's entire body is covered with *tzara'as*, he is *tahor* (pure), but if one spot on his body heals, then he is *tamei*.

2. He dresses and acts like a mourner, so that he will be influenced to grieve and repent the behavior that brought this affliction upon him *(Ibn Ezra)*.

him pronounces him *tamei*. Without this pronouncement, the person remains *tahor* (pure) and none of the laws of *tzara'as* apply. A single word spells the difference between purity and impurity. Such is the power of speech.

In the Book of *Mishlei*, Shlomo *HaMelech* states: מָוֶת וְחַיִּים בְּיַד לָשׁוֹן, *Death and life are in the hand of the tongue* (*Mishlei* 18:21). Words can destroy and words can build. People's lives can change dramatically through a single remark directed their way, as the following true stories demonstrate.

♖   ♖   ♖

Daniel is a professional who is married and raising a fine religious family in a neighborhood whose streets are dotted by *shuls* and *battei midrash*. Daniel says, "*Daf Yomi* saved my life." He explains:

"As a yeshivah high-school student, I was not very successful in my Torah studies. I had trouble grasping some of the more difficult concepts and had difficulty retaining whatever I did manage to understand.

"One day, I was studying in the yeshivah's *beis midrash* and thought of what seemed to be a good question on the *Gemara* which I was learning. I approached one of the older *beis midrash* students whom I knew well. When he heard my question, he could not help but smile. 'Daniel,' he said, 'that's a question that only an *am ha'aretz* (ignoramous) would ask. You had better start working harder at your learning, or that's exactly what you're going to grow up to be — an *am ha'aretz*.'

"His words cut through me like a knife. I assumed that his assessment of me as an *am ha'aretz* was correct, but he was wrong in thinking that I wasn't trying hard. I was, it just didn't come easy to me. I decided then and there that it was no use trying any more — I was doomed to failure.

"I graduated high school, left yeshivah, and rarely opened a *sefer* for many years. It was very painful to me when my children would ask me to help them with their learning and I could not.

"In 1982, the *siyum* (completion) of *Daf Yomi* generated great excitement worldwide. In my neighborhood, new *shiurim* (lectures) were beginning and some of my friends were joining up. I felt caught up in the excitement and decided to give it a shot. I began to attend a *shiur* and was amazed to discover that I understood it!

"To make a long story short, I now study the *daf* five times a day. I attend a *shiur* in the morning before work, listen to it again in the car on the way to work, then again on the way home from work. I then go to a second *shiur* on the same *daf* at night after work, and then I review it on my own. And guess what? Not only do I understand the *Gemara*, I even retain a lot of it.

"Yes, *Daf Yomi* saved my life."

❧ ❧ ❧

Dov is a respected member of an American Torah community. Twenty years ago, Dov was attending public school. Then, a yeshivah in his area began a "buddy" program. Every Tuesday night, boys from the local public school would be brought to the yeshivah for refreshments and half an hour of Torah study in the *beis midrash* with students of the yeshivah. It was as a result of this program that Dov became religious and began to attend yeshivah.

When Dov was already an established member of that yeshivah's *beis midrash,* he approached one of the married students and said, "You know, I never told you this, but it's thanks to you that I became religious."

The other student was taken aback. "Thanks to me? But we never even studied together!"

"I know," Dov replied, "but I can vividly recall my first night in the yeshivah. I felt so uncomfortable. All of you with your short haircuts, suits and white shirts, and me with my long hair and jeans! I liked the fellow that studied with me, but not enough to want to come back.

"As I was about to leave that night, you came over and greeted me warmly. You asked me my name and said that it was really nice having me and my friends visit your school. And you invited me to come again. I could tell that you meant it and it made me feel very good.

"That is why I came back the next week."

פרשת מצורע
Parashas Metzora

Soul Talk

זֹאת תִּהְיֶה תּוֹרַת הַמְּצֹרָע בְּיוֹם טָהֳרָתוֹ.
*This shall be the law of the metzora
on the day of his purification (Vayikra 14:2).*

Hashem would take note of the *metzora*'s repentance and heal him of his affliction. The *Kohen* would go outside the Israelite Camp to examine the *metzora*. Having been declared healed by the *Kohen,* the *metzora* would begin the purification process, which included the offering of sacrifices, as detailed in the Torah. The very complex order of purification which the *metzora* must undergo is further proof of the severity of the sin of *lashon hara.*

One may wonder why in our day those who habitually speak *lashon hara* are not stricken with *tzara'as*. In *Sefer Shemiras HaLashon,* the Chofetz Chaim cites the explanation of *Chidah*:

When Hashem punishes an individual, He does it for the person's benefit; to purify him of his sins and to stir him towards repentance. It was only while the *Beis HaMikdash* stood that a *metzora* could attain *taharah* (purification). However, today when, to our misfortune, the *Beis HaMikdash* has yet to be rebuilt, there is no sacrifice, and no way for the *Kohen* to perform the other components of the purification process. Therefore, if a person were to be afflicted with *tzara'as*, he would remain in his impure state for the rest of his life (or until the coming of *Mashiach*), without any possibility of ridding himself of it. Therefore, in our days, the impurity of *tzara'as* clings only to the soul, and not to the person's body.[1]

❧ ❧ ❧

When Rabbi Yitzchak Blazer, a leading disciple of Rabbi Yisrael Salanter, passed away, the city of Jerusalem was grief-stricken. "R' Itze'le," as he was known, was revered as both a *gaon* and *tzaddik*, and was a leader of Jerusalem's holy community. His loss was irreplaceable.

As preparations for his funeral were being made, it became known that R' Itze'le had left instructions that *hespeidim* (eulogies) not be said for him. Such has been the way of many *tzaddikim* throughout the generations. However, the scholars of Jerusalem were uncertain whether or not this request should be fulfilled. It was known that when Rabbi Yaakov Yehoshua Falk, author of *P'nei Yehoshua*, had left the same request, the renowned *Rav* of Prague, Rabbi Yechezkel Landau (author of *Noda BeYehudah*), had ruled that eulogies should be said, for the *Pnei Yehoshua* was רֹאשׁ כָּל בְּנֵי הַגּוֹלָה, *leader of the*

---

1. The Chofetz Chaim adds that the sufferings of poverty can take the place of *tzara'as*, for arrogance is the prime cause of *lashon hara* and by being dependent upon others for survival, the poor man is humbled. Moreover, he is actually afraid to speak disparagingly of others, lest they learn of his remarks and cease assisting him.

Tikkunei Zohar, as well, states that this sin can lead to poverty.

entire Diaspora [i.e. the entire generation]. Nevertheless, Rabbi Shmuel Salant, Jerusalem's venerable *Rav,* was of the opinion that R' Itze'le's request *should* be honored.

In the end, Rabbi Chaim Berlin, another of the Holy City's luminaries, spoke at the funeral and prefaced his words with the following. The Torah relates that when Sarah died, Avraham came לִסְפֹּד לְשָׂרָה וְלִבְכֹּתָה, *to eulogize Sarah and to cry for her* (*Bereishis* 23:2). R' Chaim explained that לִסְפֹּד, *to eulogize,* means to speak the praises of Sarah, while לִבְכֹּתָה, *to cry for her,* means to cry over what the generation had lost with Sarah's passing. Said R' Chaim, "In keeping with the deceased's request, I will not speak his praises, but I will express our pain over the void which his passing has created in our community."

On the following Friday night, R' Itze'le appeared to R' Chaim in a dream and said, "Thank you for not speaking my praises." R' Chaim then asked R' Itze'le to tell him of his judgment before the Heavenly Court. R' Itze'le replied that the Heavenly Court is very exacting in its judgment; nothing a person has done in his lifetime is overlooked. R' Itze'le added that, *"the judgment is particularly exacting regarding forbidden speech which the person has spoken."*

Rabbi Eliyahu Lopian would relate the above with great emotion and would conclude, "The sin of forbidden speech is exceedingly awesome! No angel will come to defend those who are guilty of this sin."

פרשת אחרי
Parashas Acharei

Between Man and His Fellow

כִּי בַיּוֹם הַזֶּה יְכַפֵּר עֲלֵיכֶם לְטַהֵר אֶתְכֶם,
מִכֹּל חַטֹּאתֵיכֶם לִפְנֵי ה' תִּטְהָרוּ.

For on this day he shall provide atonement
for you to cleanse you; from all your sins
before Hashem shall you be cleansed (Vayikra 16:30).

R' Elazar ben Azariah taught: For sins between man
and Hashem, Yom Kippur provides atonement, but for
sins between man and his fellow, Yom Kippur does not
provide atonement, until he appeases his fellow man
(Mishnah Yoma 8:9).

In the early years of this century, there lived a young couple in Jerusalem who were married for a number of years and did not have children. Both husband and wife prayed fervently that this blessing be granted them.

In those days, the only way to do laundry was by hand. After each article had been thoroughly washed and wrung out, it would be hung on an outdoor line to dry. One day, this young woman washed her laundry and, as usual, hung the items on her line outside. After she went inside, a hot-tempered woman, who lived in a neighboring apartment entered the courtyard as she returned home. As she walked, she momentarily became entangled in the laundry which hung on the line. Perhaps the laundry was hanging lower than it should have been; or it may have been that the woman was engrossed in her thoughts and simply was not looking where she was walking. Whatever the case, her reaction was inexcusable. In a rage, she rushed to her apartment and returned to the courtyard with a pair of scissors. Without a moment's thought, she cut the clothesline and all the laundry fell to the dirt.

A few minutes later, the first woman went outside to see if her laundry was dry. For a few moments she stared open-mouthed in disbelief. When she noticed how the rope had obviously been cut, tears welled up in her eyes. Silently, she gathered up her laundry and brought it inside. As she began her second wash of the day, she vowed to herself not to tell her husband what had happened. Were he to find out, he would surely be distressed, and out of concern for his wife might seek to discover the identity of the perpetrator. Strife is like fire; one must do everything in one's power to avert it. And so, when her husband came home from the *beis midrash* that evening, she said not a word.

But there was commotion in another home that night. A young child of the hot-tempered woman suddenly developed a high fever and his condition seemed serious. A doctor was summoned and the boy's father paid a visit to the city's *Rav*, Rabbi Yosef Chaim Sonnenfeld, in search of his bles-sing for the child's recovery. Hearing of the suddenness with which the child fell ill, R' Yosef Chaim asked if anything unusual had occurred at home in the hours beforehand. The husband did not know of anything, but said that he would ask his wife.

Shamefacedly, the woman told her husband of her terrible act. Soon, both husband and wife were standing before R' Yosef Chaim. Upon hearing what had transpired, the *Rav* quickly donned his hat and coat. "Come," he beckoned to them "we have no time to lose. You must beg forgiveness immediately."

He accompanied them to the woman's home. There, the woman who had cut the clothesline broke down and cried as she admitted her guilt to her neighbor. She said that Hashem had already punished her by afflicting her child with illness. Humbly, she begged forgiveness. The other woman accepted her apology and said that she forgave her with a full heart. The child's fever soon subsided.

While all this was going on, R' Yosef Chaim became aware that the husband of the woman who had hung out the laundry was totally baffled by what was taking place. "You mean to say that your wife did not inform you of what had transpired?" the *Rav* asked.

"That is correct. This is the first that I am hearing about it."

It became clear to R' Yosef Chaim that it was the woman's righteousness which had prevented her from making mention of the incident. Deeply moved, he said, "In merit of your silence, may you be blessed with a son."

One year later, the woman gave birth to a boy, whom they named Yosef Sholom. He is Rabbi Yosef Sholom Elyashev, the renowned *posek* of Jerusalem.

פרשת קדושים
Parashas Kedoshim

The Art of Reproof

הוֹכֵחַ תּוֹכִיחַ אֶת עֲמִיתֶךָ וְלֹא תִשָּׂא עָלָיו חֵטְא.

You shall reprove your fellow
and do not bear a sin because of him
(Vayikra 19:17).

Although we are commanded to reprove someone
who sins, we are not to do so in a way that will cause
him embarrassment. To embarrass someone — even
when he has clearly done wrong — is a very grave sin
(based on Rashi).

One day, when the Chofetz Chaim was already in his nineties, he informed his family that he would be journeying by train to the town of Lida, where he had lived for a time in his younger years. Despite the protests of his children that his frail health did not permit such a trip, the Chofetz Chaim was insistent. He said that he would be going there to attend an important meeting at which his presence was absolutely necessary. He drew up a list of some thirty men from Lida who he wanted present at the meeting.

On the day of the meeting, the Jews of Lida gathered at the town's train station to welcome the *tzaddik* of the generation. A horse-drawn carriage brought the Chofetz Chaim to the community building where the meeting was to take place.

All those who had been invited were in attendance. The Chofetz Chaim wasted no time in explaining the purpose of his visit.

"When a person prepares to visit a certain city, it is proper that he inform his friends and neighbors of this, to afford them the opportunity to send packages, messages, or merely regards to their acquaintances there.

"Now, I will soon be going on a trip, and this concerns all of you. I am a very old man, and I will soon be heading the way of all men, to the World of Truth.

"In my younger years, I lived in this very town, with your parents and grandparents. Surely, I will meet them in the World to Come, and they will expect me to bring regards from you.

"Daniel," the Chofetz Chaim now said turning his attention to one particular man, "what shall I tell you father, who was so dear to me? Can I give him 'good' regards and tell him that his children and grandchildren faithfully follow the path of Torah by which he lived? Tell me, my dear Daniel, what do you wish me to say?"

Tears welled up in Daniel's eyes. He said nothing.

In this way, the Chofetz Chaim addressed each man in the room, recalling his fondness for that person's ancestors, and asking what he could relate to those ancestors when he would reach the next world.

By the time the Chofetz Chaim had finished, the face of every man was wet from weeping and his heart was filled with remorse. Each one firmly resolved to mend his ways and live a life that would bring his ancestors joy and pride in the World to Come.

❃   ❃   ❃

Rabbi Aryeh Levin and a companion were once walking down a Jerusalem street on Shabbos. Walking towards them was a well-built young man smoking a cigarette. When their paths crossed, R' Aryeh said in a friendly way, "Today is Shabbos. One is not permitted to smoke on Shabbos."

"And how do you know I'm Jewish?" the man retorted.

R' Aryeh was not deterred. "You don't understand," he said. "It is only because I love you that I tell you it is Shabbos. You are my brother, and it pains a person when he sees his brother causing himself harm. This is why I took the trouble to say something to you."

The man's angry look softened. He asked quietly, "Shall I throw the cigarette down, or should I put it out?"

"Just put it down; it will go out by itself," R' Aryeh replied.

The young man did as instructed. He then said, "I have been criticized many times in my life, but this is the first time I felt that the person really meant it for my good. I am not about to say that I will keep Shabbos for the rest of my life, but I do give you my word that I will keep the remainder of this Shabbos. Please tell me what time Shabbos ends."

R' Aryeh responded, wished the man well, and continued on his way.

❀　❀　❀

It was *Tishah B'Av* afternoon and Yitzchak, a Chassidic man living in Brooklyn, opened his grocery store for the benefit of those who needed to purchase food for after the fast. Soon, two customers entered the store, a neighborhood *rav* and a non-religious Israeli girl. The girl loaded up her shopping cart with cookies, sodas and other treats. She approached the check-out counter and said defiantly, "I'm not fasting — I had a cup of coffee this morning!"

Yitzchak responded softly, "Well, you did break your fast, but you would still get a *mitzvah* if you refrained from eating from now until nightfall."

The girl was obviously taken aback by Yitzchak's soft and sincere reply. She turned to the *rav* who was now near the counter and asked, "What do you say?"

The *rav*, too, spoke in a gentle and kind tone. "The man is correct. It would be a *mitzvah* for you to refrain from eating the rest of the day."[1]

Without a word, the girl returned all her would-be purchases to their respective shelves. She left the store without another word.

The girl returned the next day. She told Yitzchak that she had not eaten the rest of the day, and in fact had refrained from eating a few hours into the night as a way of atoning for her having eaten earlier. She said, "The way in which you and the rabbi spoke to me moved me very much. I promised myself that I would never again eat on *Tishah B'Av.*"

❧ ❧ ❧

Around a century ago, there lived a *maggid* who used to travel throughout Lithuania imploring Jews to improve their observance of *mitzvos.* Once, he visited the Chofetz Chaim in Radin and poured out his frustrations. "I am coming now from a community where I was dismayed to learn of the poor level of *mitzvah* observance among many families. Shabbos morning, I stood before the *Aron HaKodesh* and spoke about the urgent need for *teshuvah.* I could not believe their reaction! Before I could finish my speech, some men charged forward and threatened to drag me away if I would not descend the pulpit on my own! What is the matter with these people? Why can't they face the truth?"

The Chofetz Chaim responded with a question of his own. "How did you speak when you delivered your reproof? Were you calm or did you get excited?"

"Why, of course I got excited!" replied the *maggid.* "Those people are sinners and they had to be told in no uncertain terms that their behavior must change! I screamed, I pounded my fist on the lectern. . .and I explained the severity of what

---

1. *Aruch HaShulchan* states: "On a day set aside for fasting. . . if one forgot and ate, or even if he has eaten intentionally — and even when he has eaten a large amount — what is done is done; he must bear his sin, but he must fast the remainder of the day" (*Orach Chaim* 568:1).

they had been doing. And I told them what's going to happen to them if they don't mend their ways!"

"Now I understand," the Chofetz Chaim responded. "Of course your words did not accomplish anything constructive. Tell me, my friend, when you put on *tefillin* in the morning, do you also shout and pound your fist? Certainly not, for that is not the way one performs a *mitzvah*. Well, offering *tochachah*[1] (reproof) to one's fellow Jew is also a *mitzvah*. Nowhere does it say that this *mitzvah* is different than any other, that it must be carried out in a manner that is insulting and belittling to the person being criticized. Next time, speak to the people in a way that shows you care for them and that you respect them. No doubt, your words will then accomplish much more."

---

1. As in הוֹכֵחַ תּוֹכִיחַ, *[lit.] reprove, you shall reprove.*

פרשת אמר
Parashas Emor

Yosse'le Ganav

וְנִקְדַּשְׁתִּי בְּתוֹךְ בְּנֵי יִשְׂרָאֵל.
*And I [Hashem] will be sanctified
among the Children of Israel (Vayikra 22:32).*

*Give yourself over [to die] and sanctify My Name
(Rashi).*

In nineteenth-century Europe, most Jewish communities did not have an organized yeshivah system for children. Parents who could afford it would get together and hire a *rebbi* to teach Torah privately to their sons. This meant that many children from poor families received no Torah education at all. And when a Jew is raised without Torah, there is no telling how low he may fall. Thus, in the city of Shpole, Russia there were some young peasant Jews who banded together to form a group of professional thieves! The leader of this group was a slight, athletic young man who was known as "Yosse'le Ganav" (Yosse'le the Thief).

It once happened that the group set its eyes upon the valuable gems and ornaments which were found in the local church. The thieves figured out that the only way they could possibly succeed at stealing this fortune was for one of them to climb up one of the church walls, and enter through a small window near the top of the building's steeple — a job, of course, for Yosse'le *Ganav*.

They waited for the end of the month when the moon disappears from view. The thieves then made their way to the church grounds in the blackness of night. As Yosse'le began his ascent, the others huddled near the wall to await Yosse'le's signal that the loot was on its way down.

Yosse'le reached the window at the top of the steeple. He pried it opened with ease and climbed inside. Meanwhile, the night watchman had come to investigate a report of suspicious noises heard around the building. As soon as the thieves saw him coming, they scattered in all directions. Yosse'le, unaware of what was transpiring outside, was busy gathering the loot. When he had gathered everything together, he spread out a large tablecloth and piled the valuables onto it. Then he tied the ends of the tablecloth together so that it served as a sack, slung it over his shoulder, and climbed back up to the window to make his escape.

Yosse'le called out a signal and waited for his comrades to respond with a signal of their own before he let the sack fall to the ground below. When there was no response, he signaled again . . . and again. Realizing that something was wrong, he began to plan his next move but did not get very far. Soon, Yosse'le found himself face to face with the watchman and a furious priest, who ordered that the Jew be cast into a dungeon.

A few days later, Yosse'le was brought before a panel of judges for sentencing. The chief judge pronounced the verdict: for daring to break into the church, the Jew would be burned alive in the city square, in the presence of the city's entire gentile population.

However, the judge continued, there was a way by which Yosse'le could save himself. If he were to publicly convert to their religion, then not only would his life be spared, but he would also be granted lavish gifts so that he would have no need to steal ever again.

Yossel'le needed no time to think it over. Drawing himself up to his full height, he declared for all to hear, "I may be a thief, I may have done plenty of wrong in my life, but never will anyone convince me to forsake my religion! Torture me if you wish — it will not make any difference. Do you think that I am out of my mind, to be willing to exchange the living G-d for some lifeless statues? I am a Jew and I will always remain a Jew."

Yossel'le was violently thrown back into his prison cell. The next day at around noon, he was brought in chains to the city square where stands which had been hastily erected were filled to capacity. The gentiles watched gleefully as Yossel'le was brought to stand next to a vat of boiling tar.

The priest turned to Yossel'le and told him that he could still "repent" and live. "Stop wasting your time," Yossel'le replied. "I told you already that I will never forsake my religion!"

The priest gave the signal and two guards lifted Yossel'le up into the air. Yosse'le's hands were slowly dipped into the boiling tar. He could not help but cry out in agony.

"You still have a chance," the priest announced. "Promise to convert and you will live, and a doctor will be called to heal your hands."

"I TOLD YOU ALREADY," Yosse'le shouted. "I AM A JEW AND I WILL ALWAYS BE A JEW! LET ME DIE AND SANCTIFY THE NAME OF THE LIVING G-D!"

That night, Yossel'le's remains were handed over to the Jewish community of Shpole. He was buried in the Jewish cemetery near the famed *tzaddik* known as the Shpole *Zeide.* A simple tombstone atop his grave bore the inscription, "Here lies the martyr, Yosse'le *Ganav.*"

※　※　※

In the fifth chapter of *Avos*, we find two consecutive *mishnayos* in which our forefather Avraham is mentioned. However, only in the second *mishnah* is he referred to as

"Avraham *Avinu,* Our father Avraham" (*Avos* 5:3). Rabbi Chaim Volozhiner explains that this *mishnah* focuses on the ten tests which Avraham withstood: "Many qualities which a *tzaddik* toils and strains to attain come naturally to his descendants, and they can achieve them with minimal effort. We see with our own eyes how so many simple Jews give their lives *al kiddush* HASHEM (for the sanctification of G-d's Name) — this quality was implanted in us by Avraham *Avinu*, who was willing to sacrifice his life for his faith in the episode at *Ur Kasdim*[1]. And so did each of Avraham's ten tests pave the way for us" *(Ruach Chaim)*.

Beautify the Mitzvah

אֵלֶּה מוֹעֲדֵי ה' מִקְרָאֵי קֹדֶשׁ אֲשֶׁר תִּקְרְאוּ אֹתָם בְּמוֹעֲדָם.
These are the appointed festivals of Hashem,
the holy convocations, which you shall designate
in their appropriate time (Vayikra 23:4).

זֶה אֵלִי וְאַנְוֵהוּ.
This is my G-d and I will glorify Him (Exodus 15:2).
וְאַנְוֵהוּ — Beauty yourself [הִתְנָאֶה] *before Him*
through mitzvos. Make a beautiful succah, a beautiful
lulav, a beautiful shofar. . . (Shabbos 133b).

R abbi Avraham Tchekenaver was one of the great Torah personalities of nineteenth-century Poland. He was revered as a great Torah scholar and a man of impeccable integrity.

---

1. See *Rashi* to *Bereishis* 11:26.

It happened one year that as the festival of Succos approached, R' Avraham still did not possess an *esrog* of a quality which satisfied him. That year, the dealers in his city had been unable to procure the high quality *esrogim* which they usually sold. R' Avraham therefore dispatched an emissary to the capital city of Warsaw to find an *esrog* that would meet with his specifications.

Sure enough, the emissary returned with an *esrog* of exceptional beauty. R' Avraham offered the man his blessings and carefully placed the *esrog* on a shelf in a bookcase of his study.

On the first morning of the *yom tov,* there was a knock on the emissary's door. R' Avraham wished to see him at once.

"Is something wrong, *Rebbe*?" the emissary was soon asking the *tzaddik*.

"Yes," R' Avraham replied, "but I'm not exactly certain what it is. There is something about this *esrog* that you have not revealed to me. What is it?"

The man was adamant. "*Rebbe,* what do you mean? The *esrog* is right here in front of us. Anyone can see that it is unusually beautiful. What could be wrong with it?"

R' Avraham looked the man squarely in the eye. "This morning, I picked up the *esrog* to recite the *berachah* and perform the *mitzvah* — and suddenly my hands began to tremble. There is something about this *esrog* that you are not telling me. Now, what is it?"

The man was silent for a few moments. He lowered his head in shame and began, "In Warsaw, I went to one of the well-known *esrog* dealers. He had good merchandise, but nothing that really satisfied me. Then, I spotted a closed box on a side shelf.

" 'What is this?' I asked the dealer.

" 'Oh, that's a real beauty,' he replied, 'but it's not for sale, someone already looked at it and asked me to put it aside for him.'

"I asked the man if I could open the box just to look, and he agreed. When I saw how beautiful this *esrog* was, I offered more than the asking price. The man refused to consider my offer. Then I said, 'Do you know for whom I am seeking an *esrog*? For R' Avraham Tchekenaver! Don't you think it is proper that *he* should have this *esrog*?' When the man heard this, he gave me the *esrog* without an argument."

R' Avraham placed the *esrog* back in its box. "Well," he said, "I certainly won't use this *esrog*. I will fulfill the *mitzvah* with another one."

❀ ❀ ❀

One year, the late Manchester *Rosh Yeshivah*, Rabbi Yehudah Zev Segal, traveled to America to spend the Pesach festival with his children. It was R' Segal's custom to eat only *matzos* which were baked under his personal supervision. Along with his suitcases, R' Segal brought to the airport a few boxes of *matzos*. As he stood on line to check his luggage, another traveler approached him. "Rabbi, I see that you have quite a bit of baggage. I'm a seasoned traveler and I can tell you that your things are going to be very much overweight — it's going to cost you a lot.

"Take my advice: Put those boxes on the side somewhere; no one will take them. When you get to the counter, just show them your suitcases. Later, when you board the plane, take the boxes with you — I assure you that no one will bother you."

R' Segal looked at the man as if he had not heard him correctly. "I don't understand — are you suggesting that I try to trick the airline personnel? How can a person do such a thing? It's dishonest!"

The boxes cost fifty British pounds in baggage fees. As he withdrew the money from his wallet, R' Segal remarked joyfully, "Another *hiddur* (beautification) in the [*mitzvah* of] *matzah!*"

There is more than one way to beautify a *mitzvah*.

פרשת בהר
Parashas Behar

Mighty Warriors

וּבַשָּׁנָה הַשְּׁבִיעִת שַׁבַּת שַׁבָּתוֹן יִהְיֶה לָאָרֶץ שַׁבָּת לַה',
שָׂדְךָ לֹא תִזְרָע וְכַרְמְךָ לֹא תִזְמֹר.

But the seventh year shall be a complete rest for the land,
a Shabbos for Hashem; your field you shall not sow
and your vineyard you shall not prune (Vayikra 25:4).

Bless Hashem, O His angels, the mighty warriors who
do His bidding, to obey the voice of His word (Tehillim
103:20). R' Yitzchak Nafcha said: This refers to those
who observe Shemittah . . . This man sees his field lie
fallow, his vineyard lie fallow — and he accepts all this
in silence! Can there be a more powerful warrior than
he? (Yalkut Shimoni, Tehillim 860).

T he Torah refers to the year of *Shemittah* as שַׁבָּת לַה', *a*
Shabbos for Hashem. The observance of Shabbos bears
testimony that Hashem created the world in six days and
rested on the seventh. Furthermore, when a person refrains
from work on Shabbos, he is demonstrating his belief that it is

Hashem Who determines whether his efforts to earn a living during the six workdays will succeed. Similarly, the observance of *Shemittah* proclaims that the land is Hashem's and that it is He Who determines whether or not the farmer's efforts during the other six years of the *Shemittah* cycle will result in good crops.

Recent *Shemittah* years have seen thousands of religious farmers lay down their plows and allow their fields to lie fallow. In a number of instances, farmers have clearly seen how the faith which they demonstrated during *Shemittah* brought blessing to their crops.

In 1949, a new Agudath Israel *kibbutz*, *Moshav Kommemius*, was founded. Since its founding, *Kommemius* has been in the forefront of *Shemittah* observance. The following is an excerpt from a letter by the settlement's legendary *Rav*, Rabbi Binyamin Mendelsohn:

"In 5717 (1957), the Jewish Agency decided to plant orchards in a number of settlements — *Kommemius* included. We agreed, but with one condition: we would keep the laws of *Shemittah* in the *Kommemius* orchard . . . .

"During the *Shemittah* year 5719 (1959), our orchards were kept in accordance with my *halachic* guidelines, though the Ministry of Agriculture representative insisted that I was endangering the orchard because the trees were not being taken care of properly. Many times I wondered how it would work out, but I found strength in my faith in the *mitzvah* of keeping *Shemittah*, and in the merit of those *poskim* (*halachic* authorities) whose words guided my decisions. . . For sure, Hashem would stand by my side . . . .

"At the end of 5719, the Ministry representative told me with great emotion that with the exception of our orchard, all the orchards under his jurisdiction had been worked as usual. The end result was that the *Kommemius* orchard prospered far, far more than all the rest. The representative asked me if I had an explanation for this.

"I told him that the first *Ani Ma'amin* (of the Thirteen Principles of Faith) is that Hashem was, is, and will be in control of all that happens. Because we fulfilled Hashem's will regarding this orchard, He guided our success with it . . . .

"The following has been entered in the registry of the Government Department of Orchards: 'The orchard of *Kommemius* was not worked during the entire year of *Shemittah,* and it prospered.' "

※   ※   ※

Yaakov cultivates aromatic flowers in Israel's Central Region. In advent of *Shemittah* 5740 (1980), Yaakov, upon the directives of *poskim,* planted his fields well in advance of Rosh Hashanah so as to permit a harvest, with distribution controlled by the local *beis din* (religious court). However, during the following summer of *Shemittah,* he was not permitted to till the soil or plant. To work the fields after *Shemittah* had ended would have been too late. His flowers have to be uprooted and planted anew each year, and so it seemed that he would have no crop at all for the year following *Shemittah.*

The local *beis din* found no loophole to allow Yaakov to plant anew. One of the *rabbis* suggested that after *Shemittah* had ended, Yaakov should water and fertilize his old plants. "Who knows?" the *rav* reasoned. "Perhaps your old plants will yield another crop."

They did. And yet another crop the following year.

Service with a Smile

וּבְאַחֵיכֶם בְּנֵי יִשְׂרָאֵל אִישׁ בְּאָחִיו לֹא תִרְדֶּה בוֹ בְּפָרֶךְ.

*And with your brethren, the Children of Israel —
a man with his brother — you shall not
rule over him overbearingly (Vayikra 25:46).*

*A Jew must not subjugate his fellow men. If his fear
is upon them, or if they are ashamed to violate his
word, then he should not command them to do
anything big or small, unless it is in accordance with
their will and to their benefit — even to warm up a flask
of water or to go on an errand to the market to buy a
loaf of bread (Sha'arei Teshuvah 3:60).*

R' Shraga Frank was one of the wealthiest Jews in Kovno, Lithuania. He owned a leather factory, a leather goods store, and a great deal of real estate. More important, he was a *talmid chacham* and *tzaddik*, and was held in high esteem by the legendary founder of the *Mussar* Movement, Rabbi Yisrael Salanter. In the attic of R' Shraga's house, R' Yisrael and his closest disciples would spend the entire month of *Elul*, in preparation for Rosh Hoshanah.[1]

R' Shraga's own approach to *Elul* can be seen from the following incident. Once, he extended a personal loan to a

---

1. R' Shraga's four sons-in-law were all outstanding *talmidei chachamim*. They were: Rabbi Moshe Mordechai Epstein, *Rosh Yeshivah* of Yeshivah Knesses Yisrael in Slobodka; Rabbi Isser Zalman Meltzer, *Rosh Yeshivah* in Slutsk and later of Yeshivah Eitz Chaim in Jerusalem (and father-in-law of Rabbi Aharon Kotler); Rabbi Baruch Hurwitz, *Rav* in Alexot, Lithuania and Chairman of Agudath Israel in Lithuania; and Rabbi Sheftel Kramer, a *Rosh Yeshivah* in Slutsk and later *Mashgiach* of one of America's first yeshivos, located in New Haven, Connecticut. (He was the father-in-law of Rabbi Yaakov Yitzchak Ruderman.)

local merchant. The man invested the money, and his investment prospered at first, but he did not repay the loan. Then, his investment floundered and he found himself penniless again. When the man requested a second loan, someone told R' Shraga, "How can you lend him again? Even when he was doing well, he didn't bother to repay the first loan!"

R' Shraga replied, "It is *Elul* now. Each year during this month, we come before Hashem and plead, 'Please grant us health and prosperity for the coming year. We promise to correct our mistakes of the past year.' When the next *Elul* comes around, we look at ourselves and realize that we have fallen far short of our spiritual goals. Yet we come before Hashem and once again we promise to improve and ask that we be granted a good year. And Hashem grants our request! Shouldn't we do the same for others?"

Once, R' Shraga was hosting some guests in the dining room of his home. When he wished to serve them tea, he rang the bell near his seat to summon the maid, but she did not appear. R' Shraga sounded the bell a few more times and received no response. One of the guests commented, "It seems that you are not tough enough with your hired help. Perhaps if your maid felt a bit of fear, she would not be so lax in her duties."

R' Shraga smiled broadly. "Ah, but it is her laxity which makes me so happy! I am forever concerned lest I be guilty of being too harsh with my hired help and thereby transgress the commandment, 'You shall not rule over him overbearingly.' When the maid fails to respond to my call, it puts me at ease."

❧ ❧ ❧

The Sephardic luminary R' Chaim Palagi related that a month after one of the Jews of his city had died, he appeared to him in a dream. The man was wearing *yom tov* finery and appeared very happy. R' Chaim asked the man how he had merited such joy in the Next World, to which the man responded, "I always treated my hired help with honor and compassion. Never was I cruel or overbearing toward them and never did I overwork them."[1]

פרשת בחקתי
Parashas Bechukosai

The Joy of Torah Study

אִם בְּחֻקֹּתַי תֵּלֵכוּ וְאֶת מִצְוֹתַי תִּשְׁמְרוּ וַעֲשִׂיתֶם אֹתָם.
וְנָתַתִּי גִשְׁמֵיכֶם בְּעִתָּם, וְנָתְנָה הָאָרֶץ יְבוּלָהּ וְעֵץ הַשָּׂדֶה יִתֵּן פִּרְיוֹ.
If you will follow My decrees and observe
My commandments and perform them.
Then I will provide your rains in their time;
the land will give its produce and the tree of the field
will give its fruit (Vayikra 26:3-4).

If you will follow My decrees — that you should toil
in the study of Torah (Rashi).

In the winter of 5728 (1968), Rabbi Meir Pam, who was then approaching ninety, fell seriously ill and had to undergo surgery. The night before he was to be admitted to the

---

1. From *Sefer Tochachos Chaim.*

hospital, R' Pam, prepared for the possibility that his end was near, gave over to his son, Rabbi Avraham Pam (*Rosh Yeshivah* of Mesivta Torah Vodaath), final instructions concerning various *tzedakah* projects.

The next morning, the two rode together in a cab to the hospital. On the way, the elder R' Pam told his son, *"Zag a vort* (Tell me a Torah thought)." His son responded by relating a difficultly asked by *Tosafos* in *Masechta Succah* and a solution to it found in *Sefer Aruch LaNer*. R' Meir Pam pondered this solution and then responded, "I am not sure that this is correct." There was no time to discuss the matter further, for they had reached the hospital and went directly to the admitting office.

The doctors decided that surgery posed too great a risk for a man in such a weakened condition. R' Meir Pam remained in the hospital, and a few days later underwent a very difficult treatment as an alternative to surgery. When he was brought back to his room, he appeared pale and extremely weak, just barely alive. R' Avraham Pam, who had been waiting in the room, was frightened by his father's appearance.

The patient motioned with his finger that his son should come to the head of his bed. R' Avraham Pam's heart was pounding, for he thought that his father wanted to relate his parting words to him. R' Pam bent down to hear what his father would say.

"Who said this?" his father whispered.

R' Pam replied, "I do not understand."

His father repeated, "Who said this?"

"I do not know to what you are referring," R' Pam responded.

"Taxi!" whispered the father.

"Ah!" R' Pam replied knowingly. "The solution of the *Aruch LaNer* which we discussed in the taxi!"

"Yes," R' Meir Pam whispered. "I have thought the matter through well. He is not right."[1]

---

1. Rabbi Avraham Pam notes that *Aruch LaNer's* solution seems to be a matter of disagreement among the later commentaries. See *Atarah L'Melech* p. 169-170.

How does a person achieve such an attachment to Torah? How can a person attain a love for Hashem's word that does not allow even the most trying situation to divert his mind from its study? R' Avraham Pam writes (in *Atarah L'Melech*) that to his mind, his father acquired this quality in his youth, through uninterrupted, in-depth Torah study, which he accomplished while in the company of other students like himself, who dedicated their minds totally to Torah. Through the joy and pleasure of toiling in Torah, one's soul becomes bound up with it.

In his youth as a *talmid* in the Slobodka Yeshivah, R' Meir Pam made it a practice to retire for the night, after a long day of intensive study, with a *sefer* in hand. In this way, he drifted off to sleep while contemplating the thoughts of *Ketzos HaChoshen*, *Noda B'Yehudah* or R' Akiva Eiger. And in the last years of his life, when his eyesight dimmed, he would strain himself by day to study from a *sefer*, and would study at night by heart. His body may have been frail, but nothing in the world could weaken his love for the word of Hashem.

☙ ☙ ☙

The following was told to Rabbi Aaron Twerski by a storekeeper who teaches a daily class in *Daf Yomi*:

"My father owned a grocery in Tel Aviv. He worked very hard to earn a living, but always arose in the wee hours of the morning to study Torah. In the store, he always kept a *Gemara* at his side. Between serving one customer and the next, he would learn.

"When my mother passed away, my father informed us that he would be selling the store so that he could devote himself to the full-time study of Torah. He was already past seventy and said that each day of old age was a special gift from Hashem and should be dedicated to His service.

"But my brother and I were afraid that our father was making a mistake. It is not easy for a man of that age to study *Gemara* all day after he has spent so many years doing business for most of the day. We respectfully suggested that our father spend a number of hours a day helping out in my brother's weaving mill, which is a bus ride away from our father's home. To this suggestion, our father replied:

" 'Listen, my children: when a person leaves this world, he has to account for how he spent his days on earth. When I am asked how I spent my days and weeks, I will have to acknowledge that much of it was spent in the grocery earning a living so that I could support my family and send my children to yeshivah. I will say that even after my children were married and on their own, I continued running the store for the sake of your mother, who very much needed to be among people and thrived on her interaction with our many customers. But what will I say about the years I was granted after your mother passed away? That I spent two hours a day riding on a bus so that I could pass the time in a weaving mill?' "

The storekeeper concluded, "For the next thirteen years of his life, my father studied Torah diligently for twelve to thirteen hours a day, and would spend his spare time doing acts of *chesed.* "[1]

Ohr HaChaim (*Devarim* 26:1) writes: "Were people to experience the sweetness and delight of Torah, they would pursue it with a madness, and all the gold and silver in the world would be nothing in their eyes."

In speaking of Torah study, the Mishnah states (*Avos* 6:4), "If you will do this . . . you are praiseworthy . . ." R' Eliyahu Lopian comments: If someone who had never tasted wine would ask you to describe that taste to him, you might say, "Did you ever taste something sweet? Did you ever taste something sour? Well, the taste of wine is a combination of sweet and sour." This explanation might be true, but it is not sufficient. The only way to really know the taste of wine is by tasting it.

And so it is with Torah. *If you will do this . . . you are praiseworthy . . . .* The joy of Torah study and the satisfaction it brings to a person's life cannot be conveyed in words. It has to be experienced.

---

1. From an article by Rabbi Twerski in *The Jewish Observer*, (February 1991).

פרשת במדבר
Parashas Bamidbar

His Children

וְאֵלֶּה תּוֹלְדֹת אַהֲרֹן וּמשֶׁה בְּיוֹם דִּבֶּר ה׳ אֶת משֶׁה בְּהַר סִינָי.
וְאֵלֶּה שְׁמוֹת בְּנֵי אַהֲרֹן הַבְּכוֹר נָדָב, וַאֲבִיהוּ אֶלְעָזָר וְאִיתָמָר.
These are the children of Aharon and Moshe
on the day Hashem spoke with Moshe at Mount Sinai.
These are the names of the sons of Aharon,
the firstborn was Nadav, and Avihu, Elazar
and Isamar (Bamidbar 3:1-2).

These are the children of Moshe and Aharon —
Though only the children of Aharon are mentioned,
they are referred to as the children of Moshe, for he
taught them Torah. This teaches that whoever teaches
another man's son Torah is considered as if he had
borne him (Rashi from Sanhedrin 19b).

Hungary during the nineteenth century was a country rich in Torah greatness. Its most famous leader was R' Moshe Sofer, author of *Chasam Sofer*. R' Chaim of Sanz, a great Chassidic leader of the following generation, once remarked, "The thoughts contained in *Sefer Chasam Sofer* are wondrous; one would think that some of them were authored by the *Rashba*."[1]

The Chasam Sofer was *Rav* of the city of Pressburg and head of the famous Pressburg Yeshivah. Under his leadership, the yeshivah became known world-wide as a glorious center of Torah. It became the pride and joy of every father and mother to be able to say that their son studied in the Chasam Sofer's yeshivah.

One of the yeshivah's outstanding students was a boy from a very poor home. The boy lived far from Pressburg and would pay for his day-to-day needs with the little money which his parents sent him. During his fourth year in the yeshivah, the boy's parents were not able to send him even that small amount. The boy had no money for cleaning his clothes, buying some food, or for anything else.

In his desperation, the boy thought of an original way of earning money. He approached a student who came from a very wealthy home and said, "I have a proposition to make: Our *Rebbi* [the Chasam Sofer] is now teaching us a topic in *Gemara* which I have studied once before. The next *shiur* (lecture) he is to deliver is one which I heard him say three years ago, my first year in the yeshivah. I remember it very well; the questions, answers, proofs and comparisons. In fact, I even remember the *Rebbi*'s gestures and facial expressions as he proceeded from point to point.

"For a modest sum of money, I will say the *shiur* for you and others, and perfectly imitate the manner in which the *Rebbe* delivered it."

The wealthy student readily agreed to the deal and the boy delivered the *shiur,* much to the delight of all those present.

Somehow, the Chasam Sofer caught wind of what had transpired. He called for an assembly of all his students, to be held the following day. The impoverished student and those who had attended his *shiur* were quite apprehensive about what the Chasam Sofer might say. It seemed obvious that they

---

1. R' Shlomo ben Aderes, one of the thirteenth century's greatest Talmudic commentators.

had demonstrated a certain lack of respect by participating in a lecture which was intended as an imitation of their *Rebbi*. Would the Chasam Sofer ask them to leave the yeshivah because of this?

The next day, the students rose in respect as the Chasam Sofer entered the room to speak. His face looked grim; he was obviously upset. He began, "My dear *talmidim*: It is impossible for me to hide my distress; I'm sure it is apparent for all of you to see. Undoubtedly, you think that what happened yesterday is the cause of my distress. You are mistaken. It is not what happened yesterday; rather, *it is what caused yesterday to happen.*

"A *talmid* of mine was desperately in need of money, so desperate that he went to extreme lengths to earn something for himself.

"But I am his *Rebbi*, his teacher, his father! Why did I not concern myself with his needs so that he should not reach such a point of desperation? Why was I unaware of how badly he needed help in caring for his needs?"

The Chasam Sofer was now weeping unabashedly, as he turned to his beloved *talmid*. "Please," the *tzaddik* begged, "please forgive me. . . ."

❦ ❦ ❦

Rabbi Shneur Kotler, who succeeded his illustrious father R' Aharon as *Rosh Yeshivah* of Beth Medrash Govoha in Lakewood, New Jersey, had a place in his heart for every Jew, and especially for his students. Under R' Shneur's leadership, the student body in Beth Medrash Govoha swelled to over one thousand students, yet R' Shneur strove to get to know each and every student. He would stop a newcomer to the yeshivah and with a genuine smile say, "Come into my office when you can and let's 'talk in learning.' " Such talks were not meant to test the *talmid*'s knowledge, but to forge a bond of Torah with him.

Amazingly, after delivering his weekly *shiur* before some 400 students who were studying a given *masechta*, R' Shneur could later recall who had been absent and would later ask the student why he had been missing.

He spoke to a young student with the respect that one would accord a famous *Rosh Yeshivah*, always referring to the student as "Reb _____." He concerned himself with the student's needs to the very best of his ability.

Once, a newly married student informed R' Shneur of his difficult financial situation and asked if he could be placed on the *kollel* payroll. R' Shneur felt very bad that he could not honor this request. For a married student to be placed on the payroll, he had to have already studied in the yeshivah for a certain amount of years, and this student had not been in the yeshivah long enough to qualify. It would be unfair to the other students for R' Shneur to make an exception.

Only a short while passed before the student was approached by a member of the yeshivah's administration. An anonymous benefactor wanted to supply a few married students with free meat for at least one year. R' Shneur had chosen this young man to be one of those selected for this gift. The young man never found out the identity of his benefactor, or if any other students also received meat. However, he knew one thing — by the time the meat supply ran out, he was already eligible for the yeshivah's payroll.

Some twenty-five years ago, a *Melaveh Malkah* was held in Camp Toras Chesed, where yeshivah students of high school and post-high school age pursue their Torah studies while benefiting from summer recreation. The *Melaveh Malkah* was graced by R' Shneur's presence.

Among those at the gathering was Rabbi Eliyahu Roman, who had studied at Beth Medrash Govoha before becoming a yeshivah *rebbi*. Despite the festive air at the *Melaveh Malkah*, R' Roman was having a hard time enjoying himself. The previous day, his young daughter had broken out with an unusual rash which covered most of her body. The doctors had recommended that she be hospitalized until they had determined the nature of the rash. Now, more than twenty-four hours later, her condition had not changed and the doctors had still not diagnosed her condition.

By the time R' Shneur arrived at the camp, the dining hall was filled. As he approached the hall, everyone rose in respect. Lively singing and clapping erupted as the students surrounded the *Rosh Yeshivah.*

Amid the tumult, R' Roman approached and extended his hand in greeting. R' Shneur did not let go of R' Roman's hand. Instead, he led his former *talmid* to a corner and asked, "What is wrong, R' Elya?"

R' Roman told R' Shneur of his daughter's condition and of the doctor's efforts thus far. R' Shneur thought for a moment and said, "She needs to be seen by Dr. Gribetz. He is a pediatric specialist and can diagnose your daughter's condition."

R' Roman thanked R' Shneur for his advice. He then asked, "May I know how the *Rosh Yeshivah* knew that something was wrong?"

"I saw it in your eyes," R' Shneur replied.

The doctor correctly diagnosed the rash as an allergic reaction, and it was cured in a very short time.

❧ ❧ ❧

In 1938, Rabbi Elchonon Wasserman came to America to raise desperately needed funds for his yeshivah in Baranovich, Poland. In 1939, as R' Elchonon prepared to return home, threatening war clouds darkened the skies over Europe. The Germans, after having seized control of Czechoslovakia, had taken Austria and were threatening to invade other countries. Those in America who were close to R' Elchonon implored him to remain with them until the situation in Europe improved. They suggested that he send for his sons to come join him in America. R' Elchonon could not consider such a proposal. "I don't have three sons; I have 400 sons — the students of my yeshivah. How can I abandon them?"

R' Elchonon returned to Poland and rejoined his beloved *talmidim,* teaching and infusing them with spiritual strength until they were forced to disperse. R' Elchonon died a martyr's death, but his memory lives on through the teachings that he transmitted to his students, many of whom are alive today.

פרשת נשא
Parashas Nasso

Seizing the Moment

דַּבֵּר אֶל בְּנֵי יִשְׂרָאֵל וְאָמַרְתָּ אֲלֵהֶם,
אִישׁ אִישׁ כִּי תִשְׂטֶה אִשְׁתּוֹ וּמָעֲלָה בוֹ מָעַל.
Speak to the Children of Israel and say to them:
Any man whose wife shall go astray and
commit treachery against him (Bamidbar 5:12).

דַּבֵּר אֶל בְּנֵי יִשְׂרָאֵל וְאָמַרְתָּ אֲלֵיהֶם,
אִישׁ אוֹ אִשָּׁה כִּי יַפְלִא לִנְדֹּר נֶדֶר נָזִיר לְהַזִּיר לַה׳.
Speak to the children of Israel and say to them:
A man or woman who shall express themselves to vow
the vow of a Nazir unto Hashem (Bamidbar 6:2).

Why is the chapter of the Nazir placed next to the
chapter of the Sotah? For whoever sees a Sotah in her
degradation should prohibit wine to himself by taking
the vow of a Nazir (Rashi from Sotah 2a).

The above teaching seems difficult to understand. If the Sotah had, in fact, been guilty of sin, then upon drinking the bitter waters in which the Name of Hashem had been erased, she would immediately die a gruesome death. It would seem that those who witnessed this sight would be petrified to follow in the *Sotah*'s sinful ways. Why then do the Sages say that one who witnessed her degradation should become a *nazir* and abstain from wine (which can cause a person to become lightheaded and ultimately to sin)? Isn't this unnecessary for those who saw what happened to the *Sotah*?

To understand the answer to this question, let us contrast the following two stories:[1]

During World War I, a young Jewish soldier in the Russian Army found himself deeply frustrated and upset. He was fighting on the front lines, where the battle raged furiously. His comrades were falling all around him; during the lulls in the fighting, he and his fellow soldiers would have to drag the dead bodies off the battlefield.

He noticed that there was one group of soldiers who were able to rejuvenate themselves when they returned to rest in their foxholes. These were religious Jews who would spend their brief rest time reciting *Tehillim*. It was obvious that the saying of *Tehillim* imbued them with faith and had a calming effect upon them.

At one point in the war, this soldier lifted his eyes to the heavens and said, "G-d, I hate being a soldier. I hate killing and being in danger of getting killed. It is not my fault that I do not pray to You, or observe the other commandments. I was never taught anything about Judaism. Please show me that You are watching over me. Cause a bullet to wound my hand so that I will no longer have to fight in this terrible war."

Moments later, the fighting came to a halt as the two sides agreed to a brief cease-fire. Then a lone shot from a German gun hit the soldier on the finger. The wound was enough to prevent him from ever returning to the front. The soldier had clearly seen Hashem's intervention. He promised himself that as soon as he returned home, he would begin to learn about Judaism and would observe all the *mitzvos*.

---

1. The first is from *The Maggid Speaks* by Rabbi Paysach J. Krohn, the second from *Lieutenant Birnbaum* by Meyer Birnbaum with Yonason Rosenblum (both published by Mesorah).

When the war ended, the soldier returned home, still determined to become religious. However, he decided that before beginning to learn about his heritage, he would first return to college for the three months of study he still needed in order to earn a degree in agriculture.

By the time those three months passed, his resolve was no longer the same. The spiritual awakening which he had experienced on the battlefield was but a distant memory. He never did return to the ways of his forefathers. Years later, in a moment of honest reflection, he said, "Had I gone to study in a yeshivah right after the war was over, I might be a different sort of person today."

❦ ❦ ❦

During the Second World War, a Canadian bomber became engaged by German war planes over France. The plane's rear gunner was a nineteen-year-old non-religious Jew who had volunteered for the Air Force in his desire to help fight the beasts who were trying to destroy his people.

By the time the air battle ended, the Canadian plane was low on gas. On its return to base in Birmingham, England, the plane was forced to circle until it had no fuel left. The pilot tried to bring the plane down safely, but it ended up crash-landing fifteen miles from the base. The plane hit the ground and rolled to a stop between two houses narrowly missing both. The impact was such that the plane was completely torn in half and its landing wheels were never recovered.

Many of the crew were knocked unconscious or suffered broken limbs. Miraculously, the rear gunner never lost consciousness and none of his bones were broken. He set out on foot in the pitch dark to get help from the base, guided only by his sense of direction. When he arrived at the base, the men there could not believe their eyes. They had been sure that all the crewmen were dead.

The boy was given a sleeping pill, and slept for twenty-four hours. As soon as he awoke, he asked to be taken to the home of Rabbi Reuven Rabinowitz, whose house was a home away from home for many Jewish soldiers. The boy was given a hero's escort as a general accompanied him to the rabbi's home. As soon as he entered the house, the boy asked that Rabbi Rabinowitz teach him how to say *Tehillim.* He began to observe the *mitzvos* and was filled with an unquenchable thirst for Torah. In time, he became fully observant.

The boy ended his military career as a captain and was awarded the Distinguished Flying Cross for his heroism at the time of the crash. Upon returning home, he lost none of his enthusiasm for Torah. Today, all his sons and sons-in-law are *bnei Torah.*

❈ ❈ ❈

When a person lives through a very inspiring experience, the memories of that event alone will not be enough to make the person a better Jew. Memories are nice but their impact fades after a while. For example, someone who has never studied Torah seriously might become very uplifted when dancing in *shul* on *Simchas Torah.* However, for *Simchas Torah* to have a lasting effect upon that person, he has to immediately begin to study Torah on a regular basis. Otherwise, the sweet memories of dancing with the Torah will fade away in a very short time.

It is true that the terrible sight of the *Sotah* in her degradation would leave anyone shaken and determined not to sin as she did. However, for the sight of the *Sotah* to have a *lasting* effect, it is crucial that the person immediately do something that will help steer him toward good and away from evil. This is what the Torah teaches us by placing the chapter of the *Nazir* next to that of the *Sotah.*

Do Whatever You Can

וַיַּקְרִיבוּ נְשִׂיאֵי יִשְׂרָאֵל רָאשֵׁי בֵּית אֲבֹתָם. . .
וַיָּבִיאוּ אֶת קָרְבָּנָם לִפְנֵי ה'. . .

*The princes of Israel, the heads of their fathers' household . . .
brought their offerings before Hashem. . . (Bamidbar 7:2-3).*

*Why did the Nesi'im (Tribal Princes) see fit to be the
first contributors at the dedication of the altar, while
they did not do so by the Mishkan's construction? [At
the time of the construction] the Nesi'im said, "Let the
people donate whatever they wish to donate, then we
will supply whatever is lacking." However, when the
people contributed all that was needed . . . the Nesi'im
said, "What is there left for us to do?" They brought the
Shoham stones . . . Therefore, they were the first to
contribute at the dedication of the altar (Rashi to
Shemos 35:27).*

Rabbi Yehudah Zev Segal noted that the *Nesi'im* were not
guilty of indolence as we know it. To be sure, their
intentions *were* meritorious. They had no idea how much or
how little would be needed to supplement the people's
contributions, yet they generously offered to provide any
missing item. Nevertheless, this approach was found wanting.
While everyone else rushed home with alacrity, they remained
in their places. Apparently, they should have taken note of the
people's eagerness to have a share in the *Mishkan* and realized
that the possibility existed that there would be nothing left for
them to bring. This oversight is recorded for eternity — for us
to learn an important lesson.

There is yet another insight that we can learn from the *Nesi'im*. Some people are quick to "throw in the towel." If they make a mistake or if they encounter difficulties in a specific area, they give up and declare failure. The *Nesi'im* were different. They made a mistake, but instead of despairing, they learned from their mistake, and did whatever they could to make up for it by being the first to bring offerings at the Altar's dedication.

❧ ❧ ❧

Rabbi Aharon Porush lived in Jerusalem in the early 1900's. He was treasurer of the Eitz Chaim Yeshivah and was an outstanding *talmid chacham*. R' Aharon delivered a daily lecture in *Gemara* to working men in the Holy City.

One day, a newly arrived immigrant began attending R' Aharon's lecture. He was an old man who had recently arrived from Russia with his wife. The man attended the lecture every day without fail, and was always there on time. He always seemed to be listening attentively — but never once did he utter a word. In a conversation with R' Aharon one day, the man related the following:

He had been drafted into the Czar's army and had been a soldier for many years. He had emerged religious, but totally ignorant of Torah. Now, as an old man, he had finally realized his lifelong dream of living in *Eretz Yisrael.*

"I am old and my mind is not what it used to be. I cannot even understand a basic Torah discussion. My time to leave this world is approaching and what have I got to show for it? I can still recite from memory the names of the Czar and all the members of his family, as I was forced to do each morning as a soldier in the Russian army.

"But when I come before the Heavenly Court, they will not be interested in hearing me recite those names. So what *will* I be able to recite? Well, I said to myself: 'If I know the names of the Czar's family, at least I should know some of the names of the great Sages of the Talmud, the distinguished members of the family of Israel!'

"That is why I attend your lecture every day. I do not understand the discussion, but I do remember the names being mentioned."

פרשת בהעלתך
Parashas Beha'aloscha

Humility and Greatness

וְהָאִישׁ מֹשֶׁה עָנָו מְאֹד מִכֹּל הָאָדָם אֲשֶׁר עַל פְּנֵי הָאֲדָמָה.
*And the man Moshe was exceedingly humble,
more than any person on the face of the earth*
(*Bamidbar* 12:3).

To be humble does not mean to think of oneself as a person without ability or accomplishment. Moshe *Rabbeinu* surely recognized that he was the greatest prophet who ever lived; after all, it was he whom Hashem had chosen to lead the Jewish people out of Egypt and transmit the Torah at Sinai. As the Steipler *Gaon*, Rabbi Yaakov Yisrael Kanievsky, explains, עֲנָוָה, *humility*, is the ability to recognize that "all one's intellect, emotions, and skills are not his own, but are loaned to him for a specific amount of time by Hashem, Who created him and Who will take back these gifts when the time comes. This can be compared to a poor man who has borrowed a rich man's clothing to wear at a festive gathering. The poor man will not pride himself over these garments, for he knows that they do not belong to him and that tomorrow he must return them" (*Chayei Olam*, p. 40).

The Steipler adds that an even higher level of humility can be attained by pondering Hashem's greatness. The greater a Jew is, the closer he feels to Hashem, and the more he comes to recognize Hashem's greatness. Additionally, the better one serves Hashem, the more he comes to recognize how utterly dependent he is upon *siyata diShmaya*, assistance from Above, and that all his abilities are gifts from his Creator.

Thus, it is not difficult to understand why Moshe was the humblest of men, and why in every generation *tzaddikim* are noted for their incredible, sincere humility.

❧ ❧ ❧

Rabbi Chaim Ozer Grodzensky was *rav* of Vilna and acclaimed giant of his generation in the years preceding the Second World War. R' Chaim Ozer was the genius among geniuses, a man whose breadth and depth of knowledge seemed limitless. His nephew, Rabbi Eliyahu Eliezer Dessler (author of *Michtav Me'Eliyahu*), said that his comprehension was indescribable and that R' Chaim Ozer also possessed the ability to think three or four unrelated thoughts simultaneously without losing track of or confusing any of them. Rabbi Dessler related to his son R' Nochum Zev (currently of Cleveland) that he had seen R' Chaim Ozer writing with both hands at the same time! He had also seen him write a responsum, compute charity amounts and discuss Torah with someone simultaneously.

R' Dessler would say that R' Chaim Ozer epitomized the quality of humility. Toward the very end of his life, when he was deathly ill, R' Chaim Ozer was unable to read the scores of letters that arrived at his door each day; it was necessary for someone to read the mail to him. One particular letter opened with an array of glorious descriptions of R' Chaim Ozer's greatness. By the time the person had completed reading these words of praise, R' Chaim Ozer was actually laughing. He explained, "In the days of the Russian revolution, the value of currency plummeted and it became virtually worthless; for a dollar, one could get a million rubles. A poor, downtrodden fellow had no difficulty becoming a 'millionaire.' Well, it seems to me, judging from this letter, that our spiritual world is experiencing this kind of gross inflation!"

R' Chaim Ozer's brother-in-law, Rabbi Elchonon Wasserman,[1] once asked him how he had fasted on Yom Kippur. R' Chaim Ozer replied, "The physical strain does not particularly affect me, but from where do I draw the spiritual strength to bear the distress of confessing my sins?" In relating this, R' Elchonon displayed his own humility by commenting, "If R' Chaim Ozer, the greatest among giants, feels this way, what can we say. . .?"

Rashi, in defining the humility of Moshe, writes: שָׁפָל וְסַבְלָן, *humble and tolerant*. A truly humble person can tolerate the wrongs directed towards him. The arrogant, on the other hand, never permit a wrong to go by unanswered.

R' Chaim Ozer once told his *rebbetzin*, "I am proud of one thing — my *savlanus* (tolerance)." His confidants would say that no one ever saw him exhibit even a trace of anger. This quality became apparent early in his career. He became *rav* of Vilna when still a young man in his twenties. Only nine years later, with the passing of the Kovno *Rav*, Rabbi Yitzchak Elchonon Spector, Reb Chaim Ozer's address became the center for all of Lithuanian Jewry. At that time, there were some "enlightened" individuals in Vilna who began to vilify the young *rav*, for they viewed him as a threat to their own activities. Placards were posted ridiculing the activities of

---

1. In the mid-1920's, after his first *rebbetzin* died, R' Chaim Ozer married a widow, Yacha Kahana. She was a daughter of the famed *Rav* of Shavli, Rabbi Meir Atlas, and a sister to the wife of R' Elchonon.

R' Chaim Ozer, who was referred to as "the new general of the black army."

R' Chaim Ozer responded with total silence. He forbade anyone from voicing any protests or defense. He said simply, "Their arrows have missed their mark."

❦ ❦ ❦

The Steipler Gaon displayed a level of humility that was unusual even among Torah leaders. His many *sefarim* on *Gemara* are studied in yeshivos throughout the world. In the preface to one of those *sefarim*, the Steipler writes: "My soul knows well the meagerness of my worth . . . The thoughts contained in this work are not to be taken as established truths, but as attempts to stimulate the mind of the student . . . It is my hope that with the help of Hashem, one will find in this work a number of good points. The author of *Chavas Da'as* has written that one good thought in a *sefer* is sufficient to make the *sefer's* publication worthwhile. This is my consolation in my poverty [of scholarship]. . ."

He expressed genuine amazement that his *sefarim* enjoyed such popularity. "What do they see in my *sefarim* more than in so many others?" he wondered aloud. He then reflected, "It's probably in merit of the blessing that my father received from his *rebbe.*"

The Steipler was a brother-in-law of the Chazon Ish. In fact, it was the Chazon Ish who, after studying the published Torah thoughts of the Steipler, arranged the match between his sister and the Steipler. And it was the Chazon Ish who orchestrated the Steipler's move from Lithuania to Bnei Brak, where the two lived in the very same house with a partition separating their apartments.

Years after the Chazon Ish's passing, the Steipler complained that it was wrong for him to be accorded the honored third *aliyah* each Shabbos at the Torah reading. "Why do they give me the third *aliyah* each week? There are many distinguished *talmidei chachamim* among the congregation who are deserving of this honor!" And for emphasis he added,

"Why, when the Chazon Ish was alive, that is how it was done — he would have the third *aliyah* one week, and I would be given it the next week. . . ." To his listeners, this bit of information reinforced their conviction that there was no one alive who was as worthy as he.

The Steipler always spoke of the Chazon Ish with immense awe, and referred to him as his teacher. His reverence for the Chazon Ish and his own lowly opinion of himself never changed.

After the Chazon Ish's death, the Steipler assumed leadership of *Kollel Chazon Ish.* He delivered *Gemara* lectures regularly until advanced age made this impossible. From that time on, he would lecture only once a year, on the Chazon Ish's *yartzeit.* The last year of the Steipler's life, the lecture was attended by an unusually large crowd. When someone commented on the crowd's size to the Steipler, he responded, "They probably came to honor the Chazon Ish."

❧   ❧   ❧

An indication of a great person's humility is his simplicity. That which others consider below the *tzaddik's* dignity is done by the *tzaddik* without a moment's hesitation.

Three years before the Steipler's passing, a young man from Jerusalem came to his door to discuss a very important matter. It was late at night and a long line of people were waiting on line to speak with the Steipler. At around midnight, the Steipler's daughter came out and announced that her father, eighty-three-years-old at the time, needed to rest and would not be seeing any more visitors that night. Everyone went home except for the young man, who had not made sleeping arrangements and had no place to go at that hour of the night. He remained in the outer hallway of the Steipler's apartment, hoping that perhaps he would somehow be able to speak with the *tzaddik.* When the Steipler's daughter came out a half hour later to say that she had to lock the outside door, the young man asked if she knew of a place where he could spend the night. She replied that she did not know of anyone who might help him at that hour, but she suggested that he go to the nearby Lederman *Shul*, where there might possibly be some people studying Torah.

Around an hour later, the door of the Lederman *Shul* opened and the Steipler, walking laboriously, entered and approached the young man. "Come," he said, "we will bring a bed into my apartment and you will sleep there. My daughter mistakenly thought that your remaining in the house posed a problem of *yichud*.[1]"

On the way home, the Steipler, breathing heavily and walking with great difficulty, was forced to sit down on a bench to rest. When the two finally arrived at the apartment, the Steipler's daughter told the young man, "I wanted to awaken the boy who sleeps in my father's room,[2] but he would not allow me to. He insisted on going himself."

As the Steipler sat catching his breath, the young man apologized for putting him through so much trouble. The Steipler replied, "I didn't do anything. People think that when a person grows old he is free of obligations."

At 2:00 A.M., the Steipler sat down to have a glass of tea with his guest and talk with him for a few minutes. He then arose and excused himself, "I must return to my *Gemara*. I have to fulfill my daily learning quotas."

The Steipler's daughter set up a bed for the young man in the room where the Steipler would learn and receive visitors. The Steipler himself brought the young man water with which to wash his hands in the morning. When the young man asked if he could use the alarm clock, the Steipler replied, "Of course," and set it for him.

At 5:30 in the morning, the young man arose to find the Steipler awake and fully dressed. When the young man returned from *shul,* the Steipler was already learning. The Steipler insisted that his guest eat breakfast at his table where he learned. While the young man ate, another visitor entered

---

1. Lit., *seclusion*, a term which refers to the laws which prohibit men and women who are not married to one another to be alone in a secluded place.
2. The Steipler's *rebbetzin* was no longer living.

to speak with the Steipler. The Steipler paused in his learning and told the young man, "Some people have private things to discuss that they don't want others to hear. You continue eating while I go to the next room to speak with this man." The young man protested that *he* should be the one to move to the next room, but the Steipler wouldn't hear of it.

When the time came for the young man to return home, the Steipler insisted that he accept two *sefarim* as a gift.

פרשת שלח
Parashas Shelach

Garment of Armor

דַּבֵּר אֶל בְּנֵי יִשְׂרָאֵל וְאָמַרְתָּ אֲלֵהֶם
וְעָשׂוּ לָהֶם צִיצִת עַל כַּנְפֵי בִגְדֵיהֶם לְדֹרֹתָם.
Speak to the Children of Israel and say to them
that they shall make themselves tzitzis
on the corners of their garments (Bamidbar 15:38).

Among the prisoners at the Auschwitz concentration camp was the Veitzener *Rav*, Rabbi Zvi Hirsh Meisels, who had served his community with distinction until the German invasion. When the Nazis forced Rabbi Meisels and his family from their home, there was little time or opportunity to take anything along. One item that the *Rav* made sure to take with him was a precious *tallis* which had been presented to him as a gift by his father-in-law. The *tallis* had belonged to the renowned *gaon* and *tzaddik* Rabbi Moshe Teitelbaum, author of *Yitav Leiv*. Our Sages teach that *tzitzis* protect a person from evil[1] and Rabbi Meisels was convinced that a *tallis* which had been worn by a *tzaddik* would provide additional protection in the dangerous times ahead.

Upon arriving at Auschwitz, the Jews were forced to surrender all their possessions. Thus, Rabbi Meisels had no choice but to hand over his precious *tallis*. He was determined, however, to do everything in his power to get it back. Through careful inquiries, he learned that all confiscated possessions had been brought to one central location in the camp. There they would be sorted; all items of substantial value would be sent to Germany for the government and army personnel to enjoy.

Somehow, Rabbi Meisels managed to join the group of prisoners that was assigned to sort these possessions. In the course of his work, he found his *tallis*. Joyously, he stuffed it inside his clothes and brought it back to his barracks. He knew that in doing so he had taken his life in his hands; if the guards found the *tallis* and realized that he taken it back without permission, he would probably be killed on the spot.

To minimize the risks, Rabbi Meisels was forced to cut the *tallis* and turn it into a *tallis katan* (small *tallis*) which he was able to wear underneath his inmates' garb. This, too, was fraught with danger; the gray inmates' clothing was very thin and upon careful inspection, anyone might notice that Rabbi Meisels's clothing looked somewhat bulkier than everyone else's. This, however, was a risk that he was willing to take.

Incredibly, he wore the *tallis katan* until the final days of the war, when he was working in a labor camp near the city of Branzweig. It was at that time that the Germans decided to

---

1. See *Menachos* 44a.

empty the labor camp of its prisoners. The sound of American gunfire could be heard in the distance, and in attempting to flee, the ruthless Nazis took with them those Jews who still remained alive. Before boarding the cattle cars for yet another time, the inmates were searched in case they had anything of value on their person. It was then that the *tallis katan* was discovered. A German guard named Willy ripped the garment off Rabbi Meisels' body and threw it into a fire as the *Rav* watched in horror.

Rabbi Meisels was devastated. He firmly believed that the *tallis katan* had been a source of protection for him. Now, with the Germans in a panic as the Americans bore down on them, the danger was perhaps greater than ever. And his *tallis katan* was gone. Still, Rabbi Meisels knew that the other Jews who had survived to that point had done so without the benefit of a *tzaddik*'s *tallis katan*. Just as Hashem had watched over them, He would continue to watch over him.

The Nazis herded their prisoners onto the cattle cars in their typically brutal way. The cars had little ventilation, and no food or water for the Jews, who were packed tightly next to one another with no room to move. Willy, the wicked guard who had destroyed the *tallis katan,* was one of those placed in charge of the car carrying Rabbi Meisels and his son, Zalman Leib. The guards made sure that conditions for themselves in the car were better than for their prisoners. They placed benches down in the center of the car and sprawled themselves out. They also made sure to have an ample supply of food and drink.

Darkness fell as the train wound its way along the countryside. Rabbi Meisels was overcome by exhaustion and attempted to sleep in the only way possible: as he stood, he turned his head to the left and rested it upon the shoulder of his son. Later, Zalman Leib would rest his head upon his father's shoulder. This was how they had slept on all their cattle car journeys since the war had begun.

Rabbi Meisels had been asleep only a few minutes when he was awakened by his son's anguished voice. "*Tatte* (Father), my shoulder hurts so much! I'm sorry, but I can't take the pain any longer." Rabbi Meisels had no choice but to raise his head, though he found his son's complaint strange, since they had slept this way many times before. Rabbi Meisels' neighbor to his right then told the *Rav* to rest his head upon his shoulder, while Zalman Leib, now also overcome by exhaustion, placed his own head upon his neighbor to his left.

Moments later, the sound of American warplanes was heard. The drone of the engines soon mixed with the sound of gunfire as the Air Force crews, mistakenly assuming that the train was carrying German soldiers, strafed the train. Suddenly, the gunfire ripped a hole in the roof of the car in which Rabbi Meisels stood, and shot directly between the tilted heads of the *Rav* and his son — hitting Willy and tearing off both his hands. Soon after, the sounds of the planes grew fainter as they headed off. The Jews in the car were all unharmed.

Willy screamed in agony and pleaded for the others to do something for him. One of the other guards called out sarcastically, "Well, Willy, I guess you won't be able to throw the Jew's prayer shawl into the fire any more."

Upon hearing these words, Willy turned to Rabbi Meisels and begged forgiveness.

Rabbi Meisels still had with him a small Book of *Tehillim*, from which he had never stopped praying since the German invasion had begun. Now, he and his son sang a chapter in unison, ". . . Behold! The Guardian of Israel does not sleep, nor does He slumber . . . ."

One of the Jews in the car, who was not religious, said to Rabbi Meisels, "Please continue to pray for us. It is obvious that G-d is watching over you. And just as He made that gunfire miss your heads and punish your persecutor, so may He soon rescue us all from these evil tyrants" (from *Sefer Mekadshei Hashem*).

פרשת קרח
Parashas Korach

Pursue Peace

וַיִּשְׁלַח מֹשֶׁה לִקְרֹא לְדָתָן וְלַאֲבִירָם בְּנֵי אֱלִיאָב, וַיֹּאמְרוּ לֹא נַעֲלֶה.
Moshe sent forth to summon Dasan and Aviram,
sons of Eliav, but they said, "We shall not go up!"
(Bamidbar 16:12).

Hillel says: Be among the disciples of Aharon, loving
peace and pursuing peace. . .(Avos 1:12).

Dasan and Aviram were among the leaders of Korach's terrible rebellion against Moshe and Aharon. Moreover, it was they who had informed on Moshe to Pharaoh, forcing Moshe to flee for his life,[1] and it was they who had flouted Moshe's word on other occasions.[2] Yet, having failed to sway Korach, Moshe appealed to them through an emissary in the hope that they might repent before it was too late. From here our Sages learn that one should always seek to end a dispute, even when he is clearly the one who is being wronged (*Rashi*).

---

1. See *Shemos* 2:15 with *Rashi*.
2. See *Shemos* 16:20 with *Rashi*.

☙ ☙ ☙

In 1908, a dispute erupted in the town of Radin between two groups who were competing for the right to serve as the Jewish community's *chevra kadisha* (burial society). As the dispute grew and threatened to engulf the entire community, the Chofetz Chaim, who resided in the town, saw that it was necessary to intervene. During the Shabbos morning prayers in Radin's main *shul,* he rose to address the congregation:

"My brothers! Were they to offer me thousands of rubles to speak in public I would refuse, for time is far more precious to me than money. But today, I feel that I have no choice but to speak.

"I have lived in this town for decades, and I remember many townspeople who used to sit here in this synagogue but are not here today. Where are they? Their tombstones can be found in the local cemetery.

"When I came to this town, some of you were not yet born, while others were but small children. May all of us be blessed with long life. Nevertheless, we cannot escape reality; eventually, every man must come before the Heavenly throne and give an accounting of all his deeds and words during his days on this earth.

"Know, my brethren! *Machlokes* (strife) is an extremely grave matter! One can perform many *mitzvos*, only to throw away their merit through strife. I am certain that when you come to the Next World and experience the fear of Heavenly judgment, you will grasp at any straw to save yourselves. You might want to claim, 'In my town there was a Jew named Yisrael Meir[1] whom we believed to be a *talmid chacham.* He saw us quarrel but said nothing!'

"Therefore, I ask of you that when your time comes, do not mention my name! I have my own burden [of sins] to worry

---

1. The Chofetz Chaim's name was Rabbi Yisrael Meir *HaKohen* Kagan. He became known for all time by the name of his first work, the classic code on the laws of forbidden speech.

about — I cannot assume responsibility for the misdeeds of others!"

With those words, the Chofetz Chaim burst into tears and his whole body trembled. Everyone present was shaken to the depths of his soul and resolved that the dispute would be settled quickly and peacefully. And so it was.

❧ ❧ ❧

Rabbi Moshe Feinstein, who was born on the birthday of Moshe *Rabbeinu*[1] and named after him, was universally recognized as the *posek hador,* the supreme judge in matters of *Halachah* in his generation. *Sefer Igros Moshe,* which contains hundreds of R' Moshe's *halachic* decisions, was already a classic during his lifetime.

It happened once that R' Moshe ruled leniently in a very delicate subject. Many great *talmidei chachamim* were surprised by the ruling and some disagreed with it. One of those who disagreed was Rabbi Yoel Teitelbaum, the saintly *Rebbe* of Satmar. It was not the only time that the two disagreed, yet despite their differences, R' Moshe and the Satmar *Rebbe* held each other in the highest regard. When some distinguished *rabbanim* suggested to the *Rebbe* that they visit R' Moshe and attempt to convince him to retract his ruling, the *Rebbe* replied that they would not succeed. R' Moshe's greatness in Torah was such that it would simply be impossible for them to disprove his opinion. The *rabbanim* did visit R' Moshe and the *Rebbe's* prediction proved correct.

There was one *rav* who publicly expressed his disagreement with R' Moshe's ruling in a way that many felt was disrespectful of R' Moshe. The following summer, R' Moshe and this *rav* spent a few weeks in the very same neighborhood in New York's Catskill Mountains region. When a committee asked R' Moshe to inspect a new *mikveh* to ensure that it met all the *halachic* requirements, he replied, "Yes, I will be happy to inspect it — but only if Rabbi . . . comes along to approve it as well."

---

1. 7 *Adar*, which is also the date of Moshe *Rabbeinu's* death.

Many were astounded. While this *Rav* was a respected *talmid chacham*, his Torah knowledge did not compare with that of R' Moshe. And moreover he had shown disrespect toward the great *tzaddik* and *posek*. Why should R' Moshe invite him to offer *his* opinion? We may suggest that this was R' Moshe's way of showing that he bore the man no ill will and that he would pursue peace in any way possible.

On another occasion, R' Moshe wrote a *haskamah* (endorsement) to a *sefer* which contained certain statements of which some disapproved. One hothead promptly wrote a pamphlet which degraded the *sefer* and its author and also contained some disrespectful comments about R' Moshe for his having endorsed the work.

A terrible rumor was spread that the pamphlet had the sanction of the Satmar *Rebbe*. Upon learning of this, the *Rebbe* dispatched a distinguished delegation to R' Moshe to assure him that the rumor was patently false.

R' Moshe received the delegation and said that he had not seen the pamphlet and would surely not believe the rumors being circulated. One of the *Rebbe's* emissaries mentioned that he had a copy of the pamphlet with him and asked if R' Moshe would care to see it. "Please do not show it to me," R' Moshe replied. "If I read it, I might become distressed. I don't want Heaven to punish the author for having caused a Jew distress."

פרשת חקת
Parashas Chukas

Dead to the World

זֹאת הַתּוֹרָה אָדָם כִּי יָמוּת בְּאֹהֶל.
*This is the teaching regarding a man
who would die in a tent (Bamidbar 19:14).*

In its plain meaning, this verse discusses the laws of *tumah* [ritual contamination] from a corpse. However, our Sages also derive a homiletical teaching from it: "Torah can endure only in a person who kills himself [כִּי יָמוּת] over it" (*Berachos* 63b).

The Chofetz Chaim explained this teaching with a parable:

There once lived a very successful textile dealer to whom customers traveled from far and wide. The business occupied the man's every waking hour; he did not even take time off to pray with a *minyan*.

Years passed; streaks of white appeared in his beard and he felt his strength weakening. He feared that his end was drawing near; the time was approaching when he would have to stand judgment for the way in which he had spent his years on earth. The man resolved that he would prepare some "food for the road," regardless of the consequences.

He decided to pray with a *minyan* each morning and remain in the *beis midrash* afterwards for two hours to study Torah. He would do this despite the fact that customers and fellow businessmen were waiting for him.

On the first day of his new schedule, the man arrived at his store three hours later than usual. His wife, greatly distressed, demanded, "Where were you? The store is packed with customers who are anxious to be on their way!"

The man replied simply, "My delay was unavoidable."

On the second morning, when the man was late again, his wife went to find him. How astounded she was to find him learning in the *beis midrash!* "What has gotten into you!" she shouted. "Have you gone mad? The store is full of customers and you are sitting and learning? Never mind the money we're losing today — you'll lose those customers forever!"

Calmly, and with a sense of conviction, the man replied, "My dear wife, allow me to ask you a question. What would you do if the Angel of Death would come to me and say, 'Come, let us go; the time has come for you to depart this world.' Would you, my dear wife, interject, 'No, not now! Not when the store is full of customers!'?

"Well, from now on, consider me dead during the first three hours of the morning. Nothing, nothing at all, should interrupt my prayers and Torah study."

This, said the Chofetz Chaim, is the meaning of our Sages' teaching: *Torah can endure only in one who considers himself as if he were dead* during his periods of Torah study. One should not allow *anything* to interfere with his study schedule, nor should he allow himself to be interrupted while in the midst of his studies.

❀   ❀   ❀

In 1967, Israel's Arab neighbors prepared for war as they threatened to "drive Israel into the sea." Tens of thousands of Arab soldiers amassed at their countries' borders as they readied for what they thought would be a swift devastation. It was then that our generation witnessed clearly what the Jewish people have always known: הִנֵּה לֹא יָנוּם וְלֹא יִישָׁן שׁוֹמֵר יִשְׂרָאֵל, *The Guardian of Israel neither sleeps nor slumbers (Tehillim 121:4).* In what became known as the Six Day War, Israel scored a lightning-quick victory and recaptured its most precious shrines, including the Western Wall, the Cave of Machpelah and the tomb of our Matriarch Rachel.

Hashem's ways are, indeed, hidden from us. No one could have predicted that the Six Day War would forever alter the fate of our (then) estranged brothers and sisters in the Soviet Union. But it did. Though the Communist propaganda machine was working overtime to malign the "Israeli aggressors" and downplay their amazing triumph, the truth could not be hidden from Soviet Jewry. The Six Day War awakened within many of them a pride in their Jewishness. In some, it inspired the first yearnings to discover the rich heritage and traditions which the Communists had tried their best to eradicate from their midst.

One of those who experienced a spiritual awakening at that time was a mathematics professor named Ilya Essas. Through tremendous determination and self-sacrifice, he mastered the Hebrew language, and in a short period of time amassed an astounding amount of Torah knowledge. Less than three months after beginning the study of *Chumash,* Ilya Essas was teaching *Chumash* to others. Today, Rabbi Eliyahu Essas is a respected *talmid chacham* who heads the Russian division of Yeshivah Ohr Somayach in Jerusalem. He is considered the *"rebbi"* of the *ba'al teshuvah* movement which arose in Russia following the Six Day War. The members of this movement studied Torah in secret under the Communists. Though well aware that their Torah study and other religious practices might lead to their arrest and imprisonment, this small, dedicated group illuminated the darkness of Communist Russia with a brilliant light.

❦   ❦   ❦

Once, a young couple, students of R' Essas, applied for visas to emigrate to the United States. The wife was granted a visa, but not the husband. The couple decided that it was wisest for the wife to take the opportunity while it was available and leave the country. Husband and wife parted tearfully, not knowing if and when they would see each other again.

The wife wrote letters to her husband regularly, but the Communists intercepted them and would not allow the letters to reach their destination. Then, the wife heard that a certain *rav* was being sent as an emissary by Agudath Israel of America to spend some time in Russia teaching Torah in secret to the *ba'alei teshuvah*. The wife wrote a letter to her husband and asked the *rav* to deliver it. He promised to try his best.

After arriving in Russia, the *rav* located the husband and rang his doorbell. When the husband came to the door, the *rav* handed him the letter and told him that it was from his wife. Tears welled up in the young man's eyes and he thanked the *rav* profusely. Then, he took the still sealed letter and placed it in his pocket.

"Aren't you going to open it?" the *rav* asked.

"Yes, but not now," came the reply. "I am in the middle of studying Torah with my *chavrusa*. When we conclude our study session, then I will open the letter."

פרשת בלק
Parashas Balak

Human Dignity

וַיִּפְתַּח ה' אֶת פִּי הָאָתוֹן, וַתֹּאמֶר לְבִלְעָם
מֶה עָשִׂיתִי לְךָ כִּי הִכִּיתָנִי זֶה שָׁלֹשׁ רְגָלִים?. . .
וַיֹּאמֶר אֵלָיו מַלְאַךְ ה', . . .אוּלַי נָטְתָה מִפָּנַי כִּי עַתָּה
גַם אֹתְכָה הָרַגְתִּי וְאוֹתָהּ הֶחֱיֵיתִי.

Hashem opened the mouth of the donkey and it said to Bilam,
"What have I done to you that you struck me these
three times?" . . . The angel of Hashem said to him [Bilam]:
"Had it [the donkey] not turned away from me,
I would now even have killed you and let it live!"
(Bamidbar 22:28, 32-33).

[The angel told Bilam:] "Now that the donkey has
spoken and rebuked you, and you could not stand up
to her rebuke, I killed her, so that people should not
say, 'This is the donkey that brought about Bilam's
downfall through her rebuke. . .' " For Hashem has
consideration for human dignity (Rashi).

A s the *Midrash* (*Bamidbar Rabbah* 20:14) relates, the emissaries sent by Balak to accompany Bilam were witness to the donkey's rebuke of him and news of the miracle surely spread. Had the donkey lived, people would have pointed to the donkey and reminded one another of how it had silenced Bilam with its rebuke.

That Hashem ordered the donkey killed for the sake of Bilam's honor is astounding. Bilam had been warned by Hashem, "Do not curse the nation, for it is blessed" (22:12). Despite this warning, Bilam set out with Balak's emissaries, his heart one with theirs. One would think that concern for כְּבוֹד הַבְּרִיּוֹת, *human dignity,* does not apply to a wicked person of this sort.

The late Manchester *Rosh Yeshivah,* Rabbi Yehudah Zev Segal, offered another point to consider: Keeping Bilam's donkey alive would have resulted in a great *kiddush Hashem* (sanctification of Hashem's Name). People would have pointed to the donkey and remembered that it had been granted a miraculous ability to speak in order to rebuke a person who sought to transgress his Creator's will. And the donkey's having spoken was one of the great wonders of Creation (see *Avos* 5:8).

All this was overlooked for the sake of Bilam's honor. Even a great *kiddush Hashem* did not justify dishonoring a thoroughly evil individual. How careful one must be with regard to the honor of others!

❧ ❧ ❧

The first World War brought enormous upheaval to the Jews of Poland and Lithuania. As the German armies continued their march, entire communities were forced to flee and cross the border into neighboring Russia. In the city of Brisk, most Jews fled, while a small percentage chose to remain behind.

When the war ended and the Jewish population returned, many problems had to be resolved. One problem concerned the slaughtering of kosher meat in the city. During the war, with no *rav* or *beis din* to lead the community, a new group of *shochtim* (slaughterers) had begun providing kosher meat for the city's Jews. Throughout its history, the G-d fearing community of Brisk had always employed *shochtim* who were acknowledged *talmidei chachamim,* known for their exactness in matters of *halachah*. The new *shochtim* did not meet this high standard.

Not long after the war, the city's regular *shochtim* returned to their positions. However, the new *shochtim* did not leave the scene. Since they were no longer permitted to slaughter in the community-controlled slaughterhouses, they took to slaughtering animals in barns and other secluded places without community approval, and then offering their meat for sale. This greatly dismayed the leaders of Brisk's Jewish population, for it meant that their high kashruth standards were being threatened. An urgent meeting of all community leaders was called, to be held in the home of the Brisker *Rav,* Rabbi Yitzchak Zev Soloveitchik.

As the meeting was about to get underway, one of the new *shochtim* entered the room and took a seat. The man had brazenly decided to come and hear what would be said about him and his friends. When someone asked the man to leave, he replied, "This is the *Rav's* house, not yours. If the *Rav* tells me to leave, I'll leave; otherwise, I'm not going anywhere." When others joined in asking the man to leave, his response was the same. At that point, someone informed the Brisker *Rav* of what was transpiring. However, instead of asking the man to leave, the *Rav* remained silent. As the minutes ticked by in silence, many grew restless and it appeared as if the gathering might disband with nothing accomplished. Finally, someone prevailed upon the man to leave peacefully.

When the man had left, the *Rav* said to those assembled: " 'Come and see how great is the power of shame! For the Holy One, Blessed is He, assisted Bar Kamtza [in his plot to take revenge for his having been shamed], and He destroyed His *Beis HaMikdash* and burned His Temple.'[1] Had I humiliated this man by ordering him to leave, we would have lost everything. No good could have resulted from a meeting that would have begun in such a way."

---

1. *Gittin* 57a

פרשת פנחס
Parashas Pinchas

A Man of Spirit

וַיְדַבֵּר מֹשֶׁה אֶל ה׳ לֵאמֹר. יִפְקֹד ה׳ אֱלֹהֵי הָרוּחֹת
לְכָל בָּשָׂר אִישׁ עַל הָעֵדָה . . . . וַיֹּאמֶר ה׳ אֶל מֹשֶׁה
קַח לְךָ אֶת יְהוֹשֻׁעַ בִּן נוּן אִישׁ אֲשֶׁר רוּחַ בּוֹ.

Moshe spoke to Hashem saying: "May Hashem,
God of the spirits of all flesh, appoint a man
over the assembly. . . .Hashem said to Moshe:
"Take to yourself Yehoshua bin Nun, a man in whom
there is spirit" (Bamidbar 27:15-16,18).

"G-d of the spirits" — Moshe said: "Ribono shel
Olam, the thoughts of each and every person are
revealed and known before You, and [it is also known
to You] that no two people think alike. Appoint a leader
for them who will be able to deal with each individual."

"[Take Yehoshua,] a man in whom there is spirit" —
:who is able to deal with each individual [according to
that person's way of thinking and needs]" (based on
Rashi).

The late Bluzhever *Rebbe*, Rabbi Yisrael Spira, is well-
known for his heroism during the Holocaust. This,
however, is only one aspect of his incredible life story. He was
a distinguished *rav* in Poland during the First World War and a

leader of Galician Jewry before the Second World War. After enduring unspeakable suffering during the Holocaust, the *Rebbe* came to America and became one of its most influential and beloved Torah leaders.

Wherever he went, scores sought the Bluzhever *Rebbe*'s blessing, encouragement and advice. He was warm, sensitive and perceptive. His advice was always on the mark; he knew what to say and how to say it.

Those who sought to develop a relationship with the *Rebbe* learned that it was very easy to feel close to him. A man who was especially close to him once remarked: "There are probably very many people who consider themselves among those closest to the *Rebbe* — and for good reason. The *Rebbe* exuded warmth, concern, and *pashtus* (simplicity), and he made you feel that you really *were* close to him."

Many stories tell of the strength with which the *Rebbe* infused others. In Bergen-Belsen, where he spent the latter part of the War, the *Rebbe* was spiritual leader of his fellow prisoners. In preparation for Chanukah, shoe dye that could serve as fuel was smuggled out of the camp factory by women inmates. Threads were pulled from sweaters by the women and spun into wicks. On the first night of Chanukah, a secret *Ma'ariv minyan* was held, led by the *Rebbe*. Scores of Jews, risking discovery, then joined together for the kindling of the Chanukah lights. The *Rebbe* recited the three blessings and lit the *menorah*.

A non-believing former Polish-Bundist leader approached the *Rebbe* and asked, "Rabbi Spira, I do not understand. I do not understand how you can bring yourself to recite the *Shehechiyanu* blessing, *Blessed are You, Hashem. . .Who has kept us alive, sustained us, and brought us to this season.* How can you offer thanks for having been kept alive to experience this horrible time of death, torture, and hunger? Haven't you made a mockery of our suffering?"

The *Rebbe* replied, "You ask a very good question. In fact, I myself was wondering how I could joyfully recite these words. But then I looked around and saw this huge assemblage of

Jews that had gathered to participate in this *mitzvah*. Despite the terrible suffering, they insist on remaining Jews, even at the risk of their lives. Have you ever in your life witnessed such a demonstration of courage and faith? For that alone it is sufficient to thank the Creator for giving us the privilege to be alive and witness the greatness of our people. No! We Jews do not give up. We are proud that we have lived to see thousands of Jews who have not given up, who will never give up, and who are living proof that we will one day rebuild anew."

Years later on a visit to Poland, an acquaintance of the *Rebbe* met this Bundist leader, who told him, "Tell Rabbi Spira that he saved my life. He will understand."

⁂ ⁂ ⁂

One of the most unusual cases to come his way occurred in the 1950's, when a woman refused the psychiatric help she desperately needed. Her family brought her to the *Rebbe* who asked the woman what was bothering her. She replied that once, while walking in the street, she had been startled by the sound of a plane flying overhead. She had expressed her outrage vehemently and, as she imagined, the plane had crashed as a result of her words. She further imagined that President Eisenhower, after learning that she had caused the crash, had sent agents to apprehend her, and she had been on the run ever since.

As she related this fantastic tale, the *Rebbe* was attentive, as if believing every word. When she finished, the *Rebbe* said, "You know, President Eisenhower, as General of the American Army, liberated me from the concentration camps. The President and I are old friends. I am certain that as a personal favor to me, he will drop all charges against you."

With that, the *Rebbe* "dialed" Washington on his phone and "chatted" with the President as one would speak with an old friend. After hanging up the phone, the *Rebbe* told the woman, "The President says that he is willing to drop all charges against you, but on one condition: that you seek psychiatric help and obey the doctor's orders."

A few days later, the *Rebbe* received a call from the woman's psychiatrist. The doctor was curious to know where the *Rebbe* had received his training in counseling. The doctor could never understand that the source of a *tzaddik's* wisdom is the Torah study in which he toils day and night.

❀ ❀ ❀

Those close to him put their total trust in his advice. A man who was very close to the *Rebbe* once asked him if he should accept a position with a certain firm. The *Rebbe* listened to the pros and cons of the matter before responding. "If you would tell me," he finally said, "that you had dreamt that someone offered you this position and that you had accepted the offer, I would say, 'Well, a dream is also worth something.' Offhand, though, it seems that this offer is not for you." The man was familiar enough with the *Rebbe*'s way of speaking to know that although he was obviously not enthusiastic about the offer, he had not totally rejected it either. Nevertheless, the man would not enter into any venture unless the *Rebbe* was firmly in favor of it, so he turned down the offer. Six months later, the firm went bankrupt.

❀ ❀ ❀

The *Rebbe* spent a number of summers vacationing in New Hampshire at a time when that area was not known as a summer resort in Orthodox circles. The *Rebbe* earned everyone's respect. While vacationing there in the 1940's, he met a Jewish secularist, an aide to President Truman. This man was so impressed with the *Rebbe* that he made a point of visiting the *Rebbe* at his Brooklyn home a number of times.

There was another secularist Jew in New Hampshire who did not have the same feelings of reverence toward the Chassidic Rabbi from New York. One day, the man walked by the *Rebbe* and openly ridiculed the *Rebbe*'s flowing *payos* and beard. In a friendly way, the *Rebbe* responded, "Do you think that I cannot afford the dollar for a trim? I certainly can. But, you see, *this*," — and the *Rebbe* tugged at his own beard — "is grown for an important reason. It has *real meaning*."

The man was taken aback by the *Rebbe*'s respectful response. He said, "Rabbi, you've got me. I'll never make a remark like that again."

The *Rebbe* once found it necessary to reprove one of his own *chassidim*. The gist of his words were: "You have such a distinguished appearance! People think very highly of you. It is crucial that you live up to your reputation, for if not, people will learn the wrong things."

❀ ❀ ❀

A man once came to the *Rebbe* complaining of a severe sinus-related problem. Doctors had advised that the man, who was of modest means, be hospitalized for a very costly procedure. The *Rebbe* told the man, "This coming Monday I have an appointment with a renowned ear, nose, and throat specialist at New York University Hospital. Come along with me; I think the doctor can help you."

The doctor examined the man, prescribed some medication and instructed him to return the following week when the *Rebbe* was scheduled for another appointment. At the next appointment, the doctor examined the man briefly, then winked to the *Rebbe* and said, "Sir, you are in need of a minor surgical procedure which I will perform here in the office right now." The procedure was performed successfully and the man was cured. After leaving the doctor's office, the man asked the *Rebbe* about the wink that he had noticed. The *Rebbe* explained, "After last week's visit, the doctor told me that he would probably have to perform the procedure. However, I elected not to inform you of this so that you would not spend an entire week worrying about what was actually minor surgery. The wink was the doctor's signal to me that his suspicions were confirmed."

The man then commented that the doctor had made no mention of a fee. The *Rebbe* replied, "It's none of your concern." The man protested, "I don't want the *Rebbe* to pay my doctor bills . . . !" The *Rebbe* responded, "When I brought you here, I made up my mind that no one would know about this — including you!" And that was the end of the matter.

פרשת מטות
Parashas Mattos

Beyond a Shadow of Doubt

וִהְיִיתֶם נְקִים מֵה׳ וּמִיִּשְׂרָאֵל.
And you shall be guiltless before Hashem and Israel (Bamidbar 32:22).

From these words our Sages derive that it is not enough for a Jew to know that his actions are proper in Hashem's eyes. A Jew must always be sure that his actions are understood as proper by the people who observe them (*Yoma* 38a).[1]

Great people often go to incredible lengths to ensure that their actions not be misunderstood and thus convey a bad impression.

1. See also *Mishnah Shekalim* 3:2.

During the Second World War, the American-based *Va'ad Hatzalah* (Rescue Committee), led by the greatest Torah personalities of the time, sent thousands of dollars to sustain the yeshivah community in Shanghai, China. The students of the Mirrer Yeshivah, *rabbanim* and their families had escaped there in their flight from Nazi persecution and Russian oppression.

Once, as the *Va'ad* prepared to send money abroad, Rabbi Aharon Kotler added some of his own money to the check that was to be sent. He explained, "A close relative of mine is among those stranded in Shanghai. I don't want it to seem as if I am using community money to support my relatives. This money which I added is for him."

❧ ❧ ❧

Rabbi Yisrael Sekula, the late Sadaver *Rav,* was a man of great Torah scholarship, warmth, kindness, and personal integrity. He went to great lengths to avoid any hint of wrong-doing, both between man and Hashem, and man and his fellow.

For many years, he was the *mashgiach* (kashrus supervisor) of a very successful Pesach hand-*matzah* bakery. It was well known that the Sadaver *Rav* employed the strictest standards in making sure that the *matzos* were kosher for Pesach beyond any doubt.

After many years, the bakery was put up for sale, and the Sadaver *Rav* decided to purchase it. It was assumed that he would remain as *mashgiach*; he was universally respected as a *talmid chacham* who could be relied upon. It seemed unnecessary to place the bakery under someone else's supervision.

The Sadaver *Rav* disagreed. "I am now running a business," he reasoned. "A businessman should not be deciding matters of *Halachah* in his own place of business." He, therefore, arranged for the renowned *posek*, Rabbi Moshe Bick, to serve as the bakery's *mashgiach*.

Toward the end of his long life, the Sadaver *Rav* suffered a stroke and was severely incapacitated. It was his custom to *"shlag kaparos"*[1] before Yom Kippur at a place only a block away from his home. In his last year, this short trip was a very strenuous journey. It took one-half hour for his sons to bring him down one flight of stairs. But the *Rav* was insistent; he would go to do the *mitzvah* as in years past, only this time in a wheelchair.

By the time the *Rav* arrived at his destination, accompanied by his distinguished sons, there stood a long line of people waiting to purchase birds for the *kaparos* ritual. The *Rav*'s sons knew that their father was in no condition to sit and wait on line for the hour or so it would take until his turn came. They suggested to their father that he allow them to wheel him to the front of the line. Surely, they reasoned, everyone would gladly allow an obviously ill person to go ahead of him.

The Sadaver *Rav* told his sons, "These people came ahead of me. I have no right to go ahead of them and make them wait that much longer. It is not worth it to do the *mitzvah* if this will cause a single Jew — even a child — any aggravation. I will wait my turn."

The *Rav*'s son, concerned that the strain was already taking its toll on him, responded that they were positive that no one would be upset. The ailing *Rav* then replied, "If I am to go ahead of them, you must wheel me down the line slowly and allow me to ask permission of each person and apologize for inconveniencing him." So, with a tube in his throat which made mere speaking a strain, the Sadaver *Rav* apologetically asked each person, including children, permission to go ahead.

When the *Rav* had completed the ritual, he said to his sons, "These people granted permission only for me to go ahead of them. You, however, were not given any such permission.

---

1. An ancient custom performed between Rosh Hashanah and Yom Kippur in which a rooster (for a male) or hen (for a female) is held above one's head while prayers are recited. The ceremony symbolizes that our sins cry out for atonement, and that our good deeds and repentance can save us from the punishment we deserve (*ArtScroll Yom Kippur Machzor*).

Please take me home now and then return to the back of the line."

☙ ☙ ☙

The world-renowned *posek*, Rabbi Yosef Sholom Elyashev of Jerusalem, was granted a fitting partner in life. *Rebbetzin* Chaya Sheina Elyashev, daughter of the renowned *tzaddik* Rabbi Aryeh Levin, dedicated herself to the Torah study of her husband and children and to acts of kindness.

R' Elyashev sets aside one hour a day to allow anyone to visit him in his small Meah Shearim apartment and ask questions in *Halachah*. People are admitted into his study on a first-come, first-served basis.

On a visit to *Eretz Yisrael*, Rabbi Nosson Scherman sought to ask R' Elyashev a *halachic* question. As R' Scherman waited his turn, along with a number of others, *Rebbetzin* Elyashev appeared. She went over to each person in the room and said, "I must ask the *Rav* something. Excuse me for going in ahead of you." Only after saying this to each person individually did *Rebbetzin* Elyashev enter her husband's study.

פרשת מסעי
Parashas Masei

The Time is Now

וְהֶעָרִים אֲשֶׁר תִּתֵּנוּ, שֵׁשׁ עָרֵי מִקְלָט תִּהְיֶינָה לָכֶם.

As to the cities that you shall designate,
there shall be six cities of refuge for you
(Bamidbar 35:13).

This teaches us that although during his lifetime
Moshe designated three refuge cities across the Jordan
River, these cities did not actually function as places of
refuge until [years later when] Yehoshua designated
the other three cities in the Land of Canaan (Rashi).

Moshe zealously took care of the matter, though he
knew that the cities would not gain their special status
until after his death. Moshe reasoned, "Whatever
mitzvah I can possibly fulfill, I will fulfill" (from Rashi to
Devarim 4:41).

Until the last few years of his life, Rabbi Moshe Feinstein would *daven* (pray) each day at Mesivtha Tifereth Jerusalem on New York's Lower East Side, where he served as *Rosh Yeshivah* for half a century. When advanced age and ill health made this impossible, a *minyan* would gather daily in his home. As time went on, it became too strenuous for R' Moshe to pray the long Shabbos morning prayers with a *minyan*. Thus, he would recite the *Shacharis* prayers alone and later a *minyan* would come to his apartment for the Torah reading and *Mussaf*.

On Shabbos *Parashas Zachor*, 5746 (1986), an *aufruf* was being held in Tifereth Jerusalem. Since those who were regularly part of R' Moshe's *minyan* would be attending the *aufruf* and would not be at his home until much later than usual, it was thought best for R' Moshe to recite *Mussaf* privately, eat the Shabbos meal and hear the Torah reading later in the day.

Rabbi Reuven Feinstein hurried to his father's home that day well before the *minyan* was to gather. R' Moshe was unaware of the plans that had been made. R' Reuven explained to his father that the *minyan* would be coming much later and only for the Torah reading.

"And why not for *Mussaf* like every week?" R' Moshe wanted to know. R' Reuven tried to explain why it would be impractical, but R' Moshe was adamant. He had to *daven Mussaf* with a *minyan* just as he did every Shabbos.

It was already past noon and most people had already recited *Mussaf,* but seeing how distressed his father was, R' Reuven made the effort to assemble a *minyan.* He was successful and R' Moshe *davened Mussaf* with a *minyan* as always.

Later, as they sat together eating the Shabbos meal, R' Moshe turned to his son and said, "*Gedenk! Men darf areinchapen viful men ken,* Remember! One must grab every *mitzvah* he possibly can!"

Reb Moshe passed away two nights later.

פרשת דברים
Parashas Devarim

Thoughtful Rebuke

אֵלֶּה הַדְּבָרִים אֲשֶׁר דִּבֶּר מֹשֶׁה אֶל כָּל יִשְׂרָאֵל
בְּעֵבֶר הַיַּרְדֵּן, בַּמִּדְבָּר בָּעֲרָבָה מוֹל סוּף בֵּין פָּארָן
וּבֵין תֹּפֶל וְלָבָן וַחֲצֵרֹת וְדִי זָהָב.

These are the words that Moshe spoke to all Israel,
on the other side of the Jordan, in the Wilderness, in Aravah,
opposite the Sea of Reeds, between Paran and Tophel and
Lavan and Chatzeiros and Di Zahav (Devarim 1:1).

Moshe spoke these words as his life in this world neared
its end. As *Rashi* explains, the names of the places
mentioned in this verse, beginning with the word בַּמִּדְבָּר, *in the*
Wilderness, actually hint to different sins committed by the
Jews during their forty years in the Wilderness. Moshe wanted
to rebuke the people before his death, but in order not to
embarrass or offend them, he only hinted to their sins rather
than mention them explicitly.

❀ ❀ ❀

As *Rav* in Prochnik, Galicia, before the Second World War, the Bluzhever *Rebbe* was once informed that a young man in his community was seen entering a movie theater. The *Rebbe* knew that he would accomplish nothing by confronting the young man directly. He therefore said nothing until the young man paid him a visit along with a friend who was known for his sterling character. The *Rebbe* turned to the friend and, pretending that he was extremely agitated, said, "What's this that I hear? Today's *bachurim* don't know what to do with their time? To movies of all things . . . movies? How can people we regard so highly even think of doing such a thing?"

The friend knew that the *Rebbe* did not mean him, while his companion got a very strong but indirect message.

The above story reflects an interpretation which the *Rebbe* suggested to the command, "Rebuke your fellow man, and you shall not bear sin because of him" (*Vayikra* 19:17). At times, said the *Rebbe,* it is necessary to rebuke in such a way that the sinner does not even realize he is being accused of sin, as if to read the verse, "Rebuke your fellow man, but do not attribute sin to him."

And other times, the way to rebuke is by speaking to the person directly, but only hinting to the wrong that has been committed, in the way of Moshe *Rabbeinu.*

Fear No Man

לֹא תַכִּירוּ פָנִים בַּמִּשְׁפָּט כַּקָּטֹן כַּגָּדֹל תִּשְׁמָעוּן,
לֹא תָגוּרוּ מִפְּנֵי אִישׁ כִּי הַמִּשְׁפָּט לֵאלֹהִים הוּא.

You shall not show favoritism in judgment,
small and great [people] alike shall you hear,
you shall not tremble before any man
for the judgment is God's (Devarim 1:17).

In nineteenth-century Eastern Europe, it was common for the government to place a tax on the sale of kosher meat. In Kovno, the government would sell the right to collect the tax to the highest bidder, in an auction held once every three years. The auction was run by the government and the bidders were Jews from the local population. The winner was obligated to use a percentage of the tax for local communal needs, and would keep the remainder for himself.

There was a certain rich family in Kovno that had access to high officials and wielded great power. This family made it known that the meat tax was theirs, and that no one was to challenge their claim to it. People who might have been in a position to bid against them were afraid to do so. The auction became a farce, with no one but this family participating.

In 1859, Rabbi Yehoshua Leib Diskin became *Rav* of Kovno. R' Yehoshua Leib was known as someone who feared only Hashem. He had earned this reputation soon after he succeeded his father as *Rav* of Lomza in 1844.

At that time, the government issued a decree calling for all schools to introduce secular studies into their curriculums. This decree was aimed against the yeshivos, which in nineteenth-century Europe taught nothing but Torah.

R' Yehoshua Leib ordered all the yeshivos in the city to ignore the order. When an informer told a government official what was transpiring, the leaders of the community were summoned. An official told them in no uncertain terms that they must obey. The Jews replied truthfully that their *Rav* had the final say in all community matters. R' Yehoshua Leib was then ordered to appear before the governor of the city.

At their meeting, the governor got straight to the point. He handed R' Yehoshua Leib a document stating that he, the *Rav* of Lomza, agreed that the Jews of his city should comply with the government's decree. The governor ordered R' Yehoshua Leib to sign the document. He refused.

The governor was furious. "I'm about to leave on an important journey. I have no time to deal with you now. But mark my words — when I return, my first order of business will be to deal with you."

The governor never had a chance to follow through on his threat. As his coach rode across a bridge on the city's outskirts, the bridge collapsed, hurling the governor and his companions to their deaths in the waters below.

When R' Yehoshua Leib was informed of the situation with the meat tax in Kovno, he rose to his full height and declared, "This shall not continue!"

As the day of the next auction neared, R' Yehoshua Leib made it known that he expected the entire community to be present. Meanwhile, he spoke with wealthy members of the community who were in a position to bid against the incumbent family.

As the auction began, the auditorium in which it was held was filled to capacity. R' Yehoshua Leib sat himself among the crowd. The bidding began with a low bid of one hundred rubles. People in the audience quickly raised it to eight thousand rubles. At this point, the incumbent family bid nine thousand rubles.

There was silence in the room. Nine thousand rubles was an unheard-of sum for the meat tax rights. For anyone to offer a

higher bid meant openly challenging the family. The auction-
eer was about to wind up the bidding when R' Yehoshua Leib
rose to his feet and bid thirty thousand rubles.

The people could not believe their ears. How could the *Rav*
bid so much? Everyone knew that he was virtually penniless.
The members of the incumbent family were laughing derisively. The rules stipulated that the winner had to put down ten
percent of his bid in cash. They were sure that R' Yehoshua
Leib could not possibly come up with such a large sum of
money. But to their utter shock, R' Yehoshua Leib calmly
made his way to the front of the room and placed three
thousand rubles on the table.

The family would not give in easily and they upped their bid
to thirty-five thousand rubles. However, the *Rav's* courage had
inspired the other wealthy community members to bid without
fear. A lively round of bidding ensued and someone finally
won the auction with a bid of seventy thousand rubles. The
monopoly had been broken.

פרשת ואתחנן
Parashas Va'eschanan

To Love Hashem

וְאָהַבְתָּ אֵת ה' אֱלֹהֶיךָ בְּכָל לְבָבְךָ וּבְכָל נַפְשְׁךָ וּבְכָל מְאֹדֶךָ
*You shall love Hashem, your God, with all your heart,
with all your soul and with all your resources (Devarim 6:5).*

וְאָהַבְתָּ אֵת ה' אֱלֹהֶיךָ, *And you shall love Hashem, your
God — [This means]* שֶׁיְּהֵא שֵׁם שָׁמַיִם מִתְאַהֵב עַל יָדֶךְ, *that
the Name of Hashem should become beloved through
you. A Jew should study Scripture and Mishnah, serve
Torah scholars and deal graciously with his fellow
man. Then others will say of him, "Fortunate is his
father who taught him Torah! Fortunate is his teacher
who taught him Torah! Woe to those who do not study
Torah! He who studies Torah — how pleasant is his
behavior and how proper are his deeds." To him may
the verse be applied: (Yeshayahu 49:3). "And He said
to me: 'You are My servant Israel, in whom I will be
glorified' " (Yoma 86a).*

Bernie, the gentile caretaker at Beth Medrash Govoha,
was devoted heart and soul to the *Rosh Yeshivah*, Rabbi
Aharon Kotler.

One Friday, Bernie was seen running at top speed toward
the yeshivah building, clutching a package in his hand. When

someone asked him if everything was all right, he replied, "The Rabbi needs this," and he continued to run.

As it turned out, all R' Aharon had needed was to know the time. However, when R' Aharon, with his broken English, had asked Bernie for the time, the caretaker had mistakenly thought that R' Aharon was asking him to purchase a certain item in a local store. Faithful servant that he was, Bernie shot out of the building like a lightning bolt before R' Aharon could stop him.

The night after R' Aharon passed away, Bernie stood in the lobby of the yeshivah with his head bowed in mourning. "The Rabbi was a saint," he told a student. "You see this coat I'm wearing? The Rabbi gave it to me."

❧ ❧ ❧

Rabbi Leibish Langer is a *rebbe* at Mirrer Yeshivah in Brooklyn and teaches one night a week at Yeshivah Darchei Torah in Far Rockaway. One night, R' Langer was on his way back to Brooklyn with a carload of *talmidim* when his car hit a pothole and stalled. He could not restart the car. The neighborhood where the mishap occurred was known to be dangerous and the boys were tense. R' Langer told the boys that they should collectively pledge money to a *R' Meir Ba'al HaNeis tzedakah*[1] and then recite a chapter of *Tehillim* together. R' Langer assured the boys that Hashem would surely watch over them.

Almost immediately, two policemen cruising by noticed the stranded car and stopped. Then a yeshivah student driving by also stopped. The police radioed a road service company, which responded that its crew could be there in one-and-a-half hours. The police could not wait there all that time, but they cautioned R' Langer that if he abandoned the car he would probably not find it intact when he returned. R' Langer asked the yeshivah student to take the boys to the nearest yeshivah while he waited for the road service. The police cautioned him to remain in the car with the doors locked.

---

1. A *segulah* (auspicious omen) when one is in need of salvation.

The other two cars drove off and R' Langer returned to his car, locked the doors from the inside and turned on a tape of a Torah lecture. Almost immediately, a car passing by came to a halt and out stepped a black fellow of imposing appearance.

"Got a problem?" the man asked.

"No, I'm fine," R' Langer replied.

"Well, I'm a mechanic and I see you've got a problem. Open the hood and I'll see what I can do."

R' Langer remained in the locked car and opened the hood.

It was obvious that the man was making a real effort to get the car started. Finally, the man came around to the driver's window and said, "The fuel is not going into the engine but I can't figure out why. Listen, you can't stay here alone — this is a very dangerous neighborhood! What are you going to do?"

Before R' Langer could respond, the man went on. "I'll tell you what to do. Come out of the car and stand next to me. You'll see, any Jew that passes by and sees you will stop to help you out. I know — you Jews are humanitarians."

As they stood there, neighborhood teenagers walking by eyed them suspiciously. The man yelled at them to stop staring and get on their way. Within a few minutes, a former yeshivah student who had studied under R' Langer pulled up. "*Rebbi,* what's the problem?"

"See!" the man shouted. "I told you someone would stop. Just wait, we'll be here long enough, they'll be twenty Jewish cars lined up to help you. I know you people. I worked for Elite Caterers, a fellow named Shlomo Katz runs it — now, that's a good man!"

While they were talking, the driver who had taken the boys to a local yeshivah returned to see if he could be of further help. R' Langer assured the gentile that he now had enough help and that the man could leave. R' Langer thanked the man and insisted that he accept some money for his services. The man left and moments later, the three got the car started. One of the other two drivers followed R' Langer in his car until they were safely out of the neighborhood.

❀ ❀ ❀

It is a mistake to think that "making Hashem's name beloved" applies only to our relationship with gentiles. To the contrary, the above teaching of our Sages seems to be describing the reaction of *other Jews* to the behavior of one who studies Torah.

In a letter written in 1929, after students of the Chevron Yeshivah were massacred by Arabs, Rabbi Elchonon Wasserman stated that we should be filled with anguish not only by the physical death of Jews, but also by the spiritual death of those who are swept away by assimilation and live a life that is devoid of Torah and *mitzvos.* If we truly care for these Jews and seek to draw them close to Hashem, then we must live a life of *kiddush Hashem,* where those who observe our behavior are moved to exclaim:

"Fortunate is his father who taught him Torah! Fortunate is his teacher who taught him Torah! Woe to those who do not study Torah! He who studies Torah — how pleasant is his behavior and how proper are his deeds."

❀ ❀ ❀

Dr. Samuel Schmidt, editor of Cincinnati's *Every Friday* Jewish weekly, was an ardent secular Zionist-Socialist. Then he came in contact with the *gaon* Rabbi Eliezer Silver, Chief Rabbi of Cincinnati and one of the founders of Agudath Israel of America. Through R' Silver's influence, Dr. Schmidt began to adopt certain religious practices.

In late 1939, The American *Va'ad Hatzalah* (Rescue Committee) decided to send a representative to Vilna to assess the situation of the thousands who had fled to that city at the outbreak of the Second World War. R' Silver, as President of the *Va'ad Hatzalah*, designated Dr. Schmidt as the committee's representative. Dr. Schmidt's meeting with Rabbi Chaim Ozer Grodzensky, *Rav* of Vilna and acknowledged leader of Lithuanian Jewry, led him to become a *ba'al teshuvah*.

In Dr. Schmidt's words:

"It was shortly after I arrived in Vilna, on a Shabbos afternoon, that I entered R' Chaim Ozer's bedroom[1] at his personal invitation. The *gaon* sat smiling pleasantly, and the atmosphere was peaceful, for he was officially not seeing visitors at that hour.

"He began to ask me about myself and listened carefully to every detail I related from my history. . . .He listened with rapt attention, and then, with a look of true friendship, said, 'Allow me, Dr. Schmidt, to address you in a familiar way, by your first name — Shmuel.'

"His words touched my heart and my tears flowed freely. 'I am not worthy of this,' I protested. He replied, 'Heaven forfend! For a Jew living in the security of America to undertake a dangerous mission and travel under wartime conditions to a faraway land in order to assist his fellow Jews and rescue the yeshivos — this is proof of his worth!'

"He continued to offer me encouragement. The next morning, I donned *tallis* and *tefillin* for the first time. . . And [ultimately,] I became observant of Torah and *mitzvos* in all their fine details."

❁ ❁ ❁

The Nazis enjoyed pitting Jew against Jew and would often appoint a Jew to supervise the work of his fellow prisoners. Many of these Jews, known as *kapos,* behaved unkindly toward their brethren out of fear for their own lives.

In the Lemberg labor camp during the Second World War, the chief work supervisor was a *kapo* named Schneeweiss. Schneeweiss did not enjoy a good reputation among his fellow Jews. As Yom Kippur approached, the Bluzhever *Rebbe*, Rabbi Yisrael Spira, made a request of Schneeweiss. "I and thirteen other Jews want to do everything possible to avoid work on our Holy Day. Please assign us work that will not involve any transgression of the laws of Yom Kippur. We are willing to do extra work on other days to make up for any work which goes

---

1. R' Chaim Ozer was ill at the time.

undone." Putting forth this request was a great act of courage on the *Rebbe's* part.

The next day, Shneeweiss informed the *Rebbe* that he had arranged for the *Rebbe* and his friends to clean the apartments of the commanding officers on Yom Kippur. The work was basically tidying and dusting, nothing that would involve any Torah prohibitions. Schneeweiss warned the *Rebbe*, "I give you no guarantees and I will not defend you if the Germans sense that something is wrong. And the apartments had better be clean."

On the day of Yom Kippur, the *Rebbe* and his friends cleaned, as the *Rebbe* led the others in reciting the Yom Kippur prayers from memory. At midday, a German came in with a tray of food for the workers. The inmates were usually served a starvation diet of coarse bread and watery soup, but the Nazis always made sure to serve good food on Yom Kippur. However, the tray of food lay untouched. All the men were fasting.

A few officers entered the apartment to inspect the work. They seemed satisfied until one of them noticed the un-touched tray. He flew into a rage. "What do you mean by not eating on this 'holy day' of yours? Stuff yourselves, Jews!"

The Bluzhever *Rebbe* calmly explained, "Today is our holy day. As you can see, we have served you loyally even on this sacred day, and our work is perfect. We are required to fast today and we ask that we be excused from eating. Our work will continue and will not be affected by our hunger."

But the officers were furious. They sent for Schneeweiss, who trembled as he entered the room. "You are responsible for these Jews. We will return in two hours. If all their food is not eaten, you will be shot."

Schneeweiss stood tall and firm as he unbuttoned his shirt. "Shoot me now, if you wish. I will not make them break their fast. In fact, I, too, am fasting on this holy day!"

One of the Nazis drew his pistol and shot Schneeweiss dead. The hated Jew had become a holy Jew. No doubt, his attitude had been profoundly affected by the courage and sacrifice of the Bluzhever *Rebbe* and his friends.

פרשת עקב
Parashas Eikev

Tefillin in the Camps

וּקְשַׁרְתֶּם אֹתָם לְאוֹת עַל יֶדְכֶם וְהָיוּ לְטוֹטָפֹת בֵּין עֵינֵיכֶם.

You shall bind them for a sign upon your arm
and let them be an ornament between your eyes
(*Devarim* 11:18).

There was no denying it. Life was becoming more frightening with each passing day. The Germans had occupied the town and the deportations to the concentration camps had begun. Mendel and Moshe were ready when their turn came.

They knew that they would not be allowed to take very much along with them. One item, however, they made sure to take — their *tefillin.* And they both vowed that come what may, they would strive to fulfill this precious *mitzvah* every single day.

It was not long before the brothers found themselves on a cattle-car bound for Auschwitz. As soon as they arrived at the camp, they were ordered to undress and their every possession, including their *tefillin,* was taken from them. Immediately, the two began searching for a way to get themselves another pair of *tefillin*. They discovered that all religious articles which the Nazis had confiscated had been thrown into a shed on camp grounds. The Nazis often saved such articles because they planned to build a "museum of the Jews" after the war, so that future generations would know that there was once a people known as "the Jews" which the Germans, the "master race," had wiped off the face of the earth, ר״ל.

Mendel noticed that one of the gentiles working at the camp seemed like a fairly decent fellow. He asked the man what his price would be to get him a pair of *tefillin* from the shed. The gentile replied that he wanted a day's food rations. Mendel quickly agreed. The next day, the man brought the *tefillin* and Mendel handed over the little bread and watery soup that was supposed to have sustained him for that day. When Mendel opened the boxes which housed the *tefillin* he became filled with dismay — they were both *tefillin shel yad* (of the arm)! He sought out the gentile and explained the problem. The gentile replied, "Look here, Jew. I took a big risk bringing you those things. And how was I supposed to know that you wanted two different boxes? If you want me to risk it again, it will cost you another day's food."

Mendel agreed. He fasted two consecutive days, but he had a pair of *tefillin*.

Mendel and Moshe shared their *tefillin* with any Jew who wanted to put them on. Before long, as many as fifty Jews a day took turns fulfilling this *mitzvah*. All were well aware that to get caught would probably mean death.

One day, a *kapo*[1] entered the barracks and asked Mendel if he could borrow the *tefillin*. Mendel had no choice but to give the *kapo* the *tefillin*. He never returned them.

The next day, news spread through the camp that a new transport of Jews would be arriving that day. Well aware of the risk involved, Mendel stood near the barbed wire fence which surrounded the camp, waiting for the transport to arrive. As soon as the frightened deportees entered the camp grounds,

---

1. See end of previous chapter.

Mendel hurried over to them. "Who has *tefillin*, who has *tefillin*?" he asked frantically, as he hurried up and down the columns of people. Finally, one man called out, "I have *tefillin*." "Then please, give them to me," said Mendel. "If you hold on to them, they will surely become lost to you, for you will be ordered to hand over your every possession. But if you give them to me, I will do my very best to guard them, and I will try to return them to you as soon as possible."

The man gave Mendel the *tefillin*. The man was old and weak and the Nazis had no use for him. They murdered him that same day. Mendel kept the *tefillin* and, as in the past, shared them with everyone.

Then one day, it happened. While one of the prisoners was wearing the *tefillin*, a Nazi entered the barracks. The Nazi flew into a rage. He demanded that the *tefillin* be handed over and asked to whom they belonged. Mendel raised his hand. "You should really die for this," the Nazi said, "but I've thought of an even better punishment. This afternoon, we're going to assemble all the prisoners in this section. They will all gather in a circle around a fire. And you," he continued, pointing to Mendel, "will throw your 'precious treasure' into the flames!" He tossed the *tefillin* back to Mendel and left.

The inmates were crestfallen. Some of them went over to comfort Mendel, while the man who had been caught wearing the *tefillin* begged forgiveness in case he had not been careful enough. Mendel assured him that there was no reason to apologize. "As for that beast's orders," he continued, "I've prepared for such a possibility." He bent down near his bed and pried up a floorboard. From underneath the floor, Mendel withdrew what looked like a pair of *tefillin*. "I made these a while back, thinking that they might come in handy some day. Today is the day."

That afternoon, the Jews assembled in a circle around a bonfire which the Nazis had set. As the Nazis looked on mockingly, Mendel threw his empty wooden boxes into the flames. The next morning, he and his friends donned the *tefillin*, just as they had the previous mornings.

It was 1945 and the war was quickly drawing to a close. The Nazis, realizing that defeat was inevitable, had stopped providing even the pitiful rations which they had given until that point. Prisoners had to fend for themselves to keep from starving.

Mendel was dreadfully weakened from all the hardships and backbreaking work he had endured. He lay on his bed with his eyes closed, barely alive. Moshe was in somewhat better health and he rushed about the camp frantically, trying to find even a crust of bread which would keep his brother alive.

A German was riding a wagon through the camp. Moshe noticed something fall off the wagon. He rushed over to pick it up — it was a lump of sugar, a precious commodity! Quickly, he hurried over to someone. "Would you trade me a few slices of bread for a lump of sugar?" The items were exchanged and Moshe ran back to his barracks. He crumbled the bread into small pieces and proceeded to place a few crumbs into his starving brother's mouth. Mendel opened his eyes and looked up at his younger brother with a mixture of love and gratitude. After swallowing a couple of mouthfuls, Mendel attempted to speak. Moshe had to bend down and place his ear near his brother's mouth to hear what he was saying.

"Moshe . . . Please bring me the *tefillin* . . . I haven't worn them today. . ."

The next day, the Allied armies took control of the camp. Mendel and Moshe eventually made their way to America, along with their precious *tefillin.*

פרשת ראה
Parashas Re'eh

A Change of Heart

כִּי יִהְיֶה בְךָ אֶבְיוֹן מֵאַחַד אַחֶיךָ בְּאַחַד שְׁעָרֶיךָ בְּאַרְצְךָ
אֲשֶׁר ה׳ אֱלֹהֶיךָ נֹתֵן לָךְ, לֹא תְאַמֵּץ אֶת לְבָבְךָ וְלֹא
תִקְפֹּץ אֶת יָדְךָ מֵאָחִיךָ הָאֶבְיוֹן.

If there shall be a destitute person among you,
any of your brethren in any of your cities,
in the Land that Hashem, your God, gives you,
you shall not harden your heart or close your hand
against your destitute brother (Devarim 15:7).

Yitzchak[1] did not want to go, but there was no choice. He had a wife and four children and he could not put bread on the table. Yitzchak lived in *Eretz Yisrael*, and since his marriage he had earned a living running a private business. Then he was called up for extended army reserve duty, and when he returned home, he found that his business had collapsed. As he tried to rebuild from scratch and at the same time provide for his family, he sank deep into debt. He finally

---

1. All names are fictitious.

came to the realization that he had no choice but to travel to America and collect *tzedakah* for himself. If he could pay off a good percentage of his debts, he might be able to succeed in business once again and lead a normal life.

Yitzchak arrived in New York and found lodging with a kindhearted family in Brooklyn. He then began the unpleasant task of ringing doorbells and begging. Each night, he would wearily count his earnings and calculate how much more he needed before he could be reunited with his family.

One night, he rang the doorbell of a beautiful three-story home. A second-floor window opened up. "Who is it?" a man asked. "I'm collecting for myself," Yitzchak began. "You see, I was in the army in Israel when . . ."

Before he could finish the sentence, something hit him on the head and then fell to the ground. It was a transit token, good for one fare on New York's buses and subways. Looking up toward the window from where it had come, Yitzchak shouted in pain, "Isn't it enough disgrace that I have to spend my days and nights begging for myself? Must you shame me even more by throwing this at me?" With that, he hurled the token back through the window and walked down the street in disgust.

Moments later, Yitzchak heard footsteps behind him. It was the man who had thrown the token. "Please," the man said, "forgive me for hurting your feelings. I should never have thrown that token, though I did not mean to hit you on the head. Please come back with me to my house and I will give you a respectable donation."

The two retraced their steps. The man led Yitzchak into his home and offered him a seat in his dining room. The man, who now introduced himself as Aaron Goldberg, served Yitzchak cake and coffee and repeated his apology. He then wrote out a check for a generous amount and handed it to Yitzchak, who expressed his gratitude. He rose to leave and Mr. Goldberg escorted him to the door. As he was about to step outside, Yitzchak turned to face his benefactor. "I hope you don't mind my asking, but what was it that made you change your attitude? Was it that you felt bad for me after I yelled back at you?"

"To tell you the truth," Mr. Goldberg replied, "I did not pay much attention to what you said. But my seven-year-old daughter did. She said to me, '*Tatte* (Father), it's such a pity on that poor man. How can we hurt his feelings by throwing coins at him?' Her simple words made me stop and think. I had become so accustomed to having poor people knock on my door, that I paid little attention to them. I had long ago stopped feeling their plight or pondering their difficult situation. My daughter's words shook me. For that moment, I saw myself in your shoes. And I knew that I had to correct what I had done."

Yitzchak returned to his lodgings feeling as if a great burden had been lifted from his heart. Meanwhile, Mr. Goldberg picked up the phone and called Eli Berger, Yitzchak's host. Yitzchak had mentioned his host's name and as Heaven willed it, he and Mr. Goldberg were friends. Mr. Goldberg related what had happened and told Mr. Berger that he was ready to help Yitzchak in any way possible.

A few weeks later, Jews everywhere celebrated the first night of Chanukah. As Yitzchak's host prepared to light the *menorah*, he sent one of his children to call Yitzchak from his room. The child returned to report, "Yitzchak is sitting on his bed, crying."

Mr. Berger hurried to Yitzchak's room and asked what was the matter. Yitzchak explained, "It is a few months now that my wife has not been feeling well. It was only out of desperation that I left her and my four children. Before leaving home, I promised my wife, 'I will be home for Chanukah.' Now, Chanukah has arrived and I have not kept my word. Worse, I cannot even call my wife and tell her when she can expect me home. You see, I cannot return home without having raised a significant sum to pay off a large portion of my debts. And I am far short of that goal."

"May I ask how much you need?" asked Mr. Berger. Yitzchak replied that he needed $3,000. Mr. Berger suggested that they light the Chanukah candles and continue their discussion later.

Later that evening, Mr. Berger phoned Mr. Goldberg. "Remember you said that you stand ready to help Yitzchak in any way possible?" Mr. Berger proceeded to explain the situation. When he finished there was silence on the other end for a few moments. Finally, Mr. Goldberg spoke. "Let's make a deal. If you raise $1500, I'll match it with the same amount." Mr. Berger agreed.

The next afternoon, Mr. Berger phoned Mr. Goldberg to say that he had raised his share. "Fine," came the reply. "Tell Yitzchak to be at my house tonight at 8:00. Oh, and tell him that he's invited for supper."

That night, Yitzchak enjoyed a delicious meal and was made to feel at home by the Goldbergs. When the meal had ended, Mr. Goldberg said, "Yitzchak, it is Chanukah and I am especially happy to have been given the opportunity to help you. Come, let us sing and dance together." Taking Yitzchak by both hands, Mr. Goldberg began to sing a *nigun* to which they danced. He then presented his new friend with a check for $1500.

The following afternoon, the second day of Chanukah, Yitzchak boarded a plane for a joyful reunion with his family.

פרשת שופטים
Parashas Shoftim

A Decision For Life

עַל פִּי הַתּוֹרָה אֲשֶׁר יוֹרוּךְ וְעַל הַמִּשְׁפָּט אֲשֶׁר יֹאמְרוּ לְךָ תַּעֲשֶׂה,
לֹא תָסוּר מִן הַדָּבָר אֲשֶׁר יַגִּידוּ לְךָ יָמִין וּשְׂמֹאל.

*According to the teaching that they will teach you
and according to the judgment that they will say to you,
shall you do; you shall not deviate from the word
that they will tell you, right or left (Devarim 17:11).*

By Torah law, an animal that is mortally wounded either through birth defect, disease or injury is deemed a *treifah* and may not be eaten.[1] There is a question whether a particular lung defect renders the animal a *treifah; Beis Yosef* (R' Yosef Karo, author of *Shulchan Aruch*) rules that it does not, while *Rama* (R' Moshe Isserles) disagrees.

Ashkenazic Jews generally follow the opinion of *Rama* when he and *Beis Yosef* disagree. However, with regard to this disagreement, one Ashkenazic *gaon* ruled according to *Beis*

---

1. Today the word *treifah* is synonymous with all unkosher food, but this is not the actual definition of the word. See *Shemos* 22:30.

Yosef. He was Rabbi Aryeh Leib Gunzberg, legendary author of *Sha'agas Aryeh* and one of the eighteenth century's greatest Torah geniuses. His *p'sak* (ruling) in this matter caused quite a stir among Ashkenazic Jews. Nevertheless, the Jews of Volozhin, where the *Sha'agas Aryeh* served as *Rav*, faithfully followed his opinion. Years later, when the *Sha'agas Aryeh*'s famed disciple, Rabbi Chaim Volozhiner, became *Rav* of Volozhin, he continued to follow his *rebbe's* ruling.

❦ ❦ ❦

In Volozhin, there lived a man who suffered from a lung disorder identical to that which was the subject of the disagreement between the *Beis Yosef* and *Rama.* The man decided that his condition would benefit from the rarified air of Switzerland and he began making plans to move his family there.

One night, the man's father, who had died some years before, appeared to him in a dream. "My son, I have come to warn you not to leave Volozhin. The illness from which you suffer is rendered life threatening by the *Rama* — and his ruling is followed by almost the entire European Jewry, including the Jewish community of Switzerland.

"It is only in Volozhin that the *Rama's* opinion is not followed, for it is there that the great *Sha'agas Aryeh* served as *Rav,* and it is he who ruled that this illness is not terminal. The *Sha'agas Aryeh*'s opinion carries great weight in Heaven. Just as the animals in Volozhin with this defect are deemed kosher and not mortally ill, so too, are you deemed capable of living many more years.

"However, if you move elsewhere, where the *Sha'agas Aryeh*'s ruling is not accepted, you will die within the year."

The man canceled his plans to move. He was never cured of is lung disorder, but he lived into his eighties.

"Father!"

וְהָיָה כְּקָרָבְכֶם אֶל הַמִּלְחָמָה, וְנִגַּשׁ הַכֹּהֵן וְדִבֶּר אֶל הָעָם.
וְאָמַר אֲלֵהֶם שְׁמַע יִשְׂרָאֵל אַתֶּם קְרֵבִים הַיּוֹם
לַמִּלְחָמָה עַל אֹיְבֵיכֶם, אַל יֵרַךְ לְבַבְכֶם אַל תִּירְאוּ
וְאַל תַּחְפְּזוּ וְאַל תַּעַרְצוּ מִפְּנֵיהֶם.

*It shall be that when you draw near to the war, the Kohen
will approach and speak to the people. He shall say to them,
"Hear, O Israel, you are coming near to the battle against your
enemies; let your heart not be faint; do not be afraid,
do not panic, and do not be broken before them
(Devarim 20:2-3).*

שְׁמַע יִשְׂרָאֵל, *Hear O Israel — Even if your only merit
is the reciting of Shema, you are worthy of Hashem's
salvation (Rashi).*

I n the Skolye *Beis Midrash* in Williamsburg, an unusual
custom was practiced every year on the eve of Yom Kippur.
As the Holy Day was ushered in, the prayers began not with *Kol
Nidrei*, but with the congregation declaring in unison: שְׁמַע
יִשְׂרָאֵל ה׳ אֱלֹהֵינוּ ה׳ אֶחָד. Before that declaration, the Skolye
Rebbe would face the open *Aron HaKodesh* and quote the
above comment of *Rashi*. He would then explain it with a
parable:

A king had an only son whom he taught great wisdom and
who was provided with his every desire. The son became
friendly with wicked people and began to stray from the proper
path. The king sent emissaries to try to convince the prince to
mend his ways, but to no avail. Finally, the king was forced to
banish his son to exile in a far-off province.

Before sending his son away, the king gave him a large amount of money and other items of value so that he could have whatever he needed even while in exile. But the prince squandered everything away. Left with nothing and living a life of degradation, the prince finally was ready to repent.

Meanwhile, the king missed his son terribly and yearned for him to return to the palace. But first, he had to be sure that the prince was ready and willing to make a new start. The king decided to travel throughout his empire, and invite his every subject to have an audience with him and put forth one request. Surely, reasoned the king, his son would hurry to see him. Then, the king would be able to judge whether or not the prince was ready to return home.

The day finally came when the king arrived at the far-off province where the prince lived. But the prince did not come forward because he had forgotten the language of the king and would not be able to communicate with him. The prince wept over his sad plight until a wise man told him, "You are mistaken. You do not need to know the language of the king. Your father has embarked on this long journey for the sole purpose of being reunited with you. Simply walk up to the throne and cry out, 'Father, Father!' and he will take you into his arms."

❀   ❀   ❀

The king alludes to Hashem, while the prince alludes to the Jewish people. Hashem taught His people the Torah, the greatest of all wisdoms. The Jews fell from their previous status of holiness and purity, and Hashem sent prophets to steer them back to the proper path. But the prophets' warnings went unheeded and the Jews were sent into exile. There, among the gentile nations, the Jews fell yet further.

After all the sufferings the Jews have endured in exile, they find it difficult to express themselves in the language of the King of kings. In a sense, they have forgotten how to communicate with Him. But they still remain His beloved nation.

When a Jew declares his belief in Hashem daily by reciting *Shema Yisrael . . .*, he is, in a sense, crying out "Father!" This declaration, says *Rashi*, was enough to gain the Jews merit to be victorious in war. And it is enough to arouse Hashem's compassion in the darkness of exile.

פרשת כי תצא
Parshas Ki Seitzei

Man of His Word

מוֹצָא שְׂפָתֶיךָ תִּשְׁמֹר וְעָשִׂיתָ.
*You shall observe and carry out
what emerges from your lips (Devarim 23:24).*

While this verse refers to a statement that has the status of a *neder* (vow), its message applies to speech in general. A Jew must weigh his words and honor them.

❧ ❧ ❧

It was a snowy winter afternoon and young Feige Kagan, youngest child of the Chofetz Chaim, had already put on her coat and was headed for the door to go visit a friend. Her father's voice stopped her.

"Feige," the Chofetz Chaim said, "please don't leave yet. I need your help. I have three sets of *Mishnah Berurah* that have to be checked for errors."

Feige's heart sank. Three sets? She knew what such "checks" involved. Her father would never sell a *sefer* without first examining each of the volume's pages for possible misprints, missing pages or other mistakes that might have crept in during the publishing process. To sell a *sefer* at the regular price when it contained even a single error would be dishonest.

Each set of *Mishnah Berurah* contains six volumes. Three sets are a total of eighteen volumes. It would take all afternoon, Feige told herself.

"*Tatte* (Father)," she said, "I was about to leave for a friend's house. But I will be sure to check the *sefarim* later!"

"Feige," the Chofetz Chaim replied, "I need these *sefarim* to be checked *now.*"

"*Tatte,*" the young girl responded, a touch of desperation in her voice, "I really want very much to visit my friend now. Tonight I'll even check *thirteen* sets of *Mishnah Berurah*!"

The Chofetz Chaim did not respond, and his daughter took this to mean that he agreed to let her leave. She headed out into the snow and returned home after dark.

A surprise greeted her upon returning home. There, on the table, were thirteen sets of *Mishnah Berurah* neatly piled up next to one another.

"*Tatte,*" she asked hesitatingly, "what's this?"

"Oh," said the Chofetz Chaim matter-of-factly, "these are the thirteen sets you promised to check when you returned home."

"But, *Tatte,*" she protested, "I didn't mean it! People say lots of things they don't really mean."

The Chofetz Chaim responded gently but firmly. "Feige, a person is responsible for every word that he says. If a person doesn't mean something, then he shouldn't say it. You said that you would check thirteen sets of *Mishnah Berurah* and you must honor your word."[1]

---

1. The Chofetz Chaim's daughter was married to Rabbi Mendel Zaks, an outstanding Torah personality. *Rebbetzin* Zaks passed away only a few years

In the early 1960's, the wife of Rabbi Chaskel Besser gave birth to a son. Rabbi Yisrael Spira, the late Bluzhever *Rebbe,* was a cousin to R' Besser and the two were close. R' Besser was also close to the late Boyaner *Rebbe*, Rabbi Mordechai Shlomo Friedman, as well. In deference to his father-in-law, who was a Boyaner *chassid*, R' Besser decided to ask the Boyaner *Rebbe* to serve as *sandak* at his son's *bris*. The Bluzhever *Rebbe* agreed wholeheartedly with R' Besser's decision, and planned to attend the *bris* in any case. However, the Boyaner *Rebbe* was forced to refuse the honor, as he had already made plans to be away that day. R' Besser again contacted the Bluzhever *Rebbe*, who now accepted the honor of *sandak*.

A case of jaundice forced the *bris'* postponement. By the time the *bris* was to take place, the Boyaner *Rebbe* had already returned from his trip. When R' Besser phoned the Bluzhever *Rebbe* regarding the time of the *bris*, the *Rebbe* said, "The Boyaner *Rebbe* will be *sandak*, for the honor was originally given to him."

However, the Boyaner *Rebbe* felt that the honor still belonged to the Bluzhever *Rebbe*. When R' Besser reported this to the Bluzhever *Rebbe*, he said, "Don't press the matter any further. I will take care of things myself."

At the *bris*, the Bluzhever *Rebbe* was announced as *sandak*. He said, "I appreciate the honor, and I now give the honor over to the *Rebbe* of Boyan." The Boyaner *Rebbe* protested, and a discussion ensued, as each *tzaddik* strove to convince the other to accept the honor. Finally, the Bluzhever *Rebbe* said, "I will tell you what we should do. You, Boyaner *Rebbe,* will be *sandak*, and I, with the help of Hashem, will officiate at this child's wedding!"

The Boyaner *Rebbe* reluctantly relented.

---

ago, leaving behind generations imbued with Torah and awe of Hashem and a legacy of *tzidkus* that made her a legend in her time.

More than twenty years later, R' Besser's son became engaged. When R' Besser visited the Bluzhever *Rebbe* shortly thereafter, the *Rebbe*, then ninety-four years old, asked, "When is your son getting married? I promised long ago that I would be the *mesader kiddushin* at his wedding."

During the following three weeks, the *Rebbe* underwent two operations. When he was visited by R' Besser after the second surgery, the *Rebbe* said, "Don't search for another *mesader kiddushin*. I'll be there."

He was.

Kosher Money

אֶבֶן שְׁלֵמָה וָצֶדֶק יִהְיֶה לָּךְ אֵיפָה שְׁלֵמָה וָצֶדֶק יִהְיֶה לָּךְ.
A perfect and honest weight shall you have,
a perfect and honest measure shall you have
(*Devarim* 25:15).

Once, Rabbi Avraham Kahaneman, President of the Ponovezher Yeshivah and son of the illustrious Ponovezher *Rav*, approached a wealthy widow for a donation to his yeshivah. The woman happily wrote out a generous check and commented that she contributed to many such causes. Curious, R' Kahaneman asked the woman which other causes she supported and she proceeded to list some of the world's finest yeshivos and organizations. R' Kahaneman was amazed. He knew that the woman's husband had died fifteen years earlier and that she had no one to advise her where to give her charity. "I hope you don't mind my asking," he said, "but how is it that you have been able to distribute your *tzedakah* so wisely without anyone advising you?"

"It's really quite simple," replied the woman. "The money my husband left me is 'kosher money' — all of it was earned honestly and none of it was earned through *chillul* (desecration of) Shabbos. I forever pray that in this merit, my *tzedakah* should end up in the right hands. Thank G-d, Hashem continues to grant my request."

❧ ❧ ❧

At the funeral of the Vilna *Gaon,* only those who could repeat Torah thoughts which they had personally heard from the *Gaon* were permitted to speak. One speaker quoted the *Gaon*'s explanation of the following Talmudic passage (*Bava Metzia* 85b):

R' Chiya once related how he had succeeded in preventing Torah from becoming forgotten. "I planted flax from which I made nets and trapped deer. I fed the deer to orphans, and from the skins I made parchment scrolls on which I wrote the Five Books of the *Chumash.* I then went to a town, taught each of the Books to five different children, and the Six Orders of the Mishnah to each of six children. . . ."

Why couldn't R' Chiya have purchased ready-made scrolls? Why did he spend so much valuable time preparing them himself? Answered the Vilna *Gaon:* For Torah study to have its desired effect, every facet of its learning must be pure. If the scrolls from which R' Chiya's students had studied would have been produced through dishonest means, then this would have had a negative effect on the children's learning. Similarly, if a person purchases a *sefer* with funds borrowed with *ribis* (interest), people who study from that *sefer* will not have proper success in their learning.

In the words of the Manchester *Rosh Yeshivah,* Rabbi Yehudah Zev Segal, "The noblest intentions do not permit taking a single dishonest cent from either the government or a private individual. In fact, the noblest goal of all is to be *mekadeish shem shamayim,* to sanctify Hashem's Name. The way to accomplish this is by strictly adhering to the Torah."[1]

---

1. See conclusion of chapter to *Parashas Emor.*

פרשת כי תבא
Parashas Ki Savo

Best Investment

אָרוּר אֲשֶׁר לֹא יָקִים אֶת דִּבְרֵי הַתּוֹרָה הַזֹּאת לַעֲשׂוֹת אוֹתָם.
*Accursed is one who will not uphold the words
of this Torah, to perform them (Devarim 27:26).*

Ramban (citing *Talmud Yerushalmi*) states that from this
verse we derive the obligation upon every Jew to
support the study of Torah.

❦ ❦ ❦

It was in 1933 that Rabbi Yaakov Yitzchok *HaLevi* Ruderman
founded Yeshivas Ner Israel in Baltimore. The yeshivah
enjoyed tremendous growth, and before long it outgrew its
original quarters. A new building was needed, and of course
this meant that money was needed. R' Ruderman was forced to
set aside precious time to go knocking on doors of Jewish
homes and stores seeking donations.

At one store, R' Ruderman received an unusual response.
The proprietor had listened respectfully as the *Rosh Yeshivah*
explained how vital it was for the Jewish community to have a

yeshivah of higher learning in its midst. When R' Ruderman finished speaking, the man said, "I'm sure, Rabbi, that whatever you have told me is true. However, before making any decisions, I must first discuss the matter with my wife. Please return tomorrow."

The next day, the man told the *Rosh Yeshivah,* "Only a few years ago, I was fabulously wealthy. I lost almost everything in the stock market crash of 1929. My wife and I learned an important lesson: when it comes to financial success and security, there are no guarantees. Money that's here today can be gone tomorrow.

"Now, all we have left in our savings account is one thousand dollars. We decided that we wanted to enjoy this money forever — by donating it to a worthy cause.

"After your visit yesterday, I repeated our discussion to my wife. We've decided to invest our thousand dollars in your 'corporation.' "

❧ ❧ ❧

Money is not the only means through which Torah study can be supported.

In 1980, the Ponovezher *Rosh Yeshivah*, Rabbi Eliezer Menachem Shach, attended the funeral of an elderly man in Bnei Brak. The funeral was held in pouring rain. Nevertheless, the aged *Rosh Yeshivah* accompanied the coffin to the cemetery on foot and he returned to yeshivah by foot as well. A *talmid* asked the *Rosh Yeshivah* why he had found it necessary to go all the way to the cemetery, and, given the weather conditions, why he had not gone by car. R' Shach replied:

In Europe, when he was a young student, he did not study in a yeshivah; there was no opportunity. He studied in a small *shul* from morning to night, and slept there, too. He was away from home and often there was no food. Occasionally, he would be invited by one of the local families for a meal. The rest of the time, he felt fortunate to obtain bread to still his hunger.

But worst of all was the frigid cold. During the day, he was so involved in his studies that he did not notice the cold, but at night it was awful. The cold wooden bench on which he sat all day served as his bed. There was a small oven in the *shul* but it did not emit much heat. The poverty was extreme and blankets were a luxury that he could not afford.

One night, a man brought him a jacket. He could wrap himself in it and keep warm as he slept. The jacket provided him with a small measure of comfort and he was able to study with greater concentration during the day.

It was this man who had brought him the coat whose funeral R' Shach had just attended.[1]

---

1. From an article by Rabbi Hillel Goldberg in *The Jewish Observer* (January 1981).

פרשת נצבים
Parashas Nitzavim

Choose Life

רְאֵה נָתַתִּי לְפָנֶיךָ הַיּוֹם אֶת הַחַיִּים וְאֶת הַטּוֹב,
וְאֶת הַמָּוֶת וְאֶת הָרָע. . . .וּבָחַרְתָּ בַּחַיִּים.
See — I have placed before you today the
life and the good, and the death and the evil . . .
and you shall choose life (Devarim 30:15,19).

There once lived a farmer who spent his entire life in the small town in which he had been born. He had never been to a big city and had never traveled by any means other than horse and wagon.

One day, a rich customer presented the farmer with a gift — a train ticket. The farmer was overjoyed. All his life he had wondered what it was like to ride a train. Now, he would finally find out.

The night before his ride, the farmer could hardly sleep. At the crack of dawn, he put on his very best clothing and anxiously watched the clock until it was time to head for the station.

At the station, the farmer stood on the platform and craned his neck so that he could see the train as soon as it appeared in the distance. Suddenly, a thought struck him. He had never seen anyone board a train before. How do you know when to board? Does the conductor come on to the platform and escort you in? Do you simply walk on?

The train was in view and the farmer was frantic. Then he had an idea. At the end of the platform stood three men who were smiling and laughing aloud. They seemed very relaxed and, as such, appeared to be seasoned travelers. The farmer hurried down the platform to stand near them. He would do whatever they did. His problem was solved.

The train pulled in to the station and its doors opened. But much to the farmer's dismay, the three men made no move at all. "Why aren't they boarding?" the farmer wondered, but he was too embarrassed to ask. The train's doors closed and its whistle blew. Still, the men made no move.

The engine started up and the train lurched forward. As the last car passed them, the three men suddenly reached out, grabbed hold of the train and hoisted themselves aboard. The farmer quickly followed suit, just barely making it onto the train.

The men entered the back car with the farmer right behind them. The farmer was aghast. The car was empty of passengers — and no wonder! It was filthy, its seats were torn, and a foul odor wafted forth from it.

"So this is what I've been waiting for?" the farmer thought in disgust. "I almost got killed jumping onto the train, and for what? To ride in a car that smells worse than my horse's stable?"

The farmer's brooding was interrupted when one of the three men shouted, "He's coming!" The three dove under the seats and were silent. The farmer did the same. "Now I've seen everything," he thought. "So the rest of the ride's gonna be on this filthy floor."

The farmer's thoughts were disturbed by a hand which yanked at his leg. "Get out from under there, you crook!"

shouted the conductor. "You thought I wouldn't notice your big legs sticking out?!" The conductor found the other three men as well.

The farmer drew himself to his full height. "Excuse me, sir, but I am *not* a crook! I work hard to earn an honest living."

"But you tried to sneak onto this train without paying!" the conductor retorted. "So you are a crook!"

The farmer reached into his pocket and pulled out his ticket. "Here's my ticket. I was not trying to sneak on."

The conductor examined the ticket. "I don't believe it!" he exclaimed. "You've got yourself a first-class ticket! You should be riding in the best car we've got — what are you doing under the seat in this dingy car?"

❅ ❅ ❅

Choose life. In today's world of sin and violence, the truth of these words is plain for all to see. The choice between a life with Torah and a life devoid of Torah is a choice between light and darkness. As the Sages teach, Torah is the key to a good life in *this* world, as well as in the next world (*Mishnah Avos* 6:4). With Torah, every moment of life is meaningful. Without Torah, life has no meaning.

A Jew who brings secular attitudes and pleasures into his life, in the belief that this will bring him happiness, is like the farmer in our parable. He could be traveling "first class" by following the way of Torah, but fails to realize how rich is his heritage and how bankrupt is the society he seeks to emulate.

פרשת וילך
Parashas Vayeilech

The Hidden Hand

וְאָנֹכִי הַסְתֵּר אַסְתִּיר פָּנַי בַּיּוֹם הַהוּא עַל כָּל הָרָעָה אֲשֶׁר עָשָׂה.
But I will utterly conceal My face on that day
because of all the evil that it [the Jewish people] did
(Devarim 31:18).

אֶסְתֵּר מִן הַתּוֹרָה מִנַּיִן? "וְאָנֹכִי הַסְתֵּר אַסְתִּיר פָּנַי."
Where is there an allusion to Esther in the Torah? "And
I will utterly conceal My face" (Chullin 139b).

The Vilna *Gaon* explained the above teaching with a parable:

A king had a son whose wayward behavior demanded harsh punishment. The king had no choice but to banish the prince to the forest. The prince thought that he had been thrown into the dangerous forest unprotected, but it was not so. The king had sent guards to hide in the forest and defend his son in case of attack.

One day, a bear appeared and was about to attack the prince. Suddenly a guard jumped out from his hiding place and killed the bear. The prince did not recognize the guard and thought that his sudden appearance was a stroke of good luck. The next day, an enemy of the prince came to attack him. Again, a guard appeared just in time to protect the defenseless prince. Now the prince understood that neither occurrence had been a coincidence. His father, while forced to punish him, had ensured his safety nonetheless. The prince became filled with a boundless love for his father and promised himself that he would mend his ways.

When the Jews are cast into exile, it appears as if Hashem has abandoned them. The Purim story is a classic illustration that this is not so. The story centered in Shushan, outside of *Eretz Yisrael*, and occured at a time when there was no *Beis HaMikdash*. The Book of Esther relates how a series of hidden miracles came together to bring about the Jews' salvation from their bitter enemies. Just as Hashem saved the Jews in the days of Queen Esther through hidden miracles, so too does He watch over us throughout the exile, even in its darkest moments. *But I will utterly conceal My face*... Hashem may conceal Himself from us, but He is always there.

❧ ❧ ❧

Many a concentration camp survivor can attest that during the dark days of the Holocaust, there were times when the hidden hand of Hashem could be clearly perceived.

Mordechai Pollan is one such survivor. He lived through the horrors of the Lodz ghetto, and then the Auschwitz and Dachau camps. Mr. Pollan was an electrician by trade and upon arriving in Dachau he was assigned to do electrical work around the camp.

Religious observance was, of course, forbidden in the camps, but this did not prevent scores of Jews from risking their lives for the sake of a *mitzvah*. One day, a Jew approached Mr. Pollan and told him that he had secretly procured a pair of *tefillin* which he was willing to sell for a dear price — eight consecutive days' bread rations.

To buy the *tefillin* involved a double risk. Anyone caught with a religious article was liable to be shot upon discovery. Perhaps even more dangerous was the possibility of death by starvation. Prisoners died every day from malnutrition, unable to survive on the camp diet of a minimal amount of coarse bread and watery soup. How was one to survive eight days without bread?

Many camp survivors would later relate that their sacrifice for *mitzvos* infused them with the spirit that carried them through those years of horror. Mr. Pollan is one of them. To him, the thought of being able to wrap himself in *tefillin* meant more than food. He agreed to the deal. The seller trusted Mr. Pollan and immediately gave him the *tefillin*. Mr. Pollan gave him that day's bread.

That same day, Mr. Pollan was approached by another Jew. A German who was himself a common laborer and was considered trustworthy had promised this man a sizable reward if he would procure an electric drill for him. Knowing that Mr. Pollan was an electrician, the Jew asked if he could obtain a drill and, in exchange, would be given half the reward.

That night, Mr. Pollan entered the supply warehouse to which he had access and slipped a drill into his tool box. He gave the drill to the Jew, who brought it to the German. Before handing it to the German, the Jew finalized the terms of the deal. The German promised that for the next eight days, he would bring the Jew *two loaves of bread a day*, one for himself and one for Mr. Pollan. And so for the next eight days, Mr. Pollan had enough bread to eat sufficiently and share with others.

He would put on the *tefillin* every morning at roll call, quickly recite the first portion of *Shema*, remove them and hurry outside. One morning, a Nazi notorious for his viciousness caught him in the act. Incredibly, the Nazi uttered a few curses and then turned around and left without even reporting what he had seen.

❧ ❧ ❧

There were Jews who even as they stood face to face with death publicly proclaimed their faith that Hashem's Presence, though concealed, was indeed with them.

It was the festival of *Simchas Torah*. As it was Sunday, the German guards at a camp factory were nowhere to be seen. Someone began to sing the holiday song *MiPi Kel* aloud: "There is none as powerful as Hashem, there is none as blessed as [Moshe] Amram's son, there is no greatness like the Torah, no one expounds it like Israel!"

Suddenly, the factory chief appeared. The singer stopped in mid-sentence.

"What is going on here? Tell me," the chief said, turning to Joseph Friedenson, "what is he singing?"

"Well, sir," Mr. Friedenson replied, "today is a Jewish holiday and I guess you can say that he was praying more than singing."

"Tell me what the words mean!"

Mr. Friedenson translated the Hebrew into German.

The German was dumbstruck. "Do you really believe those words, Friedenson?"

Before Mr. Friedenson could reply, a young, unlearned Jew jumped to his feet and said, "Yes, I believe!"

The German walked away, shaking his head and muttering, "Incredible! I am afraid that we will never succeed against you people."

Selflessness for Torah

כִּי לֹא תִשָּׁכַח מִפִּי זַרְעוֹ.

For it shall not become forgotten from
the mouth of its offspring (Devarim 31:21).

This is an assurance to the Jewish people that the
Torah will never become forgotten by its offspring
(Rashi).

O ne of the primary figures in the planting of Torah in America was the legendary *Menahel* (Principal) of Mesivta Torah Vodaath, R' Shraga Feivel Mendlowitz.[1] At R' Shraga Feivel's funeral, the late *Klausenberger Rebbe* commented, "Until the end of generations, Jewry will be indebted to him."

In fulfilling his mission on earth for the sake of Torah study, R' Shraga Feivel made enormous sacrifices to help establish and strengthen yeshivos other than his own. Rabbi Yaakov Kamenetsky once said that in selflessly giving of his time, funds and students to found other yeshivos, R' Shraga Feivel was unequaled in his generation.

In Torah Vodaath itself, all types of students felt at home. Whether Lithuanian or Chassidic, German or Sephardic, every student felt he had a place in the yeshivah and that he was respected by his peers. Torah Vodaath students were sent to found a number of new yeshivos and re-establish others that had flourished in pre-war Europe. In sending students to help

---

1. R' Shraga Feivel was brought to Torah Vodaath by the yeshiva's founder, R' Binyamin Wilhelm, whose efforts are portrayed in the chapter to *Parashas Vayakhel*.

found other yeshivos, R' Shraga Feivel always selected those most likely to adapt to the style of teaching of a particular *rosh yeshivah*.

He played a key role in the founding of Mesivta Rabbi Chaim Berlin in 1936. As the new high school prepared to open, he contacted the parents of boys from the Brownsville area who had enrolled in Torah Vodaath's ninth grade for the coming year and convinced them to transfer their sons to Chaim Berlin.

Two years earlier, Rabbi Yitzchak Hutner, a prime disciple of Rabbi Nosson Zvi Finkel (*"Der Alter"*) of Slobodka, had come to America. R' Shraga Feivel became acquainted with R' Hutner and perceived the latter's greatness in Torah and abilities as a Torah teacher and leader. When Mesivta Rabbi Chaim Berlin was founded, R' Shraga Feivel saw R' Hutner as the ideal choice to serve as *Rosh Yeshivah*. His behind-the-scenes efforts played a key role in R' Hutner's appointment — and he served as *Rosh Yeshivah* until his death almost half a century later. Under R' Hutner's leadership, Chaim Berlin developed into one of the world's premier yeshivos of higher learning. R' Hutner himself produced scores of *talmidim* who occupy positions of teaching and leadership throughout the Torah world.

Rabbi Aharon Kotler came to the United States from Europe in 1941 and immediately set out to establish a yeshivah of higher learning that would recapture the spirit of the great yeshivos of pre-War Europe.[1] The nucleus of the original group of *talmidim* at Beth Medrash Govoha in Lakewood, New Jersey, was a contingent sent from Torah Vodaath by R' Shraga Feivel. These young men were among the most gifted and diligent in Torah Vodaath, and some on the yeshivah's faculty felt that R' Shraga Feivel had given up too much in sending them to learn under R' Aharon. To these complaints, R' Shraga Feivel responded simply, "We are here to enhance the glory of Torah; this is our goal, no more and no less. It

---

1. See chapter to *Parashas Terumah*.

appears that these *bachurim* have a greater opportunity for growth by studying in Lakewood under R' Aharon. Why, then, should they *not* go there to learn?"

Of R' Shraga Feivel, R' Aharon once said, "Who can compare to him? His every act was *leshem shamayim* (for the sake of Heaven)."

Rabbi Nochum Zev Dessler, Dean of the Hebrew Academy of Cleveland, escaped the Nazi horrors via Siberia and made his way to America with the aid of documents provided him by Torah Vodaath. After arriving on these shores, R' Dessler studied for a short time at Torah Vodaath until the Telshe Yeshivah was established in Cleveland. Before leaving for Telshe, R' Dessler was told by someone, "Take my advice. Don't go there. Aren't you aware that Cleveland is a spiritual wasteland, literally?" Overhearing this, R' Shraga Feivel rose from his seat, offered his hand in parting to his student and said with emotion, "And I say that you *should* go and share in the founding of the yeshivah! Hashem will assist all of you and grant you success; the wasteland will be transformed into a renowned place of Torah " — words which proved prophetic. R' Shraga Feivel added that he would assist the new yeshivah in every way possible, which included sending some Torah Vodaath *talmidim*.

R' Shraga Feivel strove to conceal his greatness to the best of his ability. Though he had received *semichah* (rabbinic ordination) and was an outstanding *talmid chacham,* he insisted on being referred to as "Mister Mendlowitz." The Ponovezher *Rav,* R' Yosef Kahaneman, once remarked, "He is not *Mister* Mendlowitz — he is *Nistar* (The Hidden One) Mendlowitz!"

פרשת האזינו
Parashas Ha'azinu

Treasuries of Wisdom

זְכֹר יְמוֹת עוֹלָם בִּינוּ שְׁנוֹת דֹּר וָדֹר,
שְׁאַל אָבִיךָ וְיַגֵּדְךָ זְקֵנֶיךָ וְיֹאמְרוּ לָךְ.
*Remember the days of yore, understand the years
of generation after generation; ask your father
and he will relate it to you, your elders and
they will tell you (Devarim 32:7).*

There are those who think that Torah leaders are prepared to deal only with questions of *Halachah*. This is a grave error. In Torah can be found the answer to every question, the solution to every dilemma. Those who dedicate themselves to the study of Torah, tirelessly and with intense effort, are granted the wisdom to offer counsel for all situations. As the Mishnah states: "Whoever engages in Torah study for its own sake *(lishmah)* merits many things . . . . From him people enjoy counsel and wisdom, understanding and strength. . ." (*Mishnah Avos* 6:1). *Rashi* comments: "I [Hashem] am wisdom and courage to those who study [My Torah] in order that they may be able to be a help to human beings."

Remember the days of yore . . . ask your father and he will relate it to you. Torah leaders can interpret the happenings of history and teach their lessons to the current generation. They are the ones to whom Jewish activists must turn in their dealings with governments and political leaders. Those who place their faith in the guidance of the generation's luminaries are sure to succeed.

❧ ❧ ❧

During the Second World War, the Orthodox Jewish community in America performed heroically under the banner of the *Va'ad Hatzalah* (Rescue Committee). The *Va'ad* rescued many European Jews from death and provided others with desperately needed food and clothing.

In 1944, the *Va'ad* learned that the Nazis had added yet another outrage to their list of war crimes. In their Prisoner of War camps, where captured Allied soldiers were being held, the Nazis were separating Jewish soldiers from the rest, with the obvious intent of subjecting them to torture or murder.

Upon being informed of this report, Rabbi Aharon Kotler organized a delegation to go to Washington and bring the matter to the attention of President Roosevelt. Though he was ill at the time, R' Aharon insisted on leading the delegation.

As they traveled to the nation's capitol, someone showed R' Aharon a statement which the delegation would be presenting to Roosevelt. One sentence read, "After two thousand years of innocent men, women and children of our people being murdered, it is sad that now even the lives of Jewish [soldiers who are] prisoners of war are in danger." R' Aharon ordered that the sentence be deleted. "This can do more harm than good," he explained. "Roosevelt might say to himself: 'This has been going on for two thousand years? So what's the big deal if it goes on a bit longer?' "

Pondering the matter further, R' Aharon suggested that the statement be sent not to Roosevelt (who had already shown that he was not overly concerned with Jewish problems), but to

General Eisenhower, Commander of American forces in Europe.

Upon receiving the statement, Eisenhower immediately broadcast a warning that if the Nazis continued with their policy, the Allies would consider it the gravest offense of international law — and the Nazis would pay dearly for it.

The Nazis put an immediate stop to their plan.

❀ ❀ ❀

In his half-century of service to the Jewish people, Rabbi Moshe Sherer, President of Agudath Israel of America, has always sought the guidance of Torah leaders in dealing with the crises and issues with which our people have been confronted. In the last thirteen years of R' Aharon Kotler's life, Rabbi Sherer spoke with R' Aharon either by phone or in person on a regular basis.

In the summer of 1962, the United Nations Security Council voted to condemn the State of Israel for what they considered wrongful action toward its Arab neighbors. With the United States casting its vote against Israel, the vote was unanimous. This was highly unusual in those days when the threat of Communism loomed large and the United States recognized Israel as its only trustworthy ally in the Middle East. Jewish groups in the United States voiced their displeasure with the vote.

In order to mollify American Jews, President John Kennedy invited leaders of twelve Jewish organizations to join him at a confidential meeting in his Oval Office. The meeting was to be held on *Tishah B'Av*.

Of the twelve organizational leaders invited to the meeting, only R' Sherer was Orthodox. Upon being invited to the meeting, R' Sherer wasted no time in phoning R' Aharon to ask whether or not he should attend. R' Aharon told R' Sherer that although the meeting was to take place on *Tishah B'Av*, there was no doubt that he must attend for the sake of the Jews in *Eretz Yisrael*.

Now that R' Aharon had given R' Sherer the go-ahead to attend, other questions needed to be addressed. Was it permissible to shave or wear shoes on the fast in order to appear dignified when meeting with the President of the United States? R' Aharon told R' Sherer that these questions should be brought to the attention of Rabbi Moshe Feinstein, whom R' Aharon considered the *posek hador*, the generation's greatest *halachic* authority.

R' Aharon then launched into a discussion of the security problems facing Israel. This *gaon,* whose every available moment was dedicated to the diligent study of Torah, showed himself to be incredibly knowledgeable in current issues relevant to the Jewish people. As R' Sherer put it, "He kept me on the phone for an hour and a half as he gave me a lesson on the security problems facing Israel and how I should approach each problem should it come up at the meeting. I can attest to the fact that R' Aharon never listened to the radio or read a secular newspaper, yet his thorough knowledge of and insight into Israel's situation was astounding. I did attend the meeting with President Kennedy and sure enough, the points which R' Aharon asked me to present became the focal point of that discussion."[1]

---

1. Related by Rabbi Sherer as part of an address delivered in Camp Agudah, summer 1992.

פרשת וזאת הברכה
Vezos Haberachah

For Every Jewish Child

תּוֹרָה צִוָּה לָנוּ מֹשֶׁה, מוֹרָשָׁה קְהִלַּת יַעֲקֹב.
*The Torah that Moshe commanded us
is the heritage of the Congregation of Yaakov*
(Devarim 33:4).

Do not read the word מוֹרָשָׁה *(heritage), rather [read it
as if it is spelled]* מְאוֹרָסָה *[married, meaning that the
Torah is "married" to the **entire** congregation of
Yaakov] (Pesachim 49b with Rashi).*

T he Torah is like a groom and every single Jew is like its
bride. Everyone, rich and poor alike, has an equal share
in Torah and deserves an equal opportunity to study its holy
words. It is the community's responsibility to ensure that every
child, regardless of his background or abilities, is provided
with a Torah education.

❀ ❀ ❀

Rabbi Yaakov Zaretsky was an outstanding *talmid chacham*
who spent the last twenty years of his life studying in Bnei
Brak's *Kollel Chazon Ish*. He related the following:

246 / SHABBOS STORIES

He grew up in the Polish city of Lechovitch and attended the local *cheder* (elementary yeshivah). When he was eleven years old, his class was visited by a young man who looked about twenty-five years of age. The young man was on his way to the Yeshivah in Kletzk and had to switch trains in Lechovitch. His next train would not be leaving for another few hours, so he had decided to use the time to visit the local *cheder*. The young man asked permission of the class's *rebbi* to test the boys orally in their studies. His request was readily granted.

The test proved to be an uplifting experience for the class. A number of the boys showed themselves to be sharp and quite knowledgeable in their learning. Afterwards, the young man asked the *rebbi* where the boys would be continuing their learning when they would outgrow the *cheder*, which would be soon. The *rebbi* replied that, unfortunately, there was no yeshivah of higher learning in Lechovitch and the boys' parents had no intention of sending them away to study. Upon leaving the *cheder*, each boy would probably be taught a trade and hopefully would remain an observant Jew who would make Torah study a fixed part of his day.

The young man was most distressed by this answer. These precious children showed such promise in their learning — and their Torah education was going to end at such a young age? Something had to be done.

The young man looked at his watch. He still had some time to spare before his train was due to depart. He asked the *rebbi* to summon the students' parents for an emergency meeting at the *cheder*.

At the meeting, the young man told the parents how impressed he had been by the knowledge which their children had shown. These boys had great potential and were only beginning to blossom. How tragic it would be if they would not be permitted to continue their Torah education after leaving the *cheder*.

The young man offered to arrange for the boys' placement in a *yeshivah gedolah* (yeshivah of higher learning). All he asked for was their parents' consent.

The parents of six boys agreed to the young man's proposal. He took down their names, discussed some details and hurried to the train.

Each of the six boys did go on to study in a *yeshivah gedolah* and all became outstanding *talmidei chachamim*. R' Yaakov Zaretsky was one of them.

And the young man who made it all possible was none other than the Ponovezher *Rosh Yeshivah*, Rabbi Eliezer Menachem Shach.

This volume is part of
THE ARTSCROLL SERIES®
an ongoing project of
translations, commentaries and expositions
on Scripture, Mishnah, Talmud, Halachah,
liturgy, history and the classic Rabbinic writings;
and biographies, and thought.

For a brochure of current publications
visit your local Hebrew bookseller
or contact the publisher:

Mesorah Publications, ltd.

4401 Second Avenue
Brooklyn, New York 11232
(718) 921-9000